MW01409430

African American Tea Party Supporters

African American Tea Party Supporters

Explaining a Political Paradox

Kirk A. Johnson

LEXINGTON BOOKS
Lanham • Boulder • New York • London

Published by Lexington Books
An imprint of The Rowman & Littlefield Publishing Group, Inc.
4501 Forbes Boulevard, Suite 200, Lanham, Maryland 20706
www.rowman.com

6 Tinworth Street, London SE11 5AL

Copyright © 2019 by The Rowman & Littlefield Publishing Group, Inc.

Cover image © Mary Parker Marcus. Singer-songwriter Lloyd Marcus, whom *The Guardian* newspaper called the Tea Party movement's most prominent African American, addressing a rally on one of his 12 national bus tours.

All rights reserved. No part of this book may be reproduced in any form or by any electronic or mechanical means, including information storage and retrieval systems, without written permission from the publisher, except by a reviewer who may quote passages in a review.

British Library Cataloguing in Publication Information Available

Library of Congress Cataloging-in-Publication Data Available

ISBN 9781498590884 (cloth : alk. paper) | ISBN 9781498590891 (electronic)

♾️™ The paper used in this publication meets the minimum requirements of American National Standard for Information Sciences Permanence of Paper for Printed Library Materials, ANSI/NISO Z39.48-1992.

Contents

Preface		vii
1	How "Black" Are They? Black Tea Partyers Talk about Race	1
2	Does It Run in the Family? The Making of a Black Tea Partyer	41
3	"Personal Responsibility"—Panacea or Placebo?	69
4	Our First Muslim President? Black Tea Partyers Weigh In on Obama	107
5	Is This a Real Invitation? African Americans Come to the Tea Party	137
Epilogue		157
Appendix: Interview Questions		163
References		169
Name Index		191
Subject Index		193
About the Author		197

Preface

On February 27, 2009, the very first day of coast-to-coast rallies that signaled the national debut of the Tea Party movement, an African American man took the microphone at a gathering of modern-day patriots in Dallas, Texas (Berger 2009). Barely a month after Barack Obama's inauguration, Apostle Claver Kamau-Imani, the Texas-born son of two Democratic activists and civil rights veterans, reached into his suit jacket and pulled out a pocket-sized version of the US Constitution (Anon. 2009a; Anon. 2013). "It seems the farther we get from 1776, the less liberty means in this country," he told the cheering crowd (Anon. 2009a). Meanwhile, in Chicago, an African American man nodded in agreement as a white man next to him said he wasn't a fan of President Obama's "socialist agenda." Sean Carr, who identified himself as "not a Kool-Aid drinking black liberal," criticized the president's freshly signed American Recovery and Reinvestment Act of 2009, which was written to create jobs and stabilize state and local budgets during the 2007–2008 financial crisis (US Congress 2009). "Unlike a lot of people, I've read the stimulus [*sic*]. There's a lot of waste, a lot of pork. I don't think it's fair that we should have to foot the bill for other people's screw-ups" (Jacobson 2009).

These early Tea Party gatherings were genteel compared to the racial and ethnic rhetoric that flared at subsequent rallies. Fueled by an influx of southern Tea Party supporters, what began as grievances about liberty and taxes morphed into a Reconstruction Era-style racial diatribe (Maxwell 2016). Confederate flags and references to lynching and gun violence became commonplace, as did signs and posters objecting to Obama's presumptive religion ("We Need a Christian President"), depicting him as a foreigner ("'Cap' Congress and 'Trade' Obama Back to Kenya!"), and characterizing him as a Nazi ("America's Taxpayers Are the Jews for Obama's Ovens") (NAACP

2010). When African American members of Congress walked across Capitol Hill after a nearby Tea Party rally in 2010, Tea Party supporters shouted "niggers!" and one spat at them (Kane 2010). A white protester at another Tea Party rally held a cardboard placard that read, "This Sign Is the Brownest Thing on This Entire Block" (Anon. 2009b). Tea Party members circulated photoshopped images of Barack and Michelle Obama as apes, and portrayed persons of color as freeloaders who are inherently undeserving of government support (Skocpol and Williamson 2012). A fabricated Tea Party announcement canceling the Obama family's annual Easter egg hunt came with an illustration of the White House grounds covered with watermelons, a racist Civil War-era trope symbolizing African Americans' childlike "juice-dribbling" simplemindedness (Associated Press 2009; Black 2014).

Research suggests that these disturbing incidents were more than isolated anecdotes. In one study, Tea Party supporters were 25 percent more likely to be racially resentful compared to Americans who didn't support the Tea Party. Nearly three-quarters (73 percent) of Tea Party supporters (compared to 33 percent of Tea Party opponents) believed that "blacks would be as well off as whites if they just tried harder" and only 45 percent of Tea Party supporters believed African Americans are intelligent (Campo-Flores 2010; Tope, Pickett, and Chiricos 2015).

At rallies, the Tea Party also shared the podium with white supremacists, who used the opportunity to recruit disaffected whites into their organizations. The protest movement drew enthusiastic support from white nationalist groups such as the Council of Conservative Citizens, the direct descendant of the white Citizens Councils that fought to maintain Jim Crow segregation in the Deep South, and that argues that whites—who own fourteen times more wealth than African Americans on average (Amadeo 2019b)—are oppressed by black people. The Tea Party also attracted support from former Klansman David Duke and Billy Joe Roper, Jr., former leader of the National Alliance, a group dedicated to creating an all-white United States by murdering or expelling African Americans, other persons of color, and Jews (Burghart and Zeskind 2010).

Finally, like many conservatives—72 percent of its members are conservative and 66 percent vote Republican—Tea Party supporters argue for a strict constructionist interpretation of the US Constitution (*New York Times/CBS News* 2010). So when Dallas activist Apostle Claver Kamau-Imani praised the Constitution and spoke wistfully of returning to the spirit of 1776, as Tea Partyers frequently do, he referred to a document that in its original form: (1) forbade the federal government from interfering in the Atlantic slave trade for twenty years after the Constitution was ratified in 1789; (2) formalized the legal rights of slaveowners to retrieve so-called runaway slaves instead of intervening on behalf of the slaves; and (3) failed to protect free blacks from racially discriminatory antebellum state and local laws

(Horton 2018). Despite a claim by Rep. Michelle Bachmann, founder of the House Tea Party Caucus, that the Founding Fathers "worked tirelessly until slavery was no more in the United States," slavery wasn't abolished until 1865, long after the Founding Fathers had died (Serwer 2011). Indeed, five of the seven Founding Fathers (Washington, Jefferson, Franklin, Madison, and Jay) owned slaves, and a sixth—Alexander Hamilton—supported slaveowners' property rights over slaves' human rights (duRoss 2011).

Yes, the Tea Party represents a unifying political statement for people who feel aggrieved by federal overreach. But it is also a protest movement that framed the first African American president as irreconcilably illegitimate, where members peddle unsettling racial theories and rallies are safe spaces for white nationalists, and where Confederate flag wavers take wistful inspiration from a document that formalized second-class treatment of African Americans. Under the circumstances, it would be counterintuitive to find a single African American to endorse the Tea Party over President Obama, who drew 99 percent of the black vote in 2008 (Gallup 2008). "For many black people, Confederate symbols often read like Do Not Enter signs," notes *New York Times* correspondent John Eligon (2018).

Yet some did. A small but measurable number of protesters—an estimated 1 percent of the Tea Party faithful—who denounced the Obama administration in widely publicized rallies were African Americans themselves (Montopoli 2012). They launched blogs, wrote books, appeared on Fox News, and ran for public office. They went to Tea Party meetings, supported Tea Party-backed candidates, and even spoke at Tea Party rallies.

Who are these contrarians? How did they come to align with a movement that reviles President Obama, condones racial insults, endorses white supremacy, and reveres the US Constitution—a document that so enshrined black subordination that abolitionist William Lloyd Garrison called it "a covenant with death and an agreement with Hell" (Finkelman 2000)? These are the central questions in this book.

These concerns are significant because African American Tea Party supporters have little precedent in American politics. Not since black nationalist Marcus Garvey met in 1922 with the Acting Imperial Wizard of the Ku Klux Klan, whom Garvey thought would share his interest in a black exodus from the United States (Hill 1985), have blacks sought political kinship in such seemingly hostile territory. Psychologist Michael Bader (2010) says patriotic flag-waving at Tea Party events represents anxiety-fueled longing for safety and connectedness. If so, why would black Tea Party supporters seek safety where most African Americans see danger, and seek connectedness with people that most African Americans try to avoid?

The questions are also significant for their policy implications. The Tea Party represents an assault on federal programs (such as Obamacare and Head Start) and policies (such as affirmative action) that are intended to foster racial and social-class equity. That means any African American who joins the Tea Party is helping to undermine initiatives designed to benefit struggling, resource-poor African American communities. Why would any African American undercut his or her own community?

AN OVERVIEW OF BLACK CONSERVATISM

In a sense, African Americans' embrace of a conservative protest movement shouldn't be all that surprising, because conservative thought has a long history in the black community. During slavery, many free blacks saw assimilation and accommodation as routes to wealth enhancement, and identified more with white aristocrats than with enslaved Africans (Lewis 2013). Even some slaves acquiesced to "the peculiar institution": in 1787, Jupiter Hammon, the first published poet of African descent, wrote that slaves should obey their owners "and we ought to do it cheerfully, and freely" because slavery was God's will (Hammon 1787). Abolitionist Frederick Douglass believed so emphatically in self-improvement—a cornerstone of conservative thinking—that he felt a united black community could overcome every challenge, even slavery. He went so far as to argue that free blacks—not white people—were "largely responsible for [slaves'] continued enslavement" because free blacks had access to resources that were denied slaves. In his endorsement of self-help, Douglass also urged black people to push for change by joining "institutions of a complexional character" (Douglass 1848). In 1895, Booker T. Washington made a similar call for self-improvement through gradual uplift by famously advising African Americans to curb any aspirations beyond manual labor. "Our greatest danger is that in the great leap from slavery to freedom we may overlook the fact that the masses of us are to live by the productions of our hands, and fail to keep in mind that we shall prosper in proportion as we learn to dignify and glorify common labor." Washington argued that accepting the brutal reality of Jim Crow segregation and lynching was vastly preferable to protesting it. "It is at the bottom of life that we must begin, and not at the top. Nor should we permit our grievances to overshadow our opportunities" (Washington 1895). By the turn of the twentieth century, "many, if not most" African Americans agreed with Washington, viewing conservatism as the most pragmatic means of advancing the race (Bracey 2008, 27).

Booker T. Washington cast a long shadow. He influenced Marcus Garvey, who trumpeted free enterprise and racial solidarity by building a fleet of black-owned and -operated steamships and selling company shares exclusively to African Americans (Lewis 2013). By 1934, the shock of the Great Depression convinced even W. E. B. Du Bois to nod to Washington, his longtime nemesis, by accommodating segregation, thus becoming "the voice of acquiescence" compared to the fiery liberalism of his earlier years (Harrell 1968, 550). In the 1960s, journalist George Schuyler opposed the civil rights movement on the grounds that it emphasized the failures of African Americans rather than its middle-class success stories, and urged cautious incrementalism instead of dangerous marches and sit-ins (Lewis 2013). Soon after Ronald Reagan (1981) reimagined government as "not the solution to our problem" but "the problem" itself, Justice Clarence Thomas was sitting on the US Supreme Court, intellectuals Glenn Loury (1995) and Shelby Steele (2006, 1999) were attacking affirmative action, and economist Thomas Sowell (1998) was arguing, based on fifteen years of studying global inequality, that economic disparities between the "haves" and "have nots" were virtually inevitable. Shortly thereafter, economist Walter E. Williams (2011, 9) argued that racism is a red herring: it's not that racial discrimination doesn't exist, he wrote. It's just that racism isn't the root of African Americans' most difficult problems, which he argued are either self-inflicted or the result of imperfect economic markets (or, as he put it, "the power of vested interest groups to use, as a means to greater wealth, the coercive powers of government to stifle market competition"). Today, thanks to the prominence of Gen. Colin Powell; Dr. Condoleeza Rice; Dr. Ben Carson; media commentators Larry Elder and Armstrong Williams; present and former members of Congress Tim Scott, J. C. Watts, and Allen West; and many others, black conservatism feels very nearly mainstream. Indeed, an estimated 25 percent of African Americans have identified as political conservatives in nearly every year since 1980, though they are often hesitant to admit so publicly (Lewis 2013; Harris-Lacewell 2004).

Today black conservatives frequently agree on a few core principles, including individual and collective *self-advancement* through education and economic empowerment rather than government assistance; *moral rectitude* as the solution for disproportionate levels of black-community dysfunction; the widespread *availability of opportunity* in the United States, where all hard-working citizens are equally capable of success; and the *absence of racism* as a significant obstacle to black success, in part because market forces discourage employers, retailers, and others from discriminating against persons of color (Lewis 2013; Dawson 2001, 20).

Under this broad tent of interlocking ideas, there are variants. In fact, political scientist Angela K. Lewis (2013) identifies four types of conservatives: the *black right*, *Afrocentric conservatives*, *individualist conservatives*, and *neoconservatives*. The *black right*, inspired by Jupiter Hammon and Booker T. Washington, stresses upright values and moral decency—rather than attacks on white racism—as a corrective to crime, drug addiction, poverty, and other problems that fall heavily on the black community. *Afrocentric conservatives*, who also take inspiration in part from Booker T. Washington, believe in racial pride through economic self-sufficiency. In contrast to the black right, they view racism as a serious and enduring social problem that persists partly because racial inequality was built into the nation's founding documents. *Individualist conservatives* decry government intervention in people's lives, and instead believe in capitalism and the power of the marketplace. Like Walter E. Williams, individualists dismiss social welfare programs and other government interventions as fostering dependency. Finally, *neoconservatives* take issue with the civil rights movement, which they say overemphasized African Americans' progress as a group and diminished the role of individual responsibility. Like individualists, neoconservatives disdain affirmative action, antipoverty programs, and other government initiatives, believing that churches and charitable organizations are better positioned to help black people in need.

ARE BLACK TEA PARTYERS CONSERVATIVE REACTIONARIES?

The Tea Party represents many of these conservative ideals. Tea Party loyalists say the government is too powerful, too intrusive in people's daily lives, too disruptive to free-market economics, and too concerned about African Americans' problems. They argue that social welfare programs should be scaled back, burdensome regulations on business should be lifted, and taxes should be lowered (Pew Research Center 2010; Zernike and Thee-Brenan 2010; Winston 2010). Thus the rallying cry that Tea Partyers have been <u>T</u>axed <u>E</u>nough <u>A</u>lready.

But in other ways, the Tea Party ventures beyond the usual contours of conservative thinking. For one thing, conservatives—at least the moderate conservatives who have dominated the Republican Party (until the Trump presidency, at least)—have long acknowledged that government serves important functions. We need a federal, state, and local government presence to protect our common interests and maintain civil society, conservatives have argued. What's more, the government has a duty—with some limits—to support the welfare state. Tea Party patriots may bemoan social welfare programs, but it was Richard Nixon's conservative administration that launched the Supplemental Security Income (SSI) program to help people with mental and physical disabilities; expanded the federal government's role in the Food Stamp Program in 1970 and again in 1973; approved a 20 percent increase in Social Security benefits in 1972, and provided federally funded job training through the Comprehensive Employment and Training Act (Marx 2011). Historically, the size of government—a major Tea Party grievance—has never really been an issue for conservatives (Lewis 2013).

The Tea Party's small-government mantra isn't the only thing that separates its supporters from other conservatives. Tea Partyers take extreme positions on other issues. In 2011, political scientists Christopher Parker and

Matt Barreto asked a diverse group of 900 conservatives if they thought Barack Obama was destroying the country. Thirty-five percent of all conservatives said yes. Yet twice as many Tea Party conservatives (71 percent) agreed that Obama was indeed wrecking the United States, prompting Parker and Barreto (2013, 56) to conclude that the Tea Party faithful are "reactionary and therefore prone to believing conspiratorial, demagogic discourse." Historically conservatives have been incrementalists, says Parker. It's not that they don't believe things can be better; they do. But they think slow, gradual change is the best way to get there. That's not the Tea Party's cup of tea. "Tea Party rallies are not about slow, gradual change. Those people want change now," says Parker (2013). "These people aren't just conservatives. They're conservative extremists."

The final element that separates Tea Partyers from other conservatives is the puzzling racial juxtaposition that it represents. To be sure, alliances between black and white conservatives are not unheard of: Jupiter Hammon's antebellum poetry was edited by "an abler and more experienced hand" who was probably white; and journalist George Schuyler was lifelong friends with fellow social critic H. L. Mencken (Hammon, Ransom, and Wegelin 1970, 30; Williams 2007; Ontaatje 2010). But a marriage of black and white Tea Party supporters represents something new. Unlike the surely close ties between Hammon and his editor and between Schuyler and Mencken, a cross-racial Tea Party alliance represents some of the most unlikely political bedfellows imaginable. Aside from Tea Party rallies, are there many social spaces in the United States where African Americans knowingly mingle with self-avowed white separatists?

So to the extent that African American Tea Partyers are ideologically aligned with their white compatriots—and that's a big *if*, as we will discover in later chapters—their coexistence in an atypical conservative protest movement is intriguingly unprecedented.

FROM PERSONAL TO THEORETICAL

The Tea Party has been criticized from both the right and the left (e.g., Whatley 2010; James 2013; Jonsson 2010), but the most vocal critics of Black Tea Partyers are other African Americans who typically assume that movement loyalists are race traitors. Tea Party supporter Deneen Borelli (2012, 2) says her appearances on Fox News have earned her dozens of hate letters by email and Twitter, presumably from other African Americans, such as: "You can not speak for black people, so take your Stepin Fetchit ass back to your master on the plantation [*sic*]" and "[G]o find your parents and slap the shit out of them."

When I first realized there were black Tea Party supporters, I was skeptical, too. After all, I'm an African American who's probably hyperaware of racial violence. I teach at the University of Mississippi, a school that erupted in a deadly riot over the prospect of admitting its first African American student in 1962, and that acquiesced only when the Kennedy administration dispatched federal troops to protect James Meredith's right to enroll in the flagship university of his home state. In my sociology and African American Studies classes I lecture on police shootings, racial incarceration disparities, the history of lynching, and other forms of judicial and extrajudicial violence. While I recognize that no region of the United States has exclusive claim to racism, I have lived and traveled throughout the South for many years, an experience that has made me chronically hypervigilant about personal safety. When I was eight and driving through Alabama with my family in 1963, my parents cautioned me and my younger sister to be particularly well-behaved as we pulled up to the black-owned A. G. Gaston Motel, one of the few places in Birmingham where African Americans could spend the night. "There's been some trouble here," my mom explained soberly. The "trouble," I discovered as an adult, was in fact a recent riot involving "thousands of Negroes" and "more than 1,000 law officers" that erupted after the Klan bombed the motel, where Dr. King had been staying, and African American bystanders were beaten by the police (Associated Press 1963, 1).

Wary of the inherent dangers posed by white extremists, I was skeptical about the racial bona fides of any African American who would choose to ally with hostile whites over the safety and familiarity of the black community. So I hypothesized that black Tea Party supporters may show indications of *racial ambivalence* such that they identify more with other groups than they do with African Americans. That might explain their apparent disdain for President Obama.

I thought of a second, related possibility: black Tea Partyers might have *a tendency to downplay the extent and effects of racism.* For example, after Harvard professor Henry Louis Gates was arrested by a police officer as Gates tried to enter his university-owned home in 2009, some critics drew parallels with the police violence that victimizes many black people. But African American Tea Party supporter Lloyd Marcus (2010, 82) dismissed the argument that the officer's actions were racially motivated. "What on earth does arresting someone for disorderly conduct have to do with race?" he wrote. "Gates is either guilty or not guilty. His skin color is irrelevant." Accordingly, African Americans who minimize racism might dismiss accusations of police misconduct, thus questioning the need for criminal justice reform and other race-related Obama-era initiatives. They also might attend Tea Party gatherings assuming that accusations of racial intolerance at such events are not credible (Mitchell 2017).

There were other reasonable possibilities. Black Tea Partyers might have been *socialized to be hard-working and self-reliant*. This focus on self-sufficiency, a celebration of the Protestant work ethic, resonates with many conservatives (Atieh, Brief, and Vollrath 1987). As former Secretary of State Condoleeza Rice once said, "In America, with education and hard work, it really does not matter where you came from. It matters only where you are going" (Bracey 2008, 171). If black conservatives believe that hard work makes a person successful, they might also assume a reasonable-sounding—but not necessarily accurate—corollary: people are poor because they don't work very hard. This assumption about poor people could conceivably bring African Americans in alliance with white Tea Partyers who are skeptical of government programs that allow "welfare cheats" to prosper on the backs of hard-working taxpayers. African Americans could have particular reason to oppose such entitlements if the programs destroy the black family by giving women a financial incentive to live as single parents, as black conservatives often claim.

Armed with these three hypotheses—that African Americans gravitate to the Tea Party because they feel ambivalent about being black, they minimize racism, or their socialization toward self-reliance makes them skeptical of government welfare programs—I conducted open-ended semi-structured interviews from 2013 to 2018 with thirty African Americans who identify as Tea Party supporters. The group ranged in age from their early twenties to late sixties, and while they all identified as conservatives, their backgrounds and experiences were diverse. There were legislators and educators, radio personalities and military veterans, a minister, a stay-at-home mom, a cab driver, a physician, a former Nation of Islam member, and a childhood admirer of the Black Panthers. Some interviewees were referrals from a national black conservative think tank; I found others through Google searches and snowball sampling from prior interviewees. The interviews lasted between one and three hours each and were conducted by phone, Skype, FaceTime, or in people's homes and offices, and in public libraries and restaurants, in Mississippi, Georgia, Florida, Virginia, the District of Columbia, New York, Texas, Illinois, Colorado, and California. The interview questions appear in the appendix; because the interviews developed organically depending on what Rapley (2001) calls "local interactional contingencies," each conversation drew from a different set of questions, some predetermined and some spontaneous. After hand-coding the transcribed conversations, I arranged excerpts on a Microsoft Excel spreadsheet. The spreadsheet allowed me to compare subjects' responses to each question regardless of its chronological appearance in the interview, thus facilitating data condensation (Miles, Huberman, and Saldana 2014).

The process of analyzing the data brought a series of surprises that forced me to question each hypothesis. As a group, black Tea Partyers don't oppose

Obama because he's black, they didn't join the Tea Party because they're oblivious to racism, and they don't fight government assistance because they assume poor people are lazy. In fact, I discovered black Tea Partyers who are proud of Obama, who fully acknowledge racism within and beyond the Tea Party, and who empathize deeply with the multiple challenges of being poor.

Moreover, the interviews helped me understand that, contrary to their critics' claims, black Tea Partyers aren't race traitors at all. In fact, in addition to a few core principles—belief in God, love of country, respect for family—the one unifying feature of this group is their deep regard for African Americans. Beyond that, their differences in upbringing, temperament, and life experiences are striking. Some think critically about conservative orthodoxy while others are more comfortable with it; some emulate the attitudes and behaviors they grew up with while others reject them; some are lifelong conservatives while others recalled a single influential event that made them rethink liberalism. Because of this variation, black Tea Partyers defy easy description; when it comes to who they are, what they believe, and how they think, they probably challenge more stereotypes than they confirm.

Once I appreciated the diversity within the group—that there's no one way to be a black Tea Party supporter—I realized that as anomalous as their political alignments may be, they're not illogical. To the contrary, I argue that when viewed in the context of their personalities, life experiences, and socializing influences, black Tea Partyers' unusual political decisions are knowable, understandable, and rational. Beyond the cardboard caricatures of racial turncoats lie people whose reasons for aligning with the Tea Party are often surprisingly compelling and nuanced. In other words, black Tea Party supporters are often maligned for reasons that have more to do with who critics imagine them to be than who they actually are.

The implications of these mistaken assumptions loom particularly in the Trump era, in which many groups of color—Muslims, Mexicans, African Americans—are automatically presumed to be terrorizers, infiltrators, or rule-breakers. This book advises caution to those of us who make such glib assumptions about all members of any group.

THE STRUCTURE OF THE BOOK

The rationale behind African Americans' alliance with the Tea Party becomes clearer through the lenses of sociology, psychology, and political science, so I borrow concepts and research findings from these disciplines. I also lean heavily on the *sociological imagination*, a theoretical concept from acclaimed sociologist C. Wright Mills (1959). Using the sociological imagination requires investigators to explore a person's personal biography and its intersection with history to determine whether the person's actions represent *personal troubles* (personality flaws) or *public issues* (institutional failings). Thus, I have taken note of both the interviewees' personal biographies and the historical events that surround them. The narratives that emerge from this exercise do a great deal to explain the seemingly inexplicable alliance of black and white Tea Partiers. In the process, they raise important questions about African American identity, political history, and electoral participation.

Chapter 1 explores black Tea Partiers' perspectives on race. It asks how much they identify with other African Americans, and whether they view race, racism, or their relationship with the black community differently than other African Americans do. This chapter addresses the possibility that African Americans may align with the Tea Party and the Republican Party in opposition to President Obama and the Democratic Party because they feel conflicted about their blackness, they downplay the prevalence or effects of racism, or because they feel disconnected from other African Americans.

Chapter 2 explores the impact of parental interactions and family structure on African Americans' subsequent decision to support the Tea Party. This discussion addresses whether black Tea Partiers were socialized from childhood to embrace the pro-work, anti-entitlement mentality that unites most conservatives, in which case African Americans' impulse to forge a unlikely alliance with white conservatives may have begun with an equally unlikely source—their parents.

Chapter 3 considers African American conservatives' claim that longstanding problems in the black community, such as intergenerational poverty and excess incarceration, could be alleviated if more African Americans simply took responsibility for their actions. It also examines the related claim that by fostering dependency and discouraging individual initiative, government entitlement programs are counterproductive. If accurate, these arguments could explain the appeal to African Americans of a protest movement designed to encourage responsible individual behavior by reducing the role of government in people's lives.

Chapter 4 addresses the nature of black Tea Partiers' opposition to President Obama. Like many white Tea Party patriots, do they question his politics and policy choices? Do they have reservations about Obama's religion and his citizenship? Do they doubt his very legitimacy as president? To the extent that African Americans accept the conspiratorial, their alliance with conspiracy-minded whites in an insurgent protest movement may make sense. But how can African Americans say they stand with the black community if they oppose the policies and party leadership of first black president?

Chapter 5 explores what happens when African American Tea Party supporters appear at Tea Party rallies and meetings. How do the mostly white crowds react, and how do those reactions inform these African Americans' conclusions about Tea Party racism? When it comes to face-to-face interactions with white conservatives who have a reputation for racial hostility, how do black Tea Partyers explain their willingness to link arms?

ACKNOWLEDGMENTS

I am grateful for the many people who sat for interviews, suggested likely interviewees, prepared hundreds of pages of transcripts, read manuscript drafts, helped me find obscure reference materials, served as sounding boards for ideas, and graciously encouraged the growth and development of this protracted research project. These include: David Almasi, John Anthony, Joshua Black, Jennifer Carroll, Lee Cohen, Kirsten Dellinger, Coby Dillard, J. T. Edwards, Michel Faulkner, Joe Feagin, Corey Fields, Amy E. Gibson, James Golden, Sherrie Gibson, Joseph Rhea Gladden, Tess Graham, Rachel Haggard, Jason Hale, Mike Hill, Dr. Deborah Honeycutt, Andrew Honeycutt, Glenn Hopkins, Jeff Jackson, Michael Jones, Ayesha Kreutz, Lloyd Marcus, Bill Marcy, Susan Marcy, Chris McCarty, Walter Meyers III, Ron Miller, Demetrius Minor, Jill Moore, Deroy Murdock, Chris Parker, Star Parker, Joseph Pinion III, Terrence Reddick, Antonio Smart, John Sonnett, Marie Stroughter, Kim Wade, Ellis Walton, Allen West, James White, Moses Winston IV, Armstrong Williams, and Gilbert Wilkerson. Project 21 of the National Center for Public Policy Research provided interview assistance. My research was also supported by two Summer Research Grants (2009, 2015) and a Senior Summer Research Grant (2016) from the University of Mississippi College of Liberal Arts, and an Investigative Grant (2016) from the University of Mississippi Office of Research and Sponsored Programs for travel and transcription assistance.

Willa and Olivia Johnson were constant sources of support. I'm grateful for their love and encouragement.

I appreciate the author-friendly professionalism of Sarah Craig, Courtney Morales, Shelby Russell, and the rest of the production team at Lexington Books.

Finally, I'm grateful for an anonymous reviewer who read an early paper on African American Tea Party supporters that I submitted to a social science journal, which rejected it. I hadn't thought of writing this book until the reviewer commented, "I do not believe the manuscript addresses an important or interesting research question."

THE TEA PARTY SUPPORTERS AT THE TIME OF THE INTERVIEWS

Andrew, political consultant, age 65
Anne, physician, age 65
Antonio, state legislator, age 40
Ashley, chaplain, age 42
Byron, retired police officer, age 70
Charlie, Navy veteran, age 35
Claudia, Byron's spouse, age 68
Dale, political commentator, age 32
Dave, youth group director, age 32
Dean, political organizer, age 51
Elton, college student, age 20
George, court clerk, age 60
Hilton, state legislator, age 56
Isaac, pastor, age 57
Jake, cab driver, age 33
James, IT executive, age 65
Jimmy, radio producer, age 59
Joan, retired naval officer, age 56
John, business executive, age 32
Kevin, real estate broker, age 58
Len, former federal official, age 54
Lindsay, political activist, age 65
Mary, stay-at-home mom, age 53
Melvin, software developer, age 61
Ritchie, political science professor, age 55
Rod, business owner, age 53
Sally, real estate agent, age 40
Sheila, political consultant, age 42
Wallace, software executive, age 56
Whitney, state legislator, age 50

Chapter One

How "Black" Are They? Black Tea Partyers Talk about Race

> Race is just this indelible feature in our country. It's just a fact.
> —Whitney, state legislator

> You know, I've never experienced racism, ever. It's never impacted my life.
> —Len, former federal official

When Hilton[1] ran a successful campaign for a seat in his state legislature in 2013, he made history: he was the first African American since Reconstruction to represent his district, which is 78 percent white. But when he phoned black pastors to talk about policies and resources he could deliver to help the African American community, something unexpected happened. Instead of congratulating him on his unlikely victory, they shunned him. "I was saying, 'I would like to meet with you. I would like to explain to you my ideology and how I can help the black community.' I reached out to a dozen black churches. I would leave a message with the church secretary, asking for the pastor to call me back. I never heard from them," Hilton said.

In a sense, the pastors typify the disdain that many African Americans feel toward black conservatives. Conservative author Shelby Steele says he's ostracized for urging black Americans to give up their culture of "entitlement and grievance" and put their energy toward advancing their interests. "Sure, I get attacked," he told a journalist in 2006. "Any white who says these things is going to be seen as racist, and any black who says them is going to be seen as an Uncle Tom. That's because the only politically correct way to see blacks is as victims of larger forces that are constantly determining them and beating them and miring them in difficulty" (Guthmann 2006).

African Americans seem to reserve special contempt for black conservatives like Hilton who support the Tea Party. In 2012, Tea Party activist Deneen Borelli, a Fox News contributor, wrote of receiving bruising emails from other African Americans who called her everything from "a despicable piece of garbage" to "a nigger crawling back to the plantation" (Borelli 2012, 2). The presumption, as Borelli views it, is that African Americans are a monolith, and those who dare to think outside of the box are turncoats. It's not a logical way of thinking, she says. "All white people are not similarly expected to agree with Bill Clinton or George Bush" (Borelli 2012, 3).

For their part, African American skeptics see black Tea Partyers as dismissing the need for solidarity and mutual support, two deeply rooted cultural traits that helped African Americans survive slavery and Jim Crow segregation. But there's more. Barely one month after the inauguration of the first African American president, televised Tea Party rallies showed white protesters coming together, sometimes using disparaging racial imagery, to urge lawmakers to reduce taxes and downsize the federal government.

Thus, critics saw black Tea Partyers as shunning a president that most African Americans adore, questioning government programs that arguably sustain broad swaths of the black community, and preferring to hang out with racially suspect white folks over other black people. So there's more at stake here than simply Tea Partyers' apparent refusal to buy into an all-for-one, one-for-all fellowship. The overriding concern is that supporting the Tea Party might bring other African Americans harm.

Tea Party haters, like the pastors in Hilton's district and the viewers who send Borelli spiteful emails, may assume there's a simple explanation for African American behavior that so violates expectations: black Tea Partyers feel conflicted about being black. It's a daring presumption—that deep down inside, maybe in ways that they don't fully realize, anyone who cuts so hard against the African American grain must have a powerful and possibly closeted affinity for white people. But that's what historian Clarence E. Walker argues. Walker (2011) says African Americans join the Tea Party because they want to be accepted by whites, an assimilationist longing that explains why they shun the demands for justice and reliance on welfare programs that stigmatize African Americans.

Similarly, sociologists know that a person's *reference group*—the group someone uses as a measuring stick for evaluating themselves—isn't necessarily the group they belong to. Psychologists Kenneth and Mamie Clark famously demonstrated as much in the 1940s, when they found that black youngsters preferred white dolls over brown ones (Clark and Clark 1939). And it's not just children who can feel ambivalent about their blackness. Sociologist E. Franklin Frazier noted during the postwar period that inasmuch as members of the black middle class strive for acceptance in the black world, they also emphasize white values, white canons of respectability, and white standards of beauty on the assumption that these attributes will bring acceptance in the white world. When whites inevitably reject them, the rejection creates "considerable self-hatred, since it is attributed to their Negro characteristics" (Frazier 1957, 26). One recent study found that nearly 10 percent of 447 at-risk black teens in Washington, DC, had psychological profiles indicating a combination of "elevated assimilation" and "extremely high self-hatred" scores, suggesting both an aversion to their blackness and a desire to fit into a white-dominated world (Worrell, Andretta, and Woodland 2014, 574). Of course, not all African Americans feel conflicted about their skin color. But for those who do, their attitude about their skin color might affect any number of daily decisions. US Supreme Court Justice Clarence Thomas, who was mocked by childhood classmates for his dark skin, internalized an aversion to blackness, according to biographers Jane Mayer and Jill Abramson. When Anita Hill accused Thomas of sexual harassment, he asked his mother to remember the women he had dated. All of them had light skin. "So what would I want with a woman as black as Anita Hill?" he asked her (Mayer and Abramson 1994, 46).

SOLIDARITY WITH THE BLACK COMMUNITY

If black conservatives were racial turncoats, you'd expect their *reference group* to be whites. They'd feel more comfortable talking and spending time with whites than with blacks. They'd avoid living near and working with other African Americans. They might refrain altogether from talking about race except to tsk-tsk with their white neighbors about woeful levels of black gang violence and teen pregnancy.

Those were my expectations, at least. Startled by news reports of African Americans at Tea Party rallies who seemed untroubled by racial messaging that reminded me of "Birth of a Nation," I started a list of tentative, uncertain questions I wanted to ask if I ever had the opportunity to talk with a black Tea Party supporter. One of the first questions was about racial identity:

> *People of African ancestry have been referred to in lots of different ways over the years, from Negroes to blacks to African Americans. What do you call yourself?*

The question was awkward and clunky—and ultimately unnecessary, because none of the people I interviewed struck me as race traitors. I found no detectable separation between the interviewees and other African Americans. For example, John, a young business executive, explained how his racial identity complicates the most routine everyday events: "When I try to catch a cab in New York City, I'm a black man in America. When I get ogled by police, I'm a black man in America. This is an unchangeable, undeniable part of who I am. Every single day." Antonio, a Republican state legislator, makes it a practice to explain the realities of African American life to his white Republican colleagues. Democrats were stunned the first time they saw him do it, because they had assumed that any African American who chooses the Republican Party doesn't identify with other blacks. One black Democrat told him admiringly, "You're more black than any of us over here."

Elton, a junior at a historically black college, celebrates when he hears other black conservatives talking about race. If they're reluctant to tackle racial issues, he says, "that to me is a problem." When I introduced my book project to James, an IT executive, and explained I wanted to illuminate why African Americans make unusual political choices, he agreed in a way that made clear his racial allegiance. "Any time I have a chance to help out one of our people, I'm on board with that 150 percent," he said.

James's use of the first-person plural *our*, which was typical among the interviewees, indicates both his alliance with other African Americans and his willingness to embrace problems that trouble the African American community. That's not something we would expect from people who spurn their blackness or who identify more with whites than blacks. These narratives that show black conservatives taking pleasure in racial discussions rather than avoiding them, and linking their personal trajectories with a shared communal destiny, upend the notion that black conservatives are racial turncoats. "How can I be a sellout when I'm trying to get people to do better?" asked Byron, a retired police officer. I asked Byron how he answers the charge that black Tea Partyers aren't really black. "I've been black all my life!" he said, laughing.

People who question black Tea Partyers' racial bona fides undoubtedly assume that all African Americans show how they feel about being black in the same way—by voting for Democratic candidates, for example, or supporting social welfare programs. But black Tea Party sympathizers remind us that there are many ways to be black. For example, Isaac, a pastor who spoke with me in his church office, bemoaned the pack mentality that defines blackness by which political party a person supports:

> Since when does blackness have to do with political opinions, with political alliances? It has nothing to do with that. It has to do with a person's genealogy, not their ideology. If you listen to people like Jesse Jackson or Al Sharpton, most African Americans would consider you a disciple. But that would mean I'm not really black, because I don't follow the party line.

Similarly, Len objects to the compulsory homogeneity that frequently makes outcasts of black conservatives:

> People denigrate and demean and delegitimize black conservatives by saying, "I've heard you're not really black." Well, then, what is really black? Is it my

skin? Am I supposed to speak a certain way? And then they say, "Well, you don't think like we do." So what's this "we" thing? I thought that I had a brain that God gave me to make decisions on my own. I didn't know that I was supposed to be plugged into some collective.

Hilton, the state legislator, goes so far as to question the label "African American." Reverend Jesse Jackson, who called for the term in 1988, may have intended to replace the then-popular racial term "black" with an ethnic label (Martin 1991), but Hilton says the term is disempowering:

I refuse to be called an African American. I'm not. I'm an American. This is my country. Why would I not claim the most powerful, the most magnificent, the most benevolent country the world has ever seen as my own? I think we need to get away from these hyphenated names—African-American, Hispanic-American, Asian-American. That divides our country. We are one nation under God. I think there is something that is deeper about being called or wanting to belong to a group called African-Americans. What is sinister about it is it gives too many people the idea that this is not really your country.

Similarly, Lloyd Marcus, who has spoken at over 500 Tea Party rallies as president of the National Association for the Advancement of Conservative People of Color (NAACPC), introduces himself to crowds by saying, "Hello, my fellow patriots! I am NOT an African American! I am Lloyd Marcus, AMERICAN!" (Marcus 2010, 24). Marcus's declaration may sound like racial ambivalence, but it's also consistent with research showing that race is not always a black person's primary source of group identity. As psychologist William E. Cross, Jr., notes in a review of 45 studies of black identity, "Some Blacks make religion, sexual preference, socioeconomic status, simply being an 'American,' or any number of reference group orientations more salient than race" (Cross 1991, 142).

NO UNANIMITY ON RACISM

If black Tea Partyers feel uniformly comfortable in their blackness, multivalent as blackness may be, do they think in similar ways about racism as well? Before we address that question, let's define racism, because scholars and nonscholars tend to think about the word entirely differently. To most laypersons, racism simply means treating someone badly because of their skin color. This popular definition of racism is individualistic, and it hinges on a person's behavior: if someone believes white people are genetically superior to persons of color but they don't act on that belief, they're not racist (Campbell 2018). Race scholars take a more expansive approach. They realize that racism has an interpersonal dimension, but they also recognize that institutions can have racially exclusionary rules and policies. Those rules can be written (as when a school district allocates by formula more resources for white students than for black and brown students) or unwritten (as when the school board tacitly assumes that students of color are more likely than white students to be written up for behavioral disturbances). Scholars also understand that the head of an institution might be prejudiced against persons of color, such that a school board president would never consider hiring a black principal, though he or she might welcome black cafeteria workers. These examples represent *institutional racism,* a problem that's substantially more potent, though it's often difficult to spot, compared to *interpersonal racism,* which is often (though not always) obvious (Sue 2010).

"Institutions have great power to reward and punish," remind Louis L. Knowles and Kenneth Prewitt (1969, 5), authors of *Institutional Racism in America.* In the above examples, educational institutions decide whose intellect flourishes, who receives the best career opportunities, and whose self-respect gets the most encouragement. Likewise, medical institutions, financial institutions, religious institutions, media institutions, and other organizations reward and punish by distributing goods and services to some people more than others. No society distributes social benefits perfectly equitably, write Knowles and Prewitt (1969, 5–6). "But no society need use race as a criterion to determine who will be rewarded and who is punished. Any nation that permits race to affect the distribution of benefits from social policies is racist." The most cursory glimpse of the sociology literature shows that institutional racism has a very real impact on the life chances of all persons of color in the United States (Brown et al. 2003; Feagin 2006, 2000; Pollack 2008; Entman and Rojecki 2000; Alexander 2012; Bonilla-Silva 2003; Martin 2017, 2015). And because historical inequalities contribute to contemporary ones, yesterday's institutionalized policies and practices shape racial disparities today (Katznelson 2005; Fredrickson 2002; Thompson-Miller, Feagin, and Picca 2015).

In the broader, academic sense that joins interpersonal and institutional dimensions, the Tea Partyers expressed five ways of thinking about racism—a five-runged ladder, if you will—that range from outright denial to full-throated acceptance, and a bit beyond.

Racism as a Myth

Because most conservatives take a dim view of affirmative action and social welfare programs, you'd think they might flat-out deny that racism is a salient social force. That is indeed the case for some black Tea Partyers; let's call them racism *deniers.* Jake, a cab driver, denied that racism is a "thing," explaining that black people and white people have equivalent opportunities to succeed. "I don't ever see a white person treated better than I am just because they're white," he said. "I think Barack Obama is a perfect example of that. By winning the White House, Obama has done what Clinton did and what Bush did. He's getting the same praises, the same criticism. It doesn't matter that his skin is black." Similarly, Dale, a political commentator, told me he had experienced exactly one racist incident in his fifty-two years:

> The only racist thing I can point to is one night I was at a bar with some friends having drinks. I excused myself to go to the bathroom. As I go into the men's room, a white guy comes out and points down the stairs to the parking lot and says, "Oh, your bathroom's out there." Now, maybe people say nasty stuff behind my back, but that's the only time to my face. I'm lucky I haven't had to deal with racism other than that.

Len, the former federal official, did Dale one better. When I asked him whether he thinks racism is widespread, he answered, "You know, I've never experienced racism, ever? It's never impacted my life. I've never seen it. I get picked up by cabs. I don't have problems with law enforcement."

Note that all three men seem to have thought about racism solely in terms of interpersonal encounters. Blatant infringements of racial social norms are rarer today than in the past, so if your sole marker of racism is a racial epithet from a stranger or "KKK" spray-painted on your garage door, a social scientist would say you're underestimating the magnitude of the problem.

But Len went on to deny even institutional forms of racism:

> I don't believe there's institutional racism in the United States. You'd be crushed if you tried to institute racism. It may be the case that people in some communities may not like me because of the color of my skin. But if I sit down and talk with them, I believe they will understand me based on the content of my character, not the color of my skin. So I think there are some individual prejudices out there; we can't get around that. But institutionally, America's not a racist nation.

Similarly, Melvin, a sixty-one-year-old software developer, denied unequivocally the existence of institutional racism. He said if we're treated poorly by the criminal justice system, for example, it's our own fault:

> If you're asking whether black people are arrested more or sentenced to prison for longer sentences because they're black, I couldn't disagree more with that statement. We are committing those crimes. We have a history of being thugs, of doing bad things. People are less afraid of a white couple walking down the street at night than two black guys with a boombox. The likelihood of nothing happening in both of those scenarios is fairly high, but if you understand historical trends it makes sense to be more afraid of the two black guys.

More subtly, Len presented institutional discrimination as such a risky practice that no organization would engage in it. His argument was that institutions understand the legal consequences of discriminatory behavior. And the social and financial costs of corporate misbehavior loom large when every passerby owns a cell phone:

> What I'm saying is that I do not believe there is any institution in the USA that sets forth a policy that says, "We're going to discriminate against someone based upon their race." That's against the law. You cannot do that. In today's world where everyone has a cell phone camera and everything, you can't hide unfair practices. It will get out and it will crush you. Furthermore, that's what the free market does. If you expose someone for those nefarious types of practices, then they're not going to be successful.

Of course, Len is correct: outright discrimination isn't a part of a rational business plan. So no business today launches a policy—much less announces it—whose primary intent is to discriminate. Yet concern over possible lawsuits hasn't stopped hospitals from allowing physicians to order fewer tests and less top-shelf medicines for their black patients, nor from getting defensive when their discriminatory decisions are challenged (Nittle 2017; Hoberman 2012). And fear of being outed by internet-savvy whistleblowers hasn't stopped the auto industry from charging African American customers higher interest rates and offering fewer rebates than whites, even when black customers have better credit (National Fair Housing Alliance 2018). If Len sounds like a wishful thinker who feels personally protected from racism, it could be because conservatives feel more optimistic and in control of their lives compared to liberals. That's the conclusion of a 2012 study that found that conservative university students had more agency than liberals as well as "a more positive outlook . . . as indicated by greater optimism" (Schlenker, Chambers, and Le 2012, 131).

But to my surprise, very few Tea Partyers I spoke with unequivocally denied the existence of racism. It's true that conservatives typically *downplay* the power—and sometimes the very existence—of racism and other interpersonal and structural forces that can shape a person's life trajectory. "The reach of human memory is a long one, and particularly so in the case of race, which combines the remembrance of subordination with a physical marker," writes political scientist Ashleen Menchaca-Bagnulo (2018). That's "something that conservatives often deny."

Racism as an Excuse

The next rung from outright denial is the notion that African Americans use racism inappropriately as the default explanation for disappointing outcomes. In this formulation, African Americans blame white people for difficulties that too often emanate from black folks themselves. Tea Partyers who offered this explanation—let's call them racism *deflectors*—don't deny that racism exists; they simply see it as a red herring for internal problems that have little to do with white people.

Chief among these problems are alleged character flaws such as lack of accountability, poor work ethic, and a tendency to focus on the present instead of planning for the future. Dave, a thirty-two-year-old youth group worker, said African Americans need to address racism but not at the expense of taking responsibility for their actions. "I'm not willing to say that institutional racism isn't real, but I also believe we should promote accountability, because until people own their actions, they're not going to see a path forward." Similarly, Rod, a fifty-three-year-old son of a small-business owner, bemoaned African Americans' lackluster work ethic:

> Black immigrants are doing much better than African Americans. That's not necessarily racism; there's no reason why a white person would be racist toward me but not toward someone from Tanzania whose skin is much darker than mine. We have to look inward. Why are Asians doing so much better than blacks are? They face discrimination, but they work 14 hours a day just so their kid can have a better future. Next thing you know, the kids are doctors, lawyers, and engineers doing great, making $250,000 a year. We're not doing that in the black community. We have challenges that maybe white people don't have, but we're not overcoming them the way other immigrants are.

To Byron, the retired police officer, young African Americans are too present minded; they don't think enough about the long-term consequences of their decisions. But it's not entirely their fault, he says:

> Too many of our kids see no reason to be in school, and I believe that's because we ask them what they want to be when they grow up. That's the wrong question. We should ask them, "Where do you want to live? What kind of house do you want to have? What kind of lifestyle do you want?" I tell teachers that asking about a future profession is too abstract for most kids. It makes it hard for them to connect being in school today with any future moment. When we ask them what kind of life they want to lead, that's a lot more tangible.

Similarly, Tea Partyers blamed absent black men for abandoning their responsibilities as partners and fathers, a present-minded decision that can deprive children of an opportunity to learn persistence, patience, perseverance, and other important values from their fathers as well as their mothers. "I would say the breakdown of the family structure would be the number one factor in the deterioration of the black community," Reverend Isaac said.

Above all, many interviewees agreed, African Americans too often think like victims of white people instead of self-saboteurs. Lindsay, who grew up in a housing project in the 1960s, recalled how readily his fellow tenants blamed "the man" for their dilapidated living conditions. But when Lindsay and his family had excitedly moved in, the property had been pristine:

> Within a short amount of time, I saw that the building became a huge ghetto. I was only a little boy, nine or 10, and I would walk home from school, and 90 percent of the time the elevators were broke and you had to walk up the stairwell. Well, all of the lightbulbs were busted in the stairwell. So you're walking in the dark, walking on broken wine bottles and you hear that sound echoing off the walls and the smell of urine. This was a brand-new building when we got there and everybody around me kept saying it was the white man's fault. Even as a little boy I knew that wasn't right, and I sarcastically said, "Well, how do we stop these mean white people from sneaking in here and urinating in the stairwells?" I think that was the roots of my conservative point of view.

False victimhood, interviewees argued, damages the psyche because it locks black people into thinking of themselves as second-class citizens. Mary, a stay-at-home mom who home-schools her teenage children, grew up in a low-income neighborhood. But to her mind, that doesn't make her any less capable. Her conservative blog, which she started as a way of expressing her political grievances, has thousands of followers on Facebook:

> I could've played the victim card: woe is me; I'm a poor black girl from the ghetto. But that doesn't make sense. My son is struggling with math right now. Should I teach him that math is a racist construct? Should we all speak Ebonics because of colonialization? I don't think we do ourselves any favors when we fall into that mindset. There is nothing a white person can do that I can't do based on my intellect alone.

Several interviewees said that African Americans' poor decisions limit them much more than racism does. "We make unrealistic choices," Byron noted, citing how readily black parents allow their children to pursue statistically unlikely careers as professional athletes instead of encouraging them to pursue higher education. James, the IT executive, who lives in a state that allows him to openly carry his firearm, says he's never been stopped by police in his community. He says it's because he dresses well and carries himself respectably. "And then you've got thugs on the corner with their pants sagging. They're the ones who get stopped."

Finally, several people identified black cultural norms that stigmatize achievers as racial turncoats. Reverend Isaac, a former substitute teacher, recalled his students deriding their high-achieving classmates for excelling. "They had this mentality. They would say, if you're speaking proper English, then you're trying to be white. If you're trying to make the honor roll, then you're some kind of sellout and you're not really black. This was a very dominant way of thinking."

Whether they be personality characteristics, personal behavior, or cultural norms, the actual reasons that African Americans suffer high rates of unemployment or wind up behind bars has become obscured by incessant talk of racism, these Tea Partyers argue. Conservative journalist George Schuyler took a similar tack in 1967 when he criticized black leaders for rushing to defend Rep. Adam Clayton Powell, Jr., of Harlem, who was stripped of his position as chair of the powerful House Committee on Education and Labor after being accused of misappropriating funds. "Race! Race! Race! was dinned daily into the masses . . . The important thing to remember is that the Powell case is not by any means the first in which this same element [black leaders] has used race as an alibi and excuse to cover up moral dereliction" (Schuyler [1967] 2001, 107–8).

Racism as Too Broad

A third group of Tea Party sympathizers sees racism as too blunt a way of framing a social problem that is real but circumscribed. These are racism *restrictors*—people who acknowledge racism but restricted it primarily to specific circumstances. Sometimes those circumstances are historical, in which case Tea Partyers frame racism as a danger to previous generations but not contemporary ones. Byron recounted a story in which his father, who delivered ice to homes in Mississippi during the Depression, was called into the office of his employer. A white customer had complained that the black deliveryman had "looked at her a little too hard." For the moment, Byron's father defused the tension with humor. "My dad said, 'Wait a minute. Before we get too wound up in this, let's set the record straight. Miss So-and-So ain't worth looking at. She's got to be one of the ugliest women in town.'" The manager agreed. "'You're right,' he said. 'But the white guys at the feed store was talking about it, and they're saying they got to do something. I'm sending you up North to be with your relatives. I don't want anything bad to happen to you.'" Byron said he thinks about his father avoiding being lynched when he hears young people today complain about racism. "My father probably had reason to be angry with white folks. He was born in 1913. I don't understand what a young black man, who was born in 1990, who has never experienced any of that discrimination, is so angry about."

Rod, the small-business operator, says the school system in and around New York doesn't work for black kids. But he circumscribes the effects of race, suggesting that racial discrepancies in education may be the result of social-class discrimination more than racism:

> If you're a poor parent, you tend to live in a poor neighborhood and you're limited to sending your kid to a poor school. I don't think a kid going to school in Harlem is getting the same education as someone who's going to a public school in wealthy neighborhoods in Connecticut. If they're both public

schools, I don't know why there should be such a disparity. If you mail a letter, it should get to its destination in a few days regardless of whether you mail it from Harlem, New York or Edison, New Jersey. If it's a public service, there should be a level of equality.

Charlie, a young US Navy veteran, says racism is more regional than national. "Some of the Old South demographic isn't dead yet. Until these people are literally in the ground, yeah, there's always going to be an element of racism, which they pass on to their kids."

Like most Americans, Sheila, a forty-two-year-old political consultant, talks about racism more as an interpersonal problem than an institutional one. She recalls a political race in which she and her Hispanic business partner helped to run a candidate's campaign along with another consultant. The candidate and the third consultant were white males. "The two of us worked really hard," says Sheila, who holds a bachelor's degree in political science plus an MBA degree. "But we didn't get paid nearly as much as our white male counterpart, who got $300,000." Sheila was additionally alarmed when she offered their services to a gubernatorial candidate who refused to consider hiring her—or to even return her phone call. "Race still matters. There's a problem when a middle-aged white male surrounds himself with middle-aged white men." But Sheila talked about racism as an interpersonal problem—how she and her Hispanic colleague were treated by two white men—as opposed to how white-dominated political campaigns tend to exclude nonwhite voices and organizations.

Racism as All-Encompassing

A fourth contingent of Tea Partiers talked about racism as a social force that has become less blatant over time, but that continues to affect people's life chances at both the individual and institutional levels. These are the Tea Partiers who captured how most social scientists see race. "People who say institutional racism doesn't exist have their heads in the sand," says Joan, a retired naval officer. Let's call these Tea Partiers racial *realists* for accepting the presence of racism on multiple levels.

These black Tea Partiers reject conservative dogma that situates the individual—not social forces—at the helm of every person's life journey. What's their reasoning for challenging conservative racial orthodoxy? In some cases, simple self-interest has prompted Tea Partiers to think broadly about racism. Mary, the stay-at-home mom, says she's had more racist experiences than she can count, whether it's being overlooked at a restaurant or being pulled over for driving while black. For Mary, protecting herself and her family from racial harm even comes down to thinking about her adopted children's names. "We dropped my daughter's biological name because it's an ethnic-sounding name. We went with her middle name instead, because I didn't want someone to look at her resume one day and say 'no.'"

Mary may have known about a 2004 study where researchers at MIT and the University of Chicago answered "help wanted" newspaper ads with fake resumés. The resumés submitted for each position were identical except for the applicants' names, some of which sounded white and others black. White-sounding resumés attracted 50 percent more interview requests than black-sounding ones, even though the credentials on each resumé were identical (Bertrand and Mullainathan 2004). A few years later, researchers at Harvard and Princeton who sent trained volunteers to answer ads for entry-level jobs found that white men who said they had been convicted of a felony were as successful at landing a job as black and Latino men who had no criminal backgrounds. Once they were interviewed, the white ex-felons were frequently encouraged to apply for higher-level positions than the jobs they were seeking (Pager, Bonikowski, and Western 2009).

Community interest drives people to think expansively about race, too. Elton, the college student, spoke of touring two sites in Alabama where polluters had made the environment unsafe for African American residents. In north Alabama, a company had contaminated a community's water supply with chemical waste. In the coastal city of Mobile, a paper mill had polluted a historically black neighborhood:

> When we were talking to the people there, they said when they were growing up the paint used to peel off their cars. Yeah, that's how bad it was. Family members were getting cancer. Dying. All kinds of bad stuff. And people in charge didn't care that it was residents of color. Their voices weren't being listened to.

Elton proposed a two-part remedy for communities hit by environmental racism:

> I definitely think we need to critique the institutions to bring about change. But I don't think we should just blame the institution. Black people have been treated wrong since the start of this nation. If you see the government consistently treating our community wrong, we need to say, "Hey, the government's not going to help us any time soon. You know, maybe we need to help ourselves, and get ourselves straightened up, so that we can survive in this nation that treats us like a stepchild at times."

Elton's remedy blends protest, a go-to tactic of liberals, with self-help, a time-honored prescription of conservatives. In so going, he addresses racism at both the interpersonal and institutional levels.

Len, who has worked with the Tea Party Caucus and the Congressional Black Caucus—two Capitol Hill groups that rarely see eye-to-eye—explained that one of the most notorious shootings of a black teen happened because of a mix of individual and institutional racism. We had the following conversation about what happens when young black men are stopped by police:

> Me: Do you think the justice system is biased against people of color?
>
> Len: Yes, the laws are. The penalties for crack cocaine are much stiffer than for powder cocaine. Police officers assume that most crimes are committed by people of color. If everyone in a neighborhood looks alike and there's crime, you'll start to believe that all criminals look like those people. But that would happen in a white neighborhood, too. It's sad. Everybody has a role to play.
>
> Me: So you would say that the criminal justice system is at fault as an institution, but it's partly individual behavior that puts black people at risk.
>
> Len: Yes. But the institution can also be very destructive to the individual because sometimes people make mistakes and stop black folks with that perception in mind.
>
> Me: Rodney King.
>
> Len: I'm not gonna say Rodney King. I'm gonna say Trayvon Martin. George Zimmerman had been conditioned to believe that there was a black culprit in his neighborhood. The only thing he cared about was that they were black.
>
> Me: A lot of black Tea Partyers I've talked to blame Trayvon Martin for being killed.
>
> Len: Nooooo. That's not true.
>
> Me: I'll tell you their argument. They say he was wearing a hoodie, looking like a thug, and he got what was coming to him.
>
> Len: There's not an argument. He was innocent. George Zimmerman should have gone to jail. Even if Trayvon was in the wrong, Zimmerman had no right to shoot him.

Racism as Irrelevant

A fifth contingent of black Tea Partyers argued that racism has nothing whatsoever to do with African Americans' fate. But unlike racism deniers like Jake, the cab driver who felt that blacks and whites have equal opportunities, or Dale, who could recall only one racist comment directed against him, some of these Tea Partyers fully accepted the ugly pervasiveness of racism. They just didn't think it's very meaningful, given African Americans' capacity to overcome. Let's call these Tea Partyers racism *dismissers*.

Kevin, a fifty-eight-year-old real estate broker, explained, "My grandmother gave me some good advice. She said, 'We don't need you walking around angry; my generation paid the price for that. Do more with opportunities. That will make me proud, not you sitting back admitting that we went through a whole lot of hell.'" Kevin's grandmother wanted him to look beyond racism as a tactic, a way of focusing on his goals so intently that racism was a mere distant concern. "You can't change racism," Kevin said. "Why harp on something that can't be changed?"

Jimmy was even more blunt. The son of a social worker, Jimmy understands how racism factors into human misery. But he also knows that giving in to racism is suicidal. His answer is simple:

> Every problem that you can give me, I can fix in two words: *achieve anyway*. Find a way to achieve. If there's racism, you have to achieve. Racism isn't the end of the world. Talk to a fat person about discrimination. Be in the body of [the late paralyzed theoretical physicist] Steven Hawking. He achieved anyway. Some of the problems black people have are horrible problems. You have to achieve anyway.

Like Kevin, Jimmy's preeminent faith in African Americans' ability to achieve despite sometimes long odds resembles Afrocentric conservatives' endorsement of black pride, self-determination, and self-help (Lewis 2013). These are conservatives whose faith in the resilience and resourcefulness of black people represents their trump card over racism and other obstacles. Armed with this reassuring belief in the power of African American solidarity, racism becomes irrelevant.

Kevin said it best when he explained that complaints about "the man" would not have made sense in his household when he was growing up; his working-class parents had more urgent concerns. So when I asked Kevin if he feels racism is widespread, he balked at the question. "The question is irrelevant," he said. "White folks may not like us, but so what? My parents raised 11 kids in the face of racism. If my parents had said, 'The white man kicked my ass today,' my question would have been, 'Yeah, but where are the corn flakes?'"

This five-part characterization of black Tea Partyers—deniers, deflectors, restrictors, realists, and dismissers—departs from Lewis's (2013) four-part framework of black conservatives, in which racism is important to Afrocentrics but not to the black right, neoconservatives, or individualist conservatives, who view African Americans' problems as stemming from anything from problematic cultural norms to irresponsible personal behavior. It also builds on a recent analysis by sociologist Corey Fields (2013), who divides black Republicans into two camps: *raceblinds* and *racial uplift*. Raceblinds don't focus on race; they acknowledge racism but don't see much point in dwelling on it. Raceblinds are the equivalent of my dismissers, who accept racism but deny its day-to-day relevance. Fields's racial uplift group acknowledges racism as a problematic social force that's built into the structure of American society. In my sample this is true of realists and dismissers, partly true of restrictors, barely true of deflectors, and not at all true of deniers.

CHALLENGING POLITICS AS USUAL

Thus far, we've seen that African American Tea Party sympathizers defy expectations by identifying with the black community instead of with whites, and by largely acknowledging that racism is alive and well instead of denying it. Those traits disturb the stereotype that black Tea Partiers use whites as a reference group and don't believe in racism. Black Tea Partyers' perspectives on politics challenge expectations as well. Critics would expect black conservatives to dismiss the Democratic Party in their headlong rush to embrace the GOP. To the contrary, the Tea Partyers I spoke with rebuked *both* of the major political parties: they challenged African Americans' decades of loyalty to a Democratic Party that has failed them on multiple levels, and they called into question Republican policies, tactics, and racism. These challenges to politics as usual were based not on theoretical reflections or fiscal considerations but the need for racial equity, suggesting that black Tea Party supporters place the concerns of the black community ahead of party loyalty. In fact, more than one interviewee suggested that the ultimate solution to representing the political interests of African Americans is moving beyond partisanship altogether.

Democrats: A Failing Proposition

Abraham Lincoln may have signed the Emancipation Proclamation for many reasons, including military gain. Like his generals, he realized that freeing enslaved persons would both deprive the South of its labor force and allow former slaves to replace manual laborers in the Union Army, thus freeing white soldiers to fight. As one Union general argued, "Every slave withdrawn from the enemy is the equivalent of a [Confederate soldier] put *hors de combat* [out of action]" (Owens 2007).

For African Americans, the immediate effect of Lincoln's momentous 719-word decree, of course, was sudden joyous freedom. With the stroke of a presidential pen, the Republican Party established itself as African Americans' foremost political ally. That alliance started to falter during Reconstruction as northern liberals lost interest in pursuing southern racial justice, thus transforming the Republican Party into what historian Harvard Sitkoff (1978, 3) calls "shibboleths of white supremacy." Black uneasiness with Republicans intensified in the late nineteenth and early twentieth centuries, prompted by the GOP's "lily-white movement" that purged black voters and scapegoated African Americans to win election victories (Fauntroy 2011; US House of Representatives n.d.a.). Black voters began to surge toward the Democrats after 1930, when Republican President Herbert Hoover, who refused to be photographed with African Americans, nominated for the US Supreme Court a prominent Republican judge who claimed that voting rights for blacks were "a source of evil" (Daniel 2012; US Senate n.d.) Even though the New Deal amounted to "more like a raw deal for African Americans," according to historians Thomas Guglielmo and Thomas Lewis (2003, 172), because its federal relief programs greatly favored whites over persons of color (Fishel 1964–1965), African Americans were even more alarmed by southern Republicans' full-throated embrace of Jim Crow subjugation. As a result, 71 percent of the black vote went to FDR in 1936 (Jackson 2008). President Harry Truman followed by desegregating the armed forces and in 1946 establishing the President's Commission on Civil Rights, which recommended many measures—such as opening a civil rights division in the US Department of Justice—that came to fruition over the following two decades (US House of Representatives n.d.b). By the time President Lyndon Johnson signed the 1964 Civil Rights Act over the opposition of Senator Barry Goldwater, his Republican opponent, the mass defection of black voters to the Democratic Party was complete (Jackson 2008; Bump 2015; Bolce, DeMaio, and Muzzio 1992). Since then, African Americans have been an ultra-reliable voting bloc for the Democratic Party; no Democratic presidential nominee since 1960 has won less than 84 percent of the black vote (Johnson 2016). Even when given the chance to support black Republicans, African Americans stick with Democrats, suggesting that a candidate's race is less important than their party affiliation, and that black voters support what they feel is in the best interests of the African American community even though they may disagree with progressive candidates about abortion, gay rights, or other policy concerns (Huffmon, Knotts, and McKee 2016; Kidd et al. 2007).

 What have African Americans gained from fifty years of loyalty to the Democratic Party? Not much, say black Tea Partyers. In fact, they say, the Democrats have largely failed black people.

Policy Failures

Some Tea Partyers are highly critical of ideas Democrats have championed over the years. Take eugenics. This American-led pseudoscientific "study of agencies under social control that may improve or impair the racial qualities of future generations" was the basis of the Nazi extermination campaigns of the 1930s and 1940s (Freeden 1979, 645). Yet eugenics—a movement that critics, including black Tea Party activists, say targeted African American women in an effort to limit black births, in part through the efforts of Planned Parenthood founder and birth control advocate Margaret Sanger—is intertwined with the history of socialism, liberalism, and progressive politics. In other words, they say, today's Democratic Party is synonymous with historical efforts to diminish the numbers of African Americans, an effort that continues today by Democrats' staunch support for birth control. Jimmy, a radio producer, put it this way:

> In New York they found that there are more black babies that are killed in abortions than are born alive. If the KKK had planned this and said, "We're going to do a program to make sure black people don't have political power in America and we want you all to kill yourselves because we can't stand your despicable race," we would have a cow. But nobody is upset. It's astounding to me that we'll go halfway around the world and talk about genocide in Sudan. We'll get pissed off at Uganda and try to get them to pass antidiscrimination laws. But no one seems overly concerned about Democrats who push genocidal policies on the black community.

Historians dispute this depiction of Sanger as a racist, citing Dr. Martin Luther King's support for Sanger's work as well as her concern that African Americans might interpret her efforts as directed against them (Chesler 2011; Valenza 1985). But Sanger's racial ideas and even the eugenicist origins of birth control initiatives are beside the point, says Jimmy, the social worker's son. The larger issue is whether Democrats genuinely respect the meaning of the term "pro-choice":

> Pro-choice doesn't mean pro-abortion. It's pro-choice—the ability to make a variety of decisions about what a woman is going to do with the life growing inside her and her reproductive health. So if you are pro-choice, what solutions have you proposed to make it so fewer women have to make this painful decision? Not many people are asking that question. We have a lot of individuals who claim that they're pro-choice, but they're pro-choice to be pro-your-vote and not pro-choice to be in favor of what's best for those women.

Support for abortion rights is only one of several policies that Tea Partyers say place the Democrats on a collision course with the African American community. Overregulating small businesses, which Tea Partyers associate with Democrats, costs African Americans dearly, says Rod, whose father owns a liquor store and a laundromat:

> One of the hardest things about running a small business is how the government would use regulations against us. Inspectors would come into our store and determine what you're allowed to sell, what you're not. They'd shut you down for almost no reason. They would shut you down if you didn't have a welcome mat or a new paint job on the walls. It became that petty. They'd shut you down every few months because of something they didn't tell you the last time to do. It became very oppressive, in my opinion. It gave me a direction on how to feel about government. Government can be too powerful. They should give you fewer regulations and less bullying.

Anne, a physician, offered a similar complaint about government overregulation of doctors' offices: "The government has to come out and make sure the rooms are big enough, for what? Each room in a doctor's office has a sink, which is hardly used. But somebody at some time made a regulation, and once they're in place, they're there forever. They're very hard to rescind."

Nearly every Tea Party supporter I interviewed expressed reflexive concern over federal entitlement policies, which they saw as being championed by the Democratic Party. The most common argument centered on the unintended consequences of programs that guarantee cash payments to people based on their membership in a particular group, such as health care for veterans or Social Security for retirees, persons with disabilities, or survivors of a spousal death. Rev. Isaac's reasoning was typical:

> It's never good to encourage someone to depend on the government from cradle to grave for their support. It kills incentive. It kills a desire to explore and become the very best person you can be. To reach out and learn the world and see how your skills and your talents can be used. It discourages all of that. I'm against the welfare state.

Some interviewees blamed Democratic immigration policies for hurting black workers. Rod noted that Democratic candidates routinely pledge to keep our borders open to immigrants. "How does that help the black community?" he asked rhetorically. "Immigrants tend to compete for the same low-skill jobs that African Americans are competing for." Rod sent me a paper by Harvard labor economist George Borjas, Grogger, and Hanson (2010), whose analysis of fifty years of national census data found that increasing the immigration-related supply of workers of a particular skill group was associated with a 2.5 percent reduction in black wages, a 5.9 percent reduction in black employment, and a 1.3 percent increase in black incarceration. When Borjas and his colleagues tallied the numbers for white workers and compared the two groups, they found that "black unemployment and incarceration rates are more sensitive to immigration than those of whites" (Borjas, Grogger, and Hanson 2010, 256).

Strategic Failures

African American Democrats and Republicans may be united in their goal of racial equity, but the Republicans say Democrats have made woeful strategic errors along the way. Tea Partyers point to five strategic errors that alienate them from Democrats. They start with the frequent criticism that Democrats take African American votes for granted. As Antonio says, "Why do black communities across the country have so many of the same problems? Because the Democratic Party is saying, 'We know they're gonna vote for us. We don't have to worry.'" Democratic National Committee chair Tom Perez admitted as much in 2018 when he apologized to a group of affluent black donors. "I am sorry," Perez said. "We took too many people for granted" (Berman 2018).

Second, when Democrats emphasize racism, their goal becomes changing how white people think. That limits their effectiveness, say black Tea Partyers. For instance, protesting housing discrimination per se doesn't necessarily move African Americans into better housing. "When you talk endlessly about racism and discrimination, it leaves you with no endgame," explained John, the business executive. "Democrats are so busy accusing people of racism and white guilt—two things that are already well documented by social scientists—that they lose sight of the need to find actual real-world solutions to our problems."

Third, talking about discrimination promotes African American victimhood. As Antonio put it, "You can always fight the Republican Party by siding with the victims, because that pulls at the heartstrings." That's problematic on two levels, Tea Partyers say. Thinking of people as victims suggests that they lack the capacity to determine their fate. "I showed my 16-year-old a news story that a fire department was modifying a test so that more black firefighters would pass it and be promoted," says Mary, the home-schooling mother of three. "The very idea that you would need to dumb down a test so that more people of color will pass it was insulting to her. My child says, 'Throw me any test you got. I'll pass it.'" Victimhood also creates questionable notions of authenticity, Lindsay said. "With the Democrats, it's almost as though group loyalty comes from feeling victimized, and you're an Uncle Tom—you're not authentically black—unless you think of yourself as a victim of America."

Fourth, focusing on what white people are doing to black people distracts from what black people are doing to themselves, a decision that could discourage African Americans from addressing internal problems that are wholly within their ability to resolve. Take out-of-wedlock pregnancies, says Len:

> If you go back 50 years, when we start the Great Society programs, the out-of-wedlock birth rate was 6 percent. Now when you fast-forward 50 years later, the out-of-wedlock rate is 42 percent nationally and in our [the black] community I think it's 72 percent. I think we took away that sense of individual responsibility. Took away that sense of cohesive family unity. Something has happened over the years, and that's why government has a role, but government cannot play the preeminent role. As my mother would say, self-esteem comes from doing esteemable things.

Finally, the master plan of the civil-rights movement—countering Jim Crow segregation with calls for integration—has brought unintended consequences that have actually hurt the black community. Living in segregated spaces forced black Americans to be self-reliant, developing their own schools, churches, banks, newspapers, and other institutions that fostered high levels of achievement and a sense of connectedness (Litwack 2000). "[Black] schools were often sources of real and justifiable pride in some communities, teachers and principals were respected community leaders, and school was a haven for impressionable young people, a place where racism didn't intrude, and where Black role models predominated," writes Stanford law professor Richard T. Ford (TheLoop21 2012). Integration opened new paths forward for some, but it also brought unintended consequences. Black schools lost some of their most talented teachers and students to newly integrated schools that offered teachers better pay and more prestige, and gave students generous scholarships and access to more resources. Indeed, black Tea Partyers like Jimmy say integration has been a double-edged sword. Black schools may have been resource-poor, he says, but all-black enclaves offered certain advantages:

> Black teachers lived in the black neighborhood with the black students. You didn't have these white teachers who were imported in these neighborhoods who have to serve time to get their pensions and don't really care about your kids. They don't understand the culture of your kids. These kids don't learn; their behavior problems are astounding. No one's disciplining these kids. You have these entire generations of kids. They can't read; they can't write; they can't function in society. They can't do anything.

Political Failures

When Anne, a sixty-five-year-old physician, decided to run for Congress as a Republican, the political neophyte enjoyed little name recognition. "There were times when I went to speaking engagements, and people would just look at me, waiting for the other candidates to come," she said. So she began challenging the crowds:

I would say, "Why do you live in a black-dominated district where you have African American elected officials, and your school district is the one that has lost its accreditation? Why is your district the one where people are losing their homes and moving out? If voting for Democrats is so great, then why don't you have the greatest district?" People started listening then.

Anne's point relates to a national problem of black political efficacy. For example, in 1960 there were no black mayors. Today, there are over 470 of them, most of them Democrats. It's a remarkable political accomplishment enabled by landmark initiatives such as the seismic 1965 Voting Rights Act, and the subsequent mobilization of millions of African American voters (Morial 2017). What do urban residents have to show for their years of activism? Dead-end schools, not enough jobs, and too much crime, say Tea Partyers. Dale, the political commentator, says black people would question their devotion to Democrats if they asked themselves what return they're getting on their investment:

> People ask me, "How can you be a black Republican?" I say, "Listen, say what you want about the Republican Party, but tell me this: what have the Democrats done for you lately? You're a black person, you live in a black neighborhood, and you got kids. Are your kids learning anything in the local school? How's that going?" People say, "Oh no, the schools are terrible. Half of them drop out in high school." "Okay, well let's see here, how about the economy in the inner city? You got jobs thriving and new businesses opening? Oh no, you don't. You have businesses staying away, businesses closing. So that's not going well. Okay, how about the crime? Is the crime happening in the white neighborhood?" They say, "Oh no, the crime is in the black neighborhood." I say, "So, kids aren't learning, the economy's not so hot, and your neighborhoods are full of crime. Yet you have a black mayor, a black city council, and a black school board. Ninety-nine percent of the time they're Democrats, yet you keep voting for Democrats. What have the Democrats done for you lately?" I never get a good answer to that question.

Dean, a political organizer for conservative causes, says he's similarly astonished by the number of African Americans who apparently never stop to ask themselves if they're supporting the party that advances their interests. "It's one of the most shocking phenomena imaginable. We [black people] actually sit around and blame people who have no power, control, or influence, and give a complete pass to people who do have power and influence and who've been in control. It's just amazing to me."

Ironically, the practical ability of any black mayor—Democrat or Republican—to transform a city may be more modest than many people think, says UCLA political scientist Edmond J. Keller. In a 1978 study, Keller found that black mayors in six major cities wanted to boost spending on social welfare programs but faced structural and human constraints ranging from shrinking tax bases and uncooperative city councils to "parasitic" white workers who commute to and from work in the city but pay taxes in the suburbs where they live (Keller 1978, 50).

A later study of seventy-four black mayors elected from 1989 to 2006 found the same thing: black mayors didn't allocate resources any differently than white mayors do, but not because they didn't try or they weren't devoted to African Americans, their most loyal supporters. It was because they have limited power. "This period saw out-migration, deindustrialization, declining federal assistance, and increasing legal and fiscal constraints on cities, meaning that winning the mayoralty might well have been a hollow prize," wrote the authors (Hopkins and McCabe 2012, 680). Little wonder Dr. Martin Luther King said mayors were "relatively impotent figures in the scheme of national politics" (King 1986, 320). Dr. King felt that while the federal government has the firepower to transform urban life, the mayors of even the largest cities simply don't have the resources to make a meaningful difference for black people.

Personal Failures

Any political impotence does not absolve elected officials from their personal transgressions, say black Tea Partyers. None of the interviewees mentioned civil rights icons such as Dr. King, whose marital infidelities the FBI famously used to try to blackmail him (Christensen 2014). But several Tea Partyers cast scathing critiques of the present leadership, whom they consider self-interested opportunists. For example, Kevin complained that the president of the Mississippi branch of the NAACP had used the organization's funds "basically as an ATM card." In 2013, the Mississippi Secretary of State flagged the state branch of the NAACP for mishandling funds through a nonprofit organization designed to "improve the quality of life for African Americans and other disenfranchised communities." According to a consent order signed by the NAACP, the nonprofit had improperly solicited donations, paid unnecessary card fees on cash withdrawals, and used thousands of dollars to pay for trips to the NAACP Image Awards in Los Angeles and to Paris, France, in violation of state law (Office of the Mississippi Secretary of State 2013). Derrick Johnson, the president of the Mississippi State Conference NAACP at the time, is now president and CEO of the NAACP (Fortin 2017).

Is corruption a widespread problem among African American leaders, as Tea Partyers like Kevin charge? Or are black leaders the victims of heightened scrutiny by powerful people who resent black political gains? Historian George Derek Musgrove (2012), who studies the surveillance of African Americans in public life, says black public officials were targeted disproportionately by the FBI and other law enforcement agencies from the 1960s to the 1990s, but that's probably because they spoke out more often than their white counterparts for civil rights and against the Vietnam war, which made government officials nervous. "That doesn't mean, then, that every black official who's investigated for a crime isn't guilty, is being set up," Musgrove told NPR (Anon. 2012a).

Some Tea Partyers suggest that one of the most common personal flaws of leaders is misplaced priorities: black leaders care more about personal aggrandizement than community empowerment. In fact, said Len, the former federal official, the entire notion of a powerful black community threatens these leaders. "I think there's a fear. It's a fear that if our communities can stand on their own, then certain charlatans lose relevance."

Still other Tea Partyers accuse black Democrats of hypocrisy for living like conservatives but voting for liberals. After a childhood in poverty, Lindsay returned to his neighborhood to find that "a shanty shack that my mother and father kept fixing and fixing" had been replaced by a mansion. "All over the neighborhood they got these huge mansions now. These are black folks who've achieved the American dream. But I bet 99 percent of them vote Democratic and don't believe a black man can make it in America," he said. Rod says he often notices the odd disconnect between how African Americans live and how they vote. "I've always said that most black people come from blue households with red bodies." These interviewees resemble K. Carl Smith, author of *Frederick Douglass Republicans,* who wrote that God's displeasure with his practice of voting liberal but acting like a conservative was contrary to his Christian beliefs, and was enough to convert him from "politico-schizophrenia" to conservatism (Smith and Smith 2011, 1).

And some Tea Party supporters reported unpleasant interactions with progressives who seemed to undermine the Democratic Party's claim to tolerance. Antonio says he was steeped in Democratic politics as a child; as a five-year-old he knocked on doors and "hung out" with Rep. Gus Savage in Chicago. But as an older child when he started asking questions about money, the reception at campaign headquarters grew chillier:

> People began to call me Uncle Tom because I started asking questions about economics. About why is it as blacks we're always just worrying about what the government is doing for us? Why aren't we out there producing capital to help us? I didn't use the word "capital" at the time because I wasn't that smart [*laughs*]. I would always just ask questions of the Democratic Party and I kept getting pushed out and ostracized.

Ashley, a chaplain and one of the first Tea Party organizers in her city, says she grew tired of white Democrats lecturing her about what the black community needs:

You try to have a conversation about what's happening in my neighborhood and they'd say, "No, no, no. What you guys really need is . . ." And I'm like, I know how I overcame and I know what I went through. I didn't get that when I talked with white Republicans. They'd be like, "Oh, really?" It was more "You're telling me something that I didn't know," and they'd accept it.

Ashley is one of the few persons of color in her coastal hometown, an enclave of progressive white ex-hippies. It was there among liberals that she encountered frequent reminders that white people considered black people to be incapable of autonomous success:

As a child I remember them talking about us as though we weren't able to do anything on our own unless there was someone nearby to help us succeed. As I got older, I realized they were saying that I'm lazy and I can't amount to anything unless a white person comes along and motivates me. So I would challenge them. And they'd say, "That's not what I'm saying, Ashley." Or they'd say, "We would never say that about you, Ashley." It was very demeaning.

These comments from Ashley's acquaintances are textbook examples of *aversive racism,* in which people who claim to be free of prejudice toward minority groups nevertheless subconsciously harbor unfavorable attitudes or beliefs about them. Aversive racists frequently "discriminate in subtle, rationalizable ways," write psychologists John F. Dovidio and Samuel L. Gaertner, who go on to suggest that because aversive racism allows negative feelings to coexist with egalitarian beliefs, "it is presumed to characterize the racial attitudes of a substantial portion of well-educated and liberal whites in the United States" (Dovidio and Gaertner 2000, 315).

Because of these multiple failures—policy failures, strategic failures, political failures, personal failures—black Tea Partyers reject the Democratic Party out of hand. There are lots of reasons to support Republican Party, they say. Some see aligning with Republicans as a way both to make the Party more diverse and to provide a political home that represents some of the ideological diversity within the black community. Here's how young Elton put it when I interviewed him soon after Republican senators rejected President Trump's effort to eliminate Obamacare and before Congress passed the Republican tax reform bill in 2017:

The Republican Party is so diverse. It's not a monolith. Everybody isn't a hard-right extreme conservative person. You know, when they tried to pass a health care bill, we couldn't even reach consensus on that. We don't even have a solid tax reform bill right now either. We're all just different, and I just want more people to understand that. I want people to understand that it's not just white people in the Republican Party; it's Hispanics, it's Asians, it's libertarians. I know Hispanics have Republicans and Democrats, whites have Republicans and Democrats, Asian people have Republicans and Democrats. I feel like we're the only group that's just partisan. We're not on both sides. That's going to continue to hurt us, if we don't change that.

Tea Partyers like Elton also see African Americans joining the Republicans as a way to improve the Party's standing with black people. Elton says he knows many African Americans who are repelled by Republicans' reputation for racism. "I'm trying to help take that stigma away from the Party by being a part of it," he says. Tea Partyers like Elton see African American participation in Republican politics as institution building, a conscious strategy to build a more responsive political party from within.

Others view party membership transactionally: they say they support Republicans because Republicans can—and do—deliver the goods for black Americans. Republicans represent economic uplift, which black conservatives feel is a key to racial uplift. Republicans oppose abortion, which some interviewees consider white-on-black genocide. Republicans support gun rights, which Antonio, the former state assemblyman, reminded me was also a *cause célèbre* of the Black Panther Party, whose Oakland-based members carried shotguns into the California Capitol building in 1967 to protest pending gun-control legislation. The Panthers argued that they had a constitutional right to defend themselves from police violence, which was rampant in Oakland (Wing 2016). "I think back to Huey [Newton]," Antonio said. "Back in '68. As black people, we should never want anybody to take away the right to defend ourselves."

By far the most common resonance with the Republican Party is a religious connection that operates on several levels. For single-issue Tea Partyers, conservatism is consistent with their perspectives on Christianity. At one time, Mary was a staunch Democrat (and baseball fan) who said she followed two rules: "I'm pro-life and I root for the Giants," she told me. But she had difficulty finding Democratic candidates who supported her position on abortion, so as a teenager she ventured across the aisle. "When I became a Christian and became more familiar with the Bible, I found some values there that were more affirmed by conservative candidates."

Similarly, Dean was a registered Democrat until he met his future wife, "a strong Christian believer" who inspired him to have a born-again experience. "Over time, I began to realize that the things I professed to believe on Sunday and the ways I was supporting [Democratic] candidates on Tuesday were inconsistent," he recalled. "In some ways, when it's a choice between God and a political party, the decision becomes easy." That's an unusual choice: even black Christian fundamentalists—some of the most conservative black folks out there—are usually Democratic Party loyalists. "[T]he gist is that race matters more than religion in determining the partisanship of most black conservative Christians," write political scientists Glenn H. Utter and James

L. True (2004, 27). "[T]his group can embrace a liberal social issue without surrendering their conservative religious stance."

Byron explained his affinity for conservative politics by likening the Bible to the US Constitution:

> As you know, black folks are extremely religious. And so are the Tea Party people; they're very religious. Blacks think Tea Party people are all Klan members. But if you didn't call us the Tea Party and instead you called us the God and Country Party, black people would come, because that's what we believe in. The number one thing we believe in is the Constitution. It's like the Bible. As a Christian, I believe the Bible is the inspired word of the Lord. Do I understand that there are bad things in there? Absolutely. But do I take it literally? Absolutely.

Finally, Tea Partyers defended their Republican partisanship by citing what they considered ruinous effects of Democratic policies, as noted above. But in the process, some of them used religious arguments. It's not that Democrats are godless, they said. "The Republican Party is not the party of God," Dean explained. "Neither is the Democrat Party. Our relationship with God is individualistic; it's not corporate." Rather, they argued, Democratic policies have led African Americans to godless behavior—unchristian behavior that fractures families and destroys communities. Here's how Rev. Isaac put it:

> It shouldn't surprise us why they [Democrats] are having so many problems with their policies being implemented because whenever you leave God out of the equation, you invite curses upon yourself and you can quote me on that. Yes, the Democratic Party will invite many more curses on themselves unless they realign themselves with Judeo-Christian values that are based on God's scriptures.

No Free Pass for Republicans

But if black Tea Party supporters blame the Democratic Party for failing the African American community, they are no less critical of Republicans. As they explained their many frustrations over what they saw as Democratic shortcomings, they were surprisingly critical of Republicans for what they felt represents injurious policies, tactical errors, and outright racism.

Policy Mistakes

Before the Tea Party came to symbolize white people airing racial grievances, you'll recall that it was known for its opposition to big government, burdensome regulation, and of course, taxes. These concerns were on some people's minds when I spoke with them about their political choices. But when they talked about federal overreach, they didn't single out Democrats alone. They blamed Republicans, too.

Some critiqued how Republicans spend taxpayer money. Jake said Republican leaders are hypocrites for preaching fiscal restraint while voting for costly spending packages:

> The blacks that come to the Republican Party, come because they want lower taxes. And the current leadership in the Republican Party—[Jeb] Bush, [Mitch] McConnell, [John] Baynor—are all voting for spending increases that we're going to have to pay for eventually. It's guaranteed to result in high taxes. We can't keep our money in our pockets when they keeping voting the way they keep voting.

Ashley went so far as to call Republican leaders "spineless liars" for not living up to their mantra of fiscal discipline:

> You can't live in debt. We have a national debt of 13 trillion dollars or something crazy like that. But every time we go to Washington [to talk with legislators] and there's a budget fight, and the Republicans talk about shutting the government down—these are actual conversations—I tell people, "Yeah, right. They're not going to shut the government down." And my friends tell me, "Ashley, they will!" I tell them that if they ever actually follow through on their promises, you'll see me there the next time. You're telling them how bad the budget is and that we need to spend within our limits, and yet they can't even fight for it.

Beyond the Republicans' fiscal governance, interviewees critiqued policy positions that they considered philosophical and practical dead ends. Andrew, a political consultant, took issue with conservatives' insistence that people who are poor lack a work ethic ("That's not true," he said. "You can't do it by yourself. You have to have connections."). Anne said the difference between African American success stories and those who are struggling isn't dedication, integrity, or other personal values—the answer that many conservatives might offer—but "happenstance of birth. It doesn't have anything to do with the person," she said.

Whether blasting Republicans for denying climate change or for opposing a minimum-wage hike, black Tea Partyers were not shy to point out where they felt Republican orthodoxy makes little sense, even on issues—such as the right to bear arms—that most conservatives consider sacrosanct. "I do believe in the second amendment right to bear arms, but I don't believe that everyone needs an assault rifle," Mary explained. "I grew up in the projects, and I saw a fair amount of violence and saw what guns can do. So I've always been pretty adamant about gun control."

Milquetoast Tactics

The very word *conservative* indicates, among other things, respect for traditional ways—"an aversion to rapid change; a belief that tradition and prevailing social norms often contain . . . handed down wisdom" (Friedersdorf 2012). But that doesn't stop some black Tea Party supporters from endorsing tactics that would surely strike some of their fellow conservatives as militant. Here is John explaining what African Americans need to do to raise the minimum wage:

> My whole thing is as a society, as a community, we must be willing to stand shoulder to shoulder with our brothers and our sisters, and be willing to pay the price for righteousness. You say you want to get paid $15 minimum wage? We can have a philosophical conversation about that, about whether that's the right price point. To me, that's a separate issue. But if you want to talk about how to get paid $15, stop going to work! Stop showing up. Walk off the line, put up a placard, and then make sure that your brothers and sisters aren't buying there. If you're not willing to pay that price and the people who live around you aren't willing to stand in solidarity with you, I don't care who's elected, nothing's ever going to change. That's not me saying that; that's history telling us that.

The fact that leading conservatives oppose raising the minimum wage altogether makes John's call for a labor strike—a favorite tactic of labor unions, which contribute heavily to the Democratic Party—all the more remarkable (Cain 2016; Silver 2011).

Jimmy, a one-time admirer of the Black Panther Party, is even more confrontational. He was blunt as we discussed strategies to bring resources to cash-strapped black schools: "Here's my strategy: take control of your damn neighborhood. It's your neighborhood. Take control," he said. "If they're not giving you resources, march over and say, 'Where's our money?' Tax strike until money comes back into our neighborhood." Refusing to pay taxes until you get what you want may sound radical, but if done peacefully it becomes civil disobedience—not to mention reminiscent of the Boston event that gives the Tea Party its name.

Similarly, Wallace, a software executive, says tax money isn't the only thing African Americans can withhold. There's one thing political parties want more than money:

> Parents on the South side of Chicago should be saying, "We're not voting Democratic any more until our kids are going to the same quality schools as the white kids on the North side of Chicago." Why can't every parent in Ferguson, Missouri, say, "I'm not voting for a Democrat unless our schools are better"? Right now, Democrats are saying, "We don't need to give a shit about black people any more. We got the black vote locked up." I hate saying stuff

like that, but look at it. We're not even demanding that you make the system better for our kids.

Rampant Racism

If the Democratic Party takes black votes for granted, the Republican Party assumes black votes are out of reach. That's the assessment of black Tea Partyers like Dean, the political organizer, who found a novel way to prod a local GOP candidate to pay more attention to African Americans:

> I called his campaign office, because I was getting sick and tired of being sick and tired, and I said, "Republicans get a small percentage of the black vote and some of that is the Republicans' fault. You don't care. You don't show up. There's no message. We're not gonna vote for who we don't know. So if your candidate would like, I will host a meet and greet at my house. I can bring people here, church people, if he wants to come explain to us why he deserves our vote."

The Republican candidate accepted the invitation, and the event went so well that Dean decided to form a regional Tea Party group of like-minded African Americans.

But success stories like this one were outnumbered by complaints that the Republican Party simply doesn't understand black people. As a group, Republicans don't get racism—or sexism, for that matter. So says Joan, the retired naval officer who now works in politics. For years, Joan found herself as the only black person—and the only woman—at meetings:

> Early on, it used to bother me. Since I've gotten older, I told my husband, it is what it is. Throughout my years I have shared with leaders how they should have more diversity both in their campaigns and in governance, and sometimes it falls on deaf ears. Unfortunately, they don't see it. When they look at the faces around the boardroom table, it seems normal. I think about my time in the military, and I look at the boardroom table as an officer where it was very rare that you have females, let alone black females. I'm looking at a table of white males and I'm the only woman and none of them see anything odd in that picture. I equate that to my Republican colleagues. They don't see anything wrong with the picture.

At the same time, the Party is afraid to address race-related problems. "I hate this current brand of Republican leaders. They suck," said Jimmy. "They're too afraid to say the black community has lots of problems because they're afraid of being called racists."

And yet, only racists would eschew African Americans whom they view as insufficiently submissive. Kevin said his forceful take-no-prisoners personality rubs many Republicans the wrong way. "The Republican Party likes quiet, meek black people like Ben Carson and Clarence Thomas, black people who know their place and won't make a fuss. I'm not subservient enough for a lot of Republicans," said the former Nation of Islam member. "I'm not a safe Negro. I make them uncomfortable because they want someone who will validate them. I believe in chest-bumping and getting right up in their faces so they can smell my breath. I'll ask 'em, 'Is there a problem, y'all?'"

Anne saw for herself what can happen when an ambitious candidate of color—someone who's not the least bit subservient—meets the Republican establishment. In 2006 when she decided to run for US Congress as a Republican in a deeply blue district, a state party official implied that Anne was arrogant for cutting in line. "I went to the Republican Party headquarters with my money and signed the papers and they go, 'Hmmm.' Because I didn't get their permission by coming up through the ranks, and I didn't let them know I was going to run." Anne lost to the Democratic incumbent but ended up drawing 33 percent of the popular vote and raising over $1 million from small donors—impressive numbers for a political novice. "So now I'm persona non grata with the state Republican establishment," she says. In 2008, she ran for Congress again but was stymied by Republican officials who refused to support her campaign despite her obvious popularity with conservative voters. "The head of the state Republican Party actually told me, 'We can't support you because if black people come out to vote for you, then they'll also vote for Barack Obama, and we can't have that.' I'm saying to myself, 'Lady, you're stupid, because they're gonna vote for Barack Obama anyway!'" This time, Anne raised $4.7 million—four times as much as the Democratic incumbent—but without the support of the GOP state party apparatus she lost the congressional election a second time. Anne's fundraising successes did attract the attention of the national Republican Party. But when they phoned her, they weren't interested in helping her get elected. "The only thing they wanted was our donor list," she recalls. Would her fellow Republicans have dismissed a white man like they did a black woman? "I am not naïve enough to think that racism isn't out there," she says.

BEYOND PARTISANSHIP

Most of the black Tea Party supporters I interviewed are conservatives who identify strongly with the Republican Party. Like their white counterparts, they are patriotic traditionalists who celebrate what they see as the American way of life. Wallace, a software executive, captured this perspective well:

> I am a part of the conservative movement. It's people who believe in God, people who believe in the country, people who believe in patriotism and loyalty and the American way. I love those types of people. I think they represent the ideals that make America what it is. I just feel like, if you don't believe in America and our Constitution, there are a lot of other countries you can move

to. For example, Bernie Sanders, if you are so into Norway or Denmark, why don't you move to Scandinavia? I'm sure they'd be very happy. You can run their government. Don't come here poisoning and infecting America. That is why I don't like that guy. If you don't like America, leave.

These conservatives talk about their respect for *natural law*—divinely inspired principles that distinguish good from bad, right from wrong (Murphy 2011). Byron says natural law is the foundation for our entire system of government:

> I believe in the natural law. I am a Christian; I believe in the Judeo-Christian ethic. But even if I wasn't a Christian, I'd still believe in the natural law that there's something, there's an underpinning of the natural law, there's something that grounds the natural law and makes it the basis for everything else. It's like natural law is the base, and what rests on top of that is our Constitution and Declaration of Independence that depends on that foundation of the natural law. Everything else kind of just sits on top of that.

These Tea Partyers want smaller government, they venerate the US Constitution, and they advocate restraints on the government's ability to reach into citizens' lives. They are concerned about the size of the federal debt, and they say individuals likewise should live within their means. Several interviewees said African Americans can and should follow the same steps to economic self-sufficiency that have worked for other Americans. As Charlie, the Navy veteran, explained:

> What I always wanted to do with the Tea Party, as far as work with the black community goes, is start from the very, very bottom. Let me show you how to save money, balance a budget, things like that, so that you can buy your own house. Get a good job, get an education, go buy your house. Once you have your house, put some more money away, start a business. Something small. Something as small as cooking or janitorial service; just start a business.

At the same time, several interviewees—perhaps one-quarter of them—departed from Tea Party talking points in significant ways. Some felt that Tea Party doctrines were too absolutist for comfort. When I spoke with Mary, for example, she said questions about the role of the government are too complicated to warrant simple black or white responses. She had said that her politics are informed by the Bible, so I began by asking her if that means she embraces a set of core beliefs about religion and politics:

> Mary: Oh yeah. But I wouldn't say I'm a full-throated Tea Party supporter. I disagree on some issues, but I disagree with the other [liberal] side on quite a few issues, too. So, I have aligned myself with a party that most closely reflects the values that I hold and I do believe that that is the Tea

Party. And I do make that distinction between the Tea Party and the Republican Party. There's a divide between the elite class—elite Republicans, establishment Republicans—and the rest of us.

Me: So, you're a pragmatist above all.

Mary: Sure. And an optimist.

Me: Could I just name some standard Tea Party positions and ask if you could give me a thumbs up or thumbs down?

Mary: Sure.

Me: The government threatens our rights and freedoms.

Mary: See, those types of questions are hard because I don't think there are thumbs-up or thumbs-down answers. I think there's nuanced answers. When it comes to questions of conscience and faith, like whether it's OK to refuse to bake a cake for a gay wedding, or whether it's OK for a Catholic hospital to not provide contraceptives, I'm not sure there are easy answers. I do think that there are areas that the government encroaches on that it shouldn't, but can I say that they're out to take away my rights? No. Those are nuanced questions.

Me: For a lot of Tea Party supporters, that's just not the case. It is thumbs up or thumbs down.

Mary: I know! That's scary! [*laughs*]

Me: Do you think that government imposes too many regulations and tax burdens on businesses?

Mary: Yes, I do. In California, businesses are hemorrhaging to other states.

Me: Do you have a feeling about whether the government interferes too much in people's lives?

Mary: That's another hard one for me. I believe that we have a right to have some of the protections that the government rightly offers us. But in order to receive some of those protections I think you have to give up some things, and if you're a law-abiding citizen you won't protest too much.

Me: Things like privacy?

Mary: Yes.

Mary's nuanced answers may have been driven by the diversity of her news sources, which she said ranged across the political spectrum from Breitbart News and The Daily Signal on the right to Salon and Huffington Post on the left. As she explained, "I try to get all my information from a variety of sources. Do I have a confirmation bias? Sure. But you can't really have a civil discussion with someone if you don't know where they're coming from." Confirmation bias refers to people's tendency to accept new information that is consistent with their existing beliefs.

But some black Tea Partyers pushed the envelope further. Few demonstrated more dissatisfaction with conservative/Republican partisanship than Antonio, who criticized both major political parties for focusing on gamesmanship while needy people of all races are suffering:

> I believe in speaking truth to power. I don't care who the power is. Real people are dying while you want to play political games. Stop it. Stop it. We can do better. The only way we do better is if we hold both parties accountable. The only way we do better is if 90 percent of black people stop voting for one party. I guarantee that in a presidential election wherever that 90/10 ratio slips to 60/40 or 50/50, it's gonna be a wake-up call to the Democratic Party to start taking black interests more seriously. I have a friend on a radio show who poses a question to every political candidate: "What's in it for black people? You want to run for office? What are you gonna do for the black people?" Simple as that. It's bad on both sides of the aisle. I never played that game.

Antonio's philosophy of governance goes beyond nonpartisanship. When he served in his state legislature as a Republican, he recruited Republicans to vote with Democrats, thus representing a sort of *counterpartisanship*. His logic was simple: forget your patrons; forget your donors. Do what's right for your constituents:

> In the general assembly, I was a brick builder. As a former police officer, I'm a trained hostage negotiator. My job is to build bridges. Sometimes I was the lone voice of reason in these rooms, pulling Republicans over to the Democratic side of the aisle, saying, "This is a good deal. Let's vote for it. Screw who gets credit for it. It's good for the state; it's good for your district." Republicans had never voted for some of the stuff they voted for when I was there.

Antonio wasn't the only black Tea Partyer to say he supports good ideas regardless of the source. Bemoaning conventional partisanship, Charlie, the US Navy veteran, said he owes his college education to Democrats:

> Once the Republican label goes onto something, we [African Americans] want nothing to do with it. Once the Democratic label goes onto something, the Republicans want nothing to do with it. I mean, I got through school because of the Democrats' idea of giving post-9/11 veterans a GI bill. You can't tell me nothing good comes out of the Democratic Party.

Thus, black Tea Partyers defy easy description because they are not all of one type. There are Wallaces and Byrons who embrace the Republican Party and say they stand by God and their country. And there are Antonios and Charlies who chastise Republicans for choosing political causes on the basis of which party sponsors them. The ideological diversity among my interviewees became clearer as I listened closely to their self-descriptions, of which they volunteered five.

John, the business executive, identified as a *progressive conservative* who feels that conservatives should be in the business of asking difficult questions and challenging convention just as progressives do. "If Wal-Mart is paying starvation wages and Wal-Mart is being subsidized by the federal government because half of their employees are getting government benefits, then guess what?" he asked.

> Don't shop there. Every time I see a conservative voter end up back on welfare on Monday, then shop at Wal-Mart on Tuesday, to me that doesn't make any sense. Pay a little more money elsewhere. Pay the extra 10 cents or 20 cents, but don't patronize a store that treats its employees unfairly. If you do that, you forfeit the right to complain when things go badly for those workers.

Antonio says he's a *compassionate conservative,* as did former President George W. Bush. He says he believes in working with people where they are, with the issues they feel are important. Similarly, John said while he feels that some aspects of Tea Party symbolism—offensive caricatures of Barack Obama, for example—are painful to him as a black man, that doesn't stop him from understanding that other people are in pain, too, and that their needs haven't been met. "I think that one of the greatest problems today in our society is an inability to appreciate that because my pain and suffering is different from yours, it doesn't make your pain any less real," he said.

Len, the former federal official, identifies as a *constitutional conservative,* a person who took inspiration from our founding documents before the Tea Party was even underway. Speaking of CNBC editor Rick Santelli, who famously derided a federal plan to protect consumers from high-risk mortgages in February 2009, thus sparking the Tea Party movement, Len said, "I was speaking about this stuff in 2008 and the Tea Party didn't come along until 2009, 2010. Rick Santelli just really lit a fire under something that I always believed" (Etheridge 2009).

Charlie, the Navy veteran and a self-styled *national defense conservative,* says we will always need a robust military. But we also need fiscal restraint, he says, and we can start by eliminating costly defense programs:

> The one that I always like to mention is the Army's last modernization program. Hundreds of billions of dollars with little to nothing to show for it. They finally cancelled it about three years ago. Another one is a program I actually worked on, the DDG-1000 system, designing for the Navy. They wanted 25 or 33 ships for $1.3 billion apiece, and it was all technology we had never done before. They finally scaled it back to two ships. That made fiscal sense to me. We really don't know if this stuff works or not.

Whitney, a member of the corrections committee of his state legislature, says he's a *common-sense conservative.* He's as tough on crime as the next guy, he says, but he thinks his fellow red-state conservatives get it wrong when they outlaw behavior simply because they find it objectionable.

> Should we be spending money on people who make us mad? You know, I don't like people smoking weed. If you're smoking weed and you're under the influence while you're driving, we already got a law for that. But if police find some in your car—and I'm not talking about a dump truck load of it; I'm talking about a joint or a little in the floorboard—should that be against the law? Especially when police department resources are already stretched thin? I mean, in my state we have 20,000 rape-test kits that are waiting to be processed. Thousands of people are waiting for justice while we try to criminalize possession of tiny bit of marijuana. It just doesn't make sense.

When you consider the range of perspectives in Angela Lewis's four categories of African American conservatives—the *black right, individualist conservatives, Afrocentric conservatives,* and *neoconservatives*—and you layer on the above five categories that emerged spontaneously during interviews, it's clear that being an African American Tea Party supporter doesn't simply represent one way of thinking. In fact, on some issues—Mary's call for gun control, Rep. Whitney's call for lenient marijuana laws, John's support for a higher minimum wage—these Tea Partyers don't even sound like conservatives.

BLACK TEA PARTYERS RECONSIDERED

On November 10, 1963, in a speech to an enthusiastic crowd in Detroit, Malcolm X explained the difference between "house Negroes" and "field Negroes." House Negroes, who lived in a slave owner's home and were treated more humanely than their counterparts in the field, identified with white people so strongly that they lost their identity as black people: "If the master's house caught fire, the house Negro would fight harder to put the fire out than the master would," Malcolm X explained. "If the master got sick, the house Negro would say, 'What's the matter, boss? We sick?' *We* sick! He identified with his master, more than the master identified with himself" (Malcolm X 1965, 10). In Malcolm X's telling, house Negroes were entirely disinterested in the welfare of the black masses, nor in black liberation. In fact, house Negroes refused to entertain talk of running away. "'Man, you crazy. What do you mean, separate? Where is there a better house than this? Where can I wear better clothes than this? Where can I eat better food than this?'" (Malcolm X 1965, 10–11).

Some say today's black conservatives are the descendants of antebellum house Negroes. Professor of social work Ronald E. Hall suggests that living with powerful whites subjected house Negroes to psychological domination that corrupted their political orientation. "Their proximity of house Negroes to the master class required that they embrace the master's political objectives to secure their aristocratic status," writes Hall (2008, 570). "The aftermath resulted in [embracing] the master's Conservatism as a mechanism for maintaining the master class status quo to which the masses of Black folk would have objected."

But none of my interviewees seemed to identify more with white people than they did with African Americans. In fact, they gave no indication of identifying with white Americans at all. Unlike Malcolm X's house Negroes, their "we" referred to blacks, not whites, and their hours of interviews gave no indication that these Tea Partyers are brown-skinned saboteurs in league with white conservatives in a bid to undermine the black community. No one spoke of climate change, campaign finance reform, or other more-global concerns; their concern was riveted on the black community. Their chief difference from progressives was strategic, not objective.

Despite generations of dehumanization that would seem to offer African Americans ample evidence that white society does not value them, I found little evidence that black Tea Partyers are so injured by racist assumptions that they devalue themselves, as some scholars of black conservatism suggest (Orey 2004; Cross 1991). Granted, any given African American can emerge from a gauntlet of diminished expectations to feel, as Shelby Steele (1998, 41) puts it, "a lifelong sense of doubt." But the black Tea Partyers who spoke with me celebrate their blackness, and other people's as well. This finding may reflect a selection bias, since African Americans who live east of the Mississippi River—as all but two of my interviewees do—tend to identify more strongly as black than do other African Americans (Broman, Neighbors, and Jackson 1988). But it also meshes with what many scholars have found empirically—that by and large, the bruising messages about African Americans in popular culture have not lowered African Americans' self-esteem or diminished their self-worth. As communications professor Richard

L. Allen (2001, 13) notes about black self-hatred, "Research does not confirm the widespread existence of this phenomenon." Thus, while critics may condemn black Tea Party supporters as disloyal Uncle Toms who feel ambivalent about their blackness, these interviews—and some previous research—suggest that this assumption lacks solid empirical support.

CONCLUSION

In the end, do black Tea Partiers think about race or racism appreciably differently than other African Americans do? Do they see themselves as apart from the black community, or think of the African American community differently compared to other African Americans? Probably not, which means incendiary accusations of racial disloyalty hold little purchase. What, then, brings them to a protest movement that seems so inimical to the interests of black people?

The easiest explanation for why a small minority of African Americans supports a political movement of agitated white people with dubious racial motives is the simplest one, the explanation that unites their angry critics: there must be something wrong with how these black folks think. But simple explanations, helpful as they may be for making sense of the world, can turn facile on closer inspection (Chater 1997). Referring to the idea that the simplest theory is the best explanation for a phenomenon—a maxim known as Occam's Razor—physicist Lisa Randall (2015, 316) writes:

> My second concern about Occam's Razor is just a matter of fact. The world is more complicated than any of us would be likely to conceive. Some particles and properties don't seem necessary to any physical processes or properties that matter—at least according to what we've deducted thus far. Yet they exist. Sometimes the simplest model just isn't the correct one.

Politics is a leap from physics, but Randall's caution feels universal; if there are truths that unite the physical world and the social world, complexity must be one of them. Surely novelist Philip Pullman (2003, 447) was correct when he wrote, "And I came to believe that good and evil are names for what people do, not for what they are. People are too complicated to have simple labels."

Likewise, when it comes to understanding political choices, it helps to remember that people are complicated, as scholars of nonideological voters and vacillating voters know (Kinder and Kalmoe 2017; Lazarsfeld, Berelson, and Lazarsfeld 1944). What, then, is the most useful way to deconstruct such an unusual trajectory for an African American? It's a sociological truism that adults are shaped from birth by their *primary socializers*—their parents and family members. So in our search for answers it makes sense to start at the beginning of each black Tea Partyer's biography—in the home.

NOTE

1. Interviewee names are pseudonyms and appear without surnames.

Chapter Two

Does It Run in the Family? The Making of a Black Tea Partyer

> My mom always made sure I was in church on Sunday. That's one of the reasons I became a conservative.
>
> —Elton, college student

> My mother once asked me, "How did we end up with a Republican from a house full of Democrats?"
>
> —Anne, physician

Like Elton, many black Tea Party supporters trace their conservatism to their time in church. "I'm not saying you have to incorporate Christianity into the government," he explained. "But when you have a nation like ours that was built on belief in God, you want to promote a culture that incorporates Christian values." Interestingly, for an institution that's such an integral part of African American life, no Tea Partyer used our interview to blame the church for the many problems in the black community. However, they did single out poor parenting for allowing unemployment or incarceration rates to spiral out of control.

Likewise, when they talked about underperforming schools, they didn't always acknowledge how education funding disparities can put majority-black schools on life support (Bifulco 2005; Chemerinsky 2002–2003). But they did mention parents. "Teachers these days have become everything for their students—counselor, disciplinarian, sympathizer, therapist," Len said. "And because parents aren't doing their job, teachers have very little time to teach."

Sociologist Joe R. Feagin (2013), who has written more than sixty books on race and inequality, once told me that his conversations with African

Americans have taught him that black people have unparalleled insights into the social world. The reason: our survival depends on it. "I've found that all African Americans are good to excellent social scientists, regardless of their level of formal education," he said.

In their emphasis on parenting, black Tea Partyers would seem to confirm Feagin's generalization. Sociologists understand that while parents may not be a cure-all for unemployment or failing schools, mothers and fathers do much more than feed, clothe, and shelter their children. Parents have a unique role in their children's *socialization*—the complicated process, beginning at birth and spanning a lifetime, by which individuals become social beings and part of a group (Sääfström and Månsson 2004).

Mothers and fathers do most of the heavy lifting to prepare the next generation for the complexity and nuance of adulthood. As a result, parental socialization affects children in myriad and powerful ways. For example, children who are rejected by their parents go on to experience higher rates of juvenile delinquency compared to children who were raised in loving homes, according to a long-term study of Massachusetts boys. Conversely, the same study found that having a self-confident or educated mother seems to protect children from the long-term effects of growing up in an abusive or neglectful household (McCord 1983). When fathers are loving and caring parents, it reduces their children's risk of depression as young adults, according to Dutch psychologists (Taris and Bok 1997). Other research shows that simply talking with children about drinking can delay their first alcohol use, even when family members are heavy drinkers (Ennett et al. 2013).

An adult's overall approach to parenting makes a difference, too. Path-breaking work in the 1960s by developmental psychologist Diana Baumrind (1971) found several parenting styles that can influence children. So-called *authoritarian* parents, who are controlling and emotionally distant, tend to raise distrustful, unhappy children. Children of *permissive* parents, who are warm but nondemanding, tend to be incurious. *Authoritative* parents—those who are affectionate but insist on rules—provide the best outcomes, raising children who are self-reliant high achievers. While many child-development specialists agree that a combination of warmth and high expectations profit children immensely, some now endorse the idea that giving children a voice in the family can also pay dividends. The idea of letting a child participate as a stakeholder in the household comes from psychologist Laurence Steinberg and colleagues (1989, 1424), who found that adolescents who say their parents treat them "warmly, democratically, and firmly" develop positive attitudes about achievement and consequently thrive in school. However you characterize parents' personalities or their parenting styles, the central lesson of socialization is that parental interactions can have an enormous effect on a child's subsequent attitudes and behavior (Maccoby 1992). "You may not know it," write psychologists Lucy Martin and Virginia Hite (2014), "but your day-to-day behavior, from the way you drive to the tone of your voice, is shaping the way your child will act for the rest of their life."

Parental nurturing may be especially valuable for African American children, whose parents can serve the critically important function of buffering them from racism. To take but one example, consider the many benefits of instilling in children a sense of racial pride. In one study of forty-five African American parents in Atlanta, all of the mothers and fathers said they try to model personal values (e.g., being kind) and moral values (e.g., telling the truth) for their children, but many also took time to instill racial pride (Spencer 2009). That single gift—helping black children embrace their history, their culture, and themselves—could pay off in spades. Fostering racial pride can buffer the corrosive effects of racism on a black adolescent's sense of self-esteem, which can be fragile as teens come to realize the brutality of the racially stratified world they are about to enter (Harris-Britt et al. 2007). A more recent study found that when African American teens take pride in their blackness, it helps them cope with racist teachers who belittle their intelligence and act as though they are afraid of them (Schoenherr 2018).

FOLLOWING THEIR PARENTS

On Religion

Religion plays a dominant role in the lives of millions of African Americans. Whereas roughly half (56 percent) of US adults say religion is very important to them, nearly four out of five (79 percent) African Americans do (Pew Research Center 2009). No subgroup has a monopoly on these feelings; African Americans across numerous income levels—low income, modest income, and middle income—say churchgoing is very important to them (Spencer 1986).

Given how parents can shape their children, it's not surprising to find black Tea Party supporters who draw a straight line between their own parents' religious messages and the attitudes and behaviors the Tea Partyers have come to embody as adults. Many interviewees expressed their adult religious sensibilities as near-inevitable consequences of a faith-filled upbringing. "When you come up in a family that's deeply religious, how can you be against Christian values?" asked Whitney, the state legislator. Similarly, Rod admitted that his single mother wasn't a devout churchgoer, but "she prayed every night and instilled those values." Len remembers his father sharing lessons about empathy and tithing from his own father, who taught him and his ten siblings that "imagination was more important than knowledge, and faith was more important than anything else":

> My father says you're not free if you don't pay your 10 percent on Sunday. 'Cause 10 percent does not belong to you. You're not free if you don't help people along the way. You're not free if you don't empower others because you cannot empower others without empowering yourself. So philanthropy has always been a big issue in our family because our father, who was on the deacon board, always had to give the biggest slice of the pie to the church when there was a shortfall. For some reason, some people just did not believe in giving. They felt they've come so far, they're just going to keep all they can. If you keep all you can, all you'll keep will literally be nothing. You gotta give. So we learned the art of giving and sharing.

These Tea Partyers spoke of a Christian upbringing rooted in the literal interpretation of the Bible. They viewed the Bible as a wellspring of inspiration, a source of comfort and guidance whose veracity they rarely questioned, and whose precepts functioned as a unifying, all-encompassing spiritual compass. Jake's parents bought him his first Bible at age six. Soon after introducing himself to me, it was clear that his religious beliefs were an overarching scaffolding from which he drew everyday meaning and guidance. In fact, Jake mentioned God or quoted biblical verses eleven times during our three-hour conversation. "God's moral law is universal," he replied when asked for lessons he learned during his formative years. Then he described his upbringing:

> My parents are both Christians. As children we were told stories in the Bible. Very much raised in a believing family. We listened to Christian music; we listened to Christian radio. We were told which teachers to listen to and which teachers not to listen to because not everyone is Christian, and whether the pastor is really a Christian and therefore qualified to be a pastor. I went over to China in 2005 and went to an orphanage. I went straight to the nursery. The Bible says in James, chapter 1, verse 27, that true religion for God means visiting widows and orphans and the afflicted people. So I went to China to fulfill that. The goal was to show the love of God in some tangible way.

Not all Tea Partyers dwelt on religion. Jimmy, who argued that much of the dysfunction in African-American communities today is rooted in failed Democratic policies, spoke for over three hours without referring to religion at all. But those who did typically saw their brand of Christianity as a pathway to conservatism. Historian Allan J. Lichtman, author of *White Protestant Nation,* traces the merging of fundamentalist Christianity and conservative politics to the 1930s, when evangelicals protested the New Deal on the grounds that it violated Christian principles of thrift and self-sufficiency and encouraged laziness and dependence. One influential Los Angeles minister pithily captured the nexus between religion and politics in 1935 by suggesting that the welfare state represented "pagan collectivism" (Lichtman 2008, 80). The fact that most African Americans have chosen a liberal political tradition—

while white conservative Christians have sometimes championed white supremacy and racial nationalism—has not stopped African Americans from embracing biblical literalism and supporting conservative causes, though not all of the Christian conservatives I spoke with would call themselves biblical literalists.

On Work

A second piece of evidence for parental socialization concerns work. Interviewees remembered growing up in disciplined, well-ordered homes where children had clearly defined responsibilities. Anne's parents, two US Navy veterans, ran a ship-shape household where she and her younger sister had a structured upbringing:

> There was a time to get up, there was a time to go to bed, there was a time to do things. We always had chores. There were rules and regulations and people outside of our family knew we were the Smith girls. The Smith girls didn't do bad stuff. The Smith girls went to school. The Smith girls got their grades. The Smith girls weren't going to skip class. We were always told that the rules were there to protect us.

Middle-class parents weren't the only ones to establish clear structure in the home. In Kevin's working-class household, his mother, a domestic worker, constructed a similarly demanding environment. It was a household where rules were absolute, which Kevin says engendered a certain toughness in him and his ten siblings:

> We had some scrimmaging, but the rules were clear. My mom would say, "When I come home from work, I don't want to see trash in the yard." She would make us pick up paper down to the corner, whether it was our yard or not, whether or not it was our paper. She'd tell us to pick it up. We were all given a list of chores to perform and we could get out of doing it by saying, "Mom, I'm sick." She say, "Okay, so and so, you do his work." And then when she'd go to work herself, the "sick" person got tested. "Oh, you really sick, huh?" You got sibling justice! So you didn't get to B.S. for long. Being the youngest, I got a lot of perks, but it wasn't a household where if you had a skinned knee, you could bounce on Mom's lap. Unless she saw bullet holes in you, she'd tell you to walk it off.

In such households where children had regular chores and clear parental expectations, it was a short leap from household duties to actual employment. Byron's first job in 1959 came at a tender age and with a biblical send-off:

> The first job I had, I was in Chicago. My dad knew I played ball every Saturday morning; baseball was my sport. He said, "Next Saturday, you got to

go up to the J&B store. They'll be looking for you. I signed you up. You got a job." I said, "Well, Dad, that's the day I play baseball." He said, "No, that's the day you go to work." He said, "You're 13 years old. The Lord started doing his work at 13. Now it's your turn."

Others spoke of learning about work by observation. Hilton's father didn't make much money as an enlisted man in the US Air Force, so he worked two jobs. Every weekday he would return home long enough to change clothes for his night job, usually at a nearby restaurant. "That strong work ethic was placed early in me by watching him," Hilton says. What's more, Hilton's exposure to his dad's work helped him internalize the values that were important to his father, and they stayed with him through adulthood, even after the end of his own military career:

> I was exposed to people taking an oath to protect and defend the Constitution, to honor your country and your flag. I was just raised that way. Growing up and even living in other nations, I saw the exceptionalism that is in the United States. And as I traveled the world, I saw what tyranny can do in other nations. I was fortunate enough to attend the Air Force Academy and get commissioned as an officer. As an officer I said the same oath to solemnly swear to protect and defend the Constitution against all enemies foreign and domestic, to bear true faith and allegiance. I took that oath without any reservations. I served 10 years active duty, then I separated from the Air Force with an honorable discharge to begin a small business. And when I left, no one told me that you are no longer bound by that oath to protect and defend our Constitution. It's a lifetime oath, so that has always stayed with me. I've always been a conservative wanting to protect and defend our Constitution.

Rod learned by observation, too. But unlike Hilton, his lesson was practical, not ideological. As the son of a man who spent long hours tending to his family's small business, Rod found himself working from 7:00 a.m. to midnight seven days a week once he took over the business. "When you own a small business and it's a competitive industry, you have to work all the time," he said. Likewise, James's family surrounded him with three generations of unequivocal messaging on the value of hard work. His stepmother told him he could be anything he wanted if he was willing to work hard. His grandmother got up every morning, caught the bus to work, and brought home a bag of groceries for dinner—as a sixty-year-old. His great-grandmother, a full-blooded Cherokee Indian, was a strict disciplinarian. Given that lineage, James took a no-nonsense approach to working. It's diametrically different than what progressive black Democrats stand for, he said. "Democrats say the man owes them because he put black people in chains. You know what my attitude is? No one owes you a damn thing."

That was certainly the attitude around Wallace's home. Wallace grew up in a lower middle-class household in Virginia. His parents weren't the best money managers, he acknowledges. But his father, a postal worker, and his mother, a school administrator, were adamant about not accepting government assistance. "My parents worked hard," he says. "They weren't the type of people to take handouts from anybody." Conversely, they spurned people who did:

> Generally, the way that was verbalized was that my parents may mention someone who is on welfare. "Why are they on welfare?" they'd say. "Why aren't they working? Well, that's why they don't have anything, because they spend everything they have." I'd hear my parents say things like that. Now, I think my dad at one point declared bankruptcy, but the thing was, he never would depend on anyone else to rescue him. If he got himself in trouble, he'd get himself out of that trouble. He would never go looking to the government. That was just not even discussed in our family. It was always verbalized in a negative light. You got out and you worked.

As I listed to Tea Partyers talk about structured, orderly households where rules and expectations were clear, I realized their experiences weren't very different from my own strict upbringing. Both my mom and dad were hardworking churchgoing, highly principled parents—but they were unabashed liberals. So I asked the Tea Partyers if they thought liberals parented any differently than conservatives. Most people demurred, but Jimmy had a ready answer:

> Here's what I think. I think most liberals are raised with a lot less discipline than we were. We got our asses kicked if we did something wrong. Not all the time. I got talked to; I had to go pull out the Bible and read, in front of them—this is what you did. And of course, I used to try to always talk my way out of getting my butt kicked. My father was really cool because he would listen and engage me in these really long conversations and then your throat would hurt, and your eyes would be watering because he was so profound. And then after all that, he would say, "Now go get my belt." [*laughs*]

Jimmy may be on to something. According to a 2014 survey of 3,243 US adults, nearly all parents (93 percent) agree that it's important to teach children how to act responsibly. Beyond that, conservatives and liberals parent very differently. Liberals emphasize empathy, curiosity, creativity, and tolerance. Conservatives, on the other hand, emphasize teaching religious faith and obedience—the behavior Jimmy's father was trying to teach him by having the boy quote the Bible and by using corporal punishment (Anon. 2014).

On Making Principled Choices

Psychologist and parenting expert Jim Taylor (2009) says it's the nature of children to make mistakes. With few life lessons to guide them, children can seem to lurch from one bad decision to another. "The fact is it's part of your children's 'job' to do stupid things," he writes. While it's actually beneficial to let children fail if a poor decision won't harm them—a spill will teach them not to try to balance twelve cups of water on a serving tray—parents can intervene to help them make principled decisions based on moral and ethical considerations. That's a third lesson that echoed through the interviews.

The simplest principle is honoring parents by following their instruction, a moral obligation that Christians recognize as one of the Ten Commandments. Andrew referred to his parents ten times during our seventy-minute interview in his office, including during an explanation of how he approaches his moral obligations today as a landlord:

> My mother drilled in us, whatever we do, we have to be legal, moral and ethical. It's imbedded in me. I'm not going to do anything corrupt. I am not going to do any illegal practices. I'm going to take care of my tenants. I will provide for them when the roof is leaking and when the toilet isn't working, and I am not going to take advantage of people. I'm going to give to those even sometimes when they harm me. I'm never going to be petty and I won't ever complain.

Parental influence on a child usually diminishes over time, psychologists tell us (Watson and Skinner 2004). So it may be atypical for a sixty-five-year-old adult to make such frequent references to his mother and father. But Andrew wasn't the only interviewee to refer glowingly and frequently to their parents' indelible contributions to their sense of right and wrong. When Len mentioned his home life and his education, he didn't simply mention that he's married and has three advanced degrees. He credited his parents, who told him that being an educated family man was the right thing to do: "Having two parents who stressed education, I have a bachelor's and two master's degrees," he said. "They stressed family, so now I've been married 24 years to my wife."

From their parents, Tea Partyers learned to take principled stands even if those positions were unpopular. For example, Jimmy made no secret of his near-bromance with a certain brash, outspoken conservative who frequently infuriates progressives. When I met Jimmy, I was struck by his ability to stand up to African Americans who think he is out of his mind. Where does that fortitude come from? I asked him. His father, he said. "One of my earliest memories is my dad being booed at a PTA meeting. If my dad thought something was right he would stand up for it."

Rod grew up in an urban neighborhood where many African American residents struggled. Unlike Wallace's parents—the Virginia couple who claimed the moral high ground over welfare recipients—Rod's parents never told them that poor people simply aren't working hard enough. Their approach to helping Rod avoid the same fate was to keep him out of harm's way:

> My parents, I think they were more sympathetic than shaming; they didn't think some people got the breaks they did. And they would say some people made really bad choices, which my parents tried to steer me away from. In my city, there were a lot of dropouts. A lot of gangbangers. A lot of drug dealers. My mother worked really hard to keep me away from that type of life. I wasn't one of those kids allowed on the streets. I didn't grow up with street-hardening like a lot of kids in my neighborhood did. I never became a street kid. I felt pretty early on, even though it's like a medal of honor for a lot of kids who grew up in that environment to have been arrested, that it would be a mark of shame if I ever had to call my parents and say I'm in jail, or I got into a fight at a Burger King. "I'm gonna be locked up for a couple of months, Mom." I never wanted to make that call.

By teaching him that character deficiencies aren't the most robust explanation for poverty, Rod's parents departed from a well-worn path to conservatism. Conservatives frequently base their explanations of how the world works on beliefs about people's *essential* (inherent) characteristics. By this logic, the idea that people are poor because they are lazy or dull leads individuals to favor conservative politics over more-progressive alternatives (Hussak and Cimpian 2018). There's just one problem: black Tea Partyers don't seem to essentialize people any more than other African Americans do. Unlike many conservatives, they don't seem willing to categorize people's circumstances as an automatic reflection of the people themselves, perhaps because of Tea Partyers' (and their parents') first-hand experiences with powerful social forces, like poverty and racism, that can severely limit a person's chances in life. By insulating Rod from a risky environment, his parents placed him in a position where he could make decisions based on lasting principles they were trying to inculcate in him—the importance of family, the value of hard work—rather than on short-term exigencies of the streets.

Similarly, Antonio had a moment of reckoning as a young man that may have saved him from disaster. Living with his mother and stepfather, both crack addicts, and ridiculed by family members because of his light complexion, he had grown suicidal. One day his best friend's aunt spotted him in a group of his friends and asked him to approach her.

> She called me over and she said—it shook my world—she said, "You know, I see everything that you're doing. But Antonio, you just got so much potential."

Then she said three words that just shook me to my core. I had never heard them before. Growing up, I didn't hear it from my parents. I was an honors student in school, but I never heard it from my teachers. She said, "You matter, Antonio." I wasn't really that close to her, but to hear somebody I knew tell me that really got to me. She saw something in me, and when she said that, I think that was the beginning of a change in how I view the world. Because after that I said to myself, "I have a purpose."

Antonio went on to become the bridge-building state legislator whose mission became helping white Republicans understand the black condition. Psychologists might say that his principled decision to be a political mediator rather than a garden-variety partisan was possible because his friend's aunt helped him establish an *internal locus of control*—the sense that Antonio, not forces outside of his influence, was in charge of his fate (Rotter 1966).

ACTING LIKE A TEA PARTYER

These conversations make clear that Tea Partyers credit their parents with influencing their *belief in God*, the *value of hard work*, and the *importance of principled decision making*. Given the history of conservative thought, it's easy to see why black Tea Partyers, like most conservatives, would emphasize these three items. Political theorist Russell Kirk (1993), author of the widely acclaimed *The Conservative Mind*—a book Richard Nixon reportedly said made him a Russell Kirk fan—wrote that conservatism is guided by ten principles, among them time-honored convention (of which belief in God is certainly one); the ability to retain the fruits of one's labor (from hard work); and belief in a moral order that separates right from wrong (as shown by principled decision making).

The life lessons people learned at home were all-encompassing, extending far beyond ideas about religion, work, and making good decisions. Their parents' conservative values were evident across the board. In Anne's household, a conservative emphasis on frugality and living within one's means was on full display. Anne remembers her grandmother's old-fashioned strategy for making sure she covered her monthly debts. "She would put money in jars for rent and utilities," she says. "That taught me the value of careful money management. In the end, my family was able to build houses without incurring any debt."

Similarly, Len's parents lived in Dr. Martin Luther King's Atlanta neighborhood and were diehard Democrats who supported civil rights icon Rep. John Lewis. But they *acted* like conservatives, structuring his life with order and discipline. "In the morning, don't sleep in. Get up and do your chores. Sit with the family. Crank up the lawn mower and cut the grass. Then earn some money cutting other people's grass." In Len's view, it's no accident that he ended up serving in the US Army. "As it says in Proverbs, train up a child in the way he should go and when he is older he will not depart from it," he told me.

In other families, the parents' own support of conservative political candidates and conservative causes made it easy for the children to follow suit. When I asked Dave for the source of his conservatism, he talked about his father:

> My dad is a Republican and I remember during the Vietnam war we'd have dinner at my grandparents' house. All of us would get together—grandpa, grandma, my family, aunts, uncles, cousins—every Sunday. It was 15, 18 people at the table. And at some point, either my dad would start, or my uncle would start yelling about Nixon or Vietnam or Watergate. My dad always took Nixon's side. My mother was not very political. I'd say she probably was a Democrat but ended up supporting Reagan.

From those lively dinner-table conversations Dale went on to volunteer for Ronald Reagan's presidential campaign in 1979. "I've been part of the conservative free-market movement ever since," he says.

Thus, the Tea Party's way of thinking may seem like a recent invention to most people but not to us, these African Americans said. Len said the Tea Party is old news to him, because it represents a repackaging of generations of black parenting wisdom:

> Principles are principles. It doesn't matter whether you're in Nigeria or Italy. Principles are the same. Work ethic. Discipline. Less government. Personal responsibility and accountability. The government can be a stopgap for people in need, but permanent help should not be your destiny. Those are just common principles and values that built this country and built other nations. They're nothing new. The Tea Party is just taking these principles and making them their own. My parents taught these principles before the existence of the Tea Party.

Len all but said that the premise of my book was backwards: it wasn't black folks who had come to the Tea Party; the Tea Party had come to them.

Parents also seemed instrumental in shaping their sons' and daughters' ideas about race. Studies show that some 50 to 80 percent of African American parents engage in racial socialization, a process by which they teach their children how to maintain their equilibrium in a racially hostile world (Parham and Williams 1993; Sanders Thompson 1994; Peters 1985). Not every parent sends the same racial messages. When African American psychologist Margaret Beale Spencer (1990, 124) asked forty-five African American parents what message they've given their children about race, racial equality, or black culture, some took what developmental psychologist David H. Demo and sociologist Michael Hughes (1990) term a *cautious/*

defensive attitude by teaching the importance of deferring to whites, whose racism makes them in the wrong but who have the upper hand in racial interactions and thus should be viewed warily.

Still others adopted an *integrative/assertive* attitude by instilling racial pride while encouraging their children to find ways to coexist with white people. This perspective resonates with something Rev. Isaac was taught by his parents. When he was preparing to immigrate to the United States as a young man in the 1960s, his parents were frank about the racial tensions he might encounter during the height of civil rights revolution. Sure enough, one day as he was searching for a place to start a church, he found an unoccupied building that seemed ideal until he spotted a sign on the front door: "Coloreds Not Welcome." But it didn't faze him, partly because his integrative/assertive parents had raised him to hold his head high. Anne's mother took a similar integrative/assertive tack by trying to prepare her daughter for the resistance she felt Anne would face in a white-dominated world. "I remember my mother teaching me that it's not a lie if you lie to white people," she said. "I have learned since that a lie is a lie is a lie, but that helped me learn how to be able to tell as much of the truth I felt is necessary at the time. I'm not saying it's good, but it was a survival thing."

While it's clear that black Tea Partyers can have divergent perspectives on racism, as we learned in chapter 1, most of the people who mentioned learning about race from their parents seemed to adopt a third perspective: an *individualistic/universalistic* attitude in which children are simply encouraged to work hard, feel good about themselves, and be good citizens. Unlike cautious/defensive or integrative/assertive parenting, this perspective doesn't mention race at all. Socialization by omission, you might call it—teaching about race by downplaying race. On the few count-them-on-one-hand occasions when interviewees' parents mentioned racism at all, it was to reject the notion that all white people were racist. Here's how Mary described the racial messages she heard as a girl:

> If you can't tell by looking at me, I'm half white, half black. So even though I grew up in a predominantly African American area, my mom raised me almost to be colorblind. I don't really like the term "colorblind" because I think you do need to honor traditions people have and their culture and that sort of thing, but colorblind in the sense that she always told me to treat people as they treat you and not based on anything else. You know, just interact with people and see how they treat you and then respond in kind. So those were the big messages I got.

Kevin, whose parents rarely complained about racism, told a similar story. When Kevin joined the Nation of Islam as a young man, he was drawn to the group by its message of black self-empowerment, not by Minister Louis Farrakhan's famous claim, "The white man is the devil" (Lusher 2016):

I had never been indoctrinated that white people were the source of your problems. And so Mr. Farrakhan's message about community, fixing and repairing and restoring, that's what appealed to me. The "white man is the devil" stuff was secondary. As a matter of fact, Elijah Mohammed explained why he used that. He said the black man has to be shaken by the lapels. You got to get the fear out. I know with my people you got to be bold. So, that's why when that was said, Elijah Mohammed was trying to get their attention and Mr. Farrakhan was doing the same thing. In fact, the devil is a spirit. It's not a race; it's a spirit-type thing at the end of the day.

Andrew's parents rarely mentioned race either. His father—a man who introduced Andrew to Republican arch-segregationist Senator Strom Thurmond, who later hired the young man—refused to call white people racist even when they vandalized his family's thriving farm:

There was a lot of jealously, on both sides, black and white, over the success of my father's farm. In the 1970s we had these fine horses. One morning we woke to find the horse stables were burned down and as we rushed out of the bed we saw these three white gentlemen walking away with gas canisters in their hands. Yes, we witnessed that and we were so angry. My brother said, "Daddy, you think these white people like you but they hate us. Look at what they've done. They want to destroy you." My father said, "Look, those are not three white men, those are three individuals filled with hatred. Don't ever judge them by the same standards they judge us. We are individuals, not groups. We'll go after those individuals, not white people." I said to myself, Whoa! I'll never forget that lesson. I think about it often. That's one of my few and only lessons from my parents about race.

It happened in interview after interview: as the parents downplayed racism, so too did their sons and daughters. Lindsay said that when his father integrated his city's fire department in 1952, the white firefighters "treated him like dirt." At one point, they so insisted on maintaining segregation that they wouldn't let his father use their silverware. One day his dad couldn't find the "black spoon" and grabbed a "white spoon" to stir his coffee. A white firefighter took the spoon and flung it into the sink, warning him to "keep his black hands off of their spoons." Yet two years later when Lindsay's father's oxygen mask malfunctioned during a blazing fire, the same firefighter entered the burning building and carried him out, saving his life. The two became lifelong friends. Lindsay's father even spoke at the man's funeral. That story dovetailed with Lindsay's own adult experience:

I spent two years in the Army and one thing I learned is just because you share someone's skin color does not make them your friend or your brother. I just judge each individual for who they are. I've been criticized my whole life for that, accused of having too many white friends. I don't think all white folks are bad. I don't think all people of any race are bad. I think if you're a black jerk or a white jerk, I don't want you in my life. If you're a good person and you're purple, I don't care. When I was in the Army, there were no white guys in my neighborhood trying to sleep with my girlfriend. It was all brothers.

Like Lindsay's firefighter father, Byron's father had a compelling racial epiphany that served as a lasting lesson to his son about the value of considering all people even-handedly regardless of skin color. Shortly after returning to his boyhood state of Mississippi to purchase a home, Byron's father found that his African American neighbors on both sides of his property were disputing the land sale. The neighbors claimed (falsely) that the seller, an elderly African American woman, had no right to sell the property because she didn't own it. In a move that startled his neighbors, Byron's father hired a local white attorney who was reviled—and feared—in the black community for having defended several white men who were eventually convicted of committing a notorious civil rights atrocity. The lawyer visited the lot and moved the property markers to their rightful positions, telling the neighbors, "Y'all move another one of those survey sticks and y'all are gonna have to answer to me." The neighbors backed off. When the lawyer brought the paperwork to finalize the sale, Byron watched his father make a painful admission. He acknowledged that he couldn't pay the attorney for the extra time it had taken to resolve the dispute:

> My dad said, "I might not have all your money because I don't know what you're gonna charge me, but I'm good for it." The lawyer sat there and he said, "Fred, let me tell you something. We were looking for folks like you to come back home. You know something, I'm not concerned about my bill." He took his bill and tore it up. He said, "Fred, I would rather have your friendship than your money." I looked at my father and I saw a tear come to the corner of his eye. The lawyer said, "There was a part of my life where I did things that I am not proud of." He was talking about defending those white men. "But I want your friendship," he said. My dad accepted his offer. The two of them used to get together and talk about world problems. My father remained friends with him until they both passed away.

Like his father did before him, Byron has an innocent-until-proven-guilty attitude toward white people. Like Mary, whose mother taught her to be colorblind, and Andrew, whose father the horse breeder saw arson as a crime but not a hate crime, and Lindsay, whose firefighter father saw the redemptive potential in even the most hardened racist, Byron isn't so naïve that he assumes there are no bad white people. But he doesn't assume people are bad because they're white.

As children and young adults, these black Tea Partyers were exposed to their parents' race-neutral attitudes in different ways. Mary was told to treat all people with equal respect unless they disrespected her. Kevin's parents didn't complain about racism. Andrew's, Lindsay's, and Byron's fathers showed their sons the importance of relating to white people as individuals, not as members of a group. The overriding lesson was there is little to gain by dwelling on racism: you shouldn't treat white people with particular deference simply because they are white, nor should you expect to be treated poorly because you're black. Sometimes this lesson came with a painful corollary about African Americans: just as all white people aren't necessarily your enemies, don't expect all black people to be your friend just because you're black. Lindsay learned that lesson himself when his friends tried to sleep with his girlfriend, as did Byron from the next-door neighbors who tried to undercut his father.

The many life lessons Tea Partyers learned from parents and other family members came through multiple paths, as suggested by the examples above. Sometimes advice came in the form of explicit instruction, as when Anne's mother schooled her in the art of practical prevarication. At other times, such as when parents led by example, guidance was implied. Mary's mother was such a dedicated worker that the daughter thought her mom might have a touch of obsessive-compulsive disorder. "She didn't miss a day of work in 40 years," Mary said. "It was just, you show up to work. Rules are there and they're rigid. So, I saw the value that she put in hard work and how she valued a work ethic and being there, being on time. Putting in a hard day's work was really important and I saw that every day."

Even when parents and other family members didn't seem to model behavior intentionally, their sons and daughters learned by watching family members interact among themselves and others, and forming their own conclusions. For example, Byron first became concerned that people can overrely on government aid programs by watching his parents raise his younger sister. He said his parents were struggling financially when he was born but they had more money by the time his sister came along. As a result, they spoiled her. Today, his fifty-eight-year-old sister "still thinks momma should take care of her." Their mother, who lives in a nursing home, is ninety-four years old.

Byron's learning through childhood observation resembles an experience of black Tea Party supporter Kevin Jackson (2009). Jackson grew up in a Texas household where his mother's white beauty shop clients gave him generous Christmas gifts as a boy. Meanwhile, his inattentive father was a habitual liar, a scam artist—and a staunch Democrat. Jackson's conclusions, which would help bring him to conservatism as an adult, were simple: (1) white people aren't racist; and (2) Democrats don't believe in self-sufficiency.

Sometimes simply knowing information about a parent's life experiences has a powerful impact on a child's turn to conservatism. Two interviewees, both of them men, oppose abortion today because they themselves were nearly statistics. As Antonio explained, "My mom wanted to abort me when she found out she was pregnant, and that's one of the reasons I'm a strong pro-life person today."

THE LIMITS OF SOCIALIZATION

Socialization limits people. It constrains a person's free will. By privileging the group's ideas about what is good or bad, socialization sacrifices the individual on the altar of the collective. Renowned German sociologist Georg Simmel (1950, 101) put it this way: "A group secures the suitable behavior of its members through custom, where legal coercion is not permissible and individual morality not reliable." Other observers of socialization are more blunt. "The individual is an ass, and yet the whole is the voice of God," composer Carl Maria von Weber wrote sarcastically (Simmel 1950, 35). As von Weber would undoubtedly agree, socialization isn't always logical. In fact, it may not even be moral: the late Polish sociologist Zygmunt Bauman (1991, 144) went so far as to say that socialization actually neutralizes the "disruptive and deregulating impact of moral behaviour" by forcing individuals to relinquish their personal sense of right and wrong. That's why socialization can be "devastating for . . . human . . . individuality," say education specialists Carl Anders Säafström and Niclas Månsson (2004, 253).

But socialization also has limits. If it didn't, people would never deviate from the norm. Students would always obey their teachers, teens would never defy authority figures, and there'd be no crime (outside of families where criminal parents teach their children to break the law). Not all behavior can be controlled simply by invoking social norms, as anyone with a loved one who abuses drugs—or people—knows all too well.

Black Tea Partyers show the limits of socialization in several ways. First are the families where the parents' conservatism didn't rub off on their children. Dave, the Tea Partyer whose Sunday dinners with his large family invariably became raucous political free-for-alls, says his Nixon-loving father and Reagan-loving mother supported him when he attended the 1980 Republican convention, and they flew him to Washington, DC, to witness President Reagan's inauguration. He's been a political extrovert since high school, running for student council and attending Republican events. Yet Dave's younger sisters are cut from different cloth: one, a former conservative, has in Dave's words "slithered to the other side" after years of living in San Francisco; the other is so taciturn that family members don't know her politics. I asked Dave how two conservative parents managed to raise a conservative, a liberal, and a political enigma. "I don't know if I can say my parents had much to do with it one way or the other," he said, suggesting that his close and supportive community of fellow conservatives is probably more responsible than anything for nurturing and sustaining his political sensibilities.

The second indication of the limits of socialization are Tea Party supporters whose politics took a sharp right turn from their liberal mothers and fathers. Their decision sometimes mystifies their parents. Anne's mother once asked her, "How did we end up with a Republican from a house full of Democrats?" Hilton, the state legislator who was shunned by area ministers because he's a Republican, comes from a family of Democrats, too. When I asked Hilton how his politics happened to diverge from his family's, his answer, excerpted in the previous chapter, merged into a rationale for conservatism itself:

Hilton: My mother was a very liberal Democrat. She was involved with the local Democratic Party. I never challenged her views. I just simply observed them. I have brothers and sisters who are liberal Democrats. I have one brother who's politically moderate, but most of my family, they're liberal Democrats.

Me: How do you think that happened?

Hilton: Actually, individualism. We're each all our separate persons. I defy someone to place me into a box, saying you must behave this way because you're a black person. In fact, I refuse to be called an African American. I'm not. I'm an American. This is my country. Why would I not claim the most powerful, the most magnificent, most benevolent country the world has ever seen as my own? I think we need to get away from these hyphenated names—African-American, Asian-American, Hispanic-American. That divides our country; it works against thinking we're one nation under God. Actually, I think there's something sinister about these labels, because it gives too many people the idea that this not really your country. Your allegiance is not really here; it's to Africa or elsewhere, where your descendants are from. It's because of that understanding that there's a tendency to not act as an owner, but instead as a renter, because this is not your place. And anyone who has owned property or rented knows that renters do not take care of the property the same way you do as an owner. We need to get more of the black community to see this as our country, to seize the opportunities that are here, and to see that they don't need to depend on the government to provide for them, but instead their own work ethic can provide for them and their families.

John laughs when he says his liberal mother pegged him as a pint-sized political rebel after he accompanied her one day as a toddler to a voting booth and insisted on pulling the lever for a Republican. Like Anne and

Hilton, he grew up around liberals; his mother, grandmother, and aunt were staunch Democrats, and his father volunteered with the Student Nonviolent Coordinating Committee (SNCC), the civil rights organization that played pivotal roles in the 1963 March on Washington, the Mississippi Freedom Summer voter registration campaign in 1964, and community organizing throughout the South. In retrospect, he says living with liberals helped him sharpen his political beliefs: "I always tell people I am a better conservative because I grew up in a liberal household. I've been forced to really think through my convictions and consider not just what I believe, but why I believe it." He calls himself the black sheep of the family, but he says he sees the logic of being a conservative when he thinks about the disparate organizations that joined to create the civil rights movement. The movement, he says, was a rope made of contrasting ideological strands:

> The reality is there were all these disparate voices, disparate groups within this movement for change. You had a Southern Baptist preacher [Dr. King], you had SNCC, but you also had the Nation of Islam and Malcolm X. The unspoken truth is that there were many times when they couldn't stand each other. We forget about the fact that Coretta Scott King and Betty Shabazz had to backchannel to make sure that their husbands, possibly the two most influential men in the history of civil rights in the United States, could even have a conversation.

David J. Garrow, author of *Bearing the Cross: Martin Luther King, Jr., and the Southern Christian Leadership Conference,* disputes John's claim that the March 27, 1964, meeting on Capitol Hill between Malcolm X and Dr. King—the only time the two leaders ever met—was arranged by their wives. "I'm 100 percent sure that was a completely happenstance encounter," he wrote in an email to me (personal communication, Sept. 30, 2018). But John's main point is an appeal to diversity: if civil rights organizations can agree on overall objectives even if they disagree on how to reach them, then surely there's room for black Republicans, Democrats, and Independents to unite behind shared goals even though they may disagree on strategy.

John's case highlights a third limit of socialization: personal experience. Regardless of how tight-knit a family might be, parents and children inevitably have different day-to-day experiences, which can affect their political inclinations. For example, John's father came of age in the 1960s, when American racism was more prominent than it is today:

> My father's time with SNCC feels weird to me because I had different experiences with racism. I wasn't necessarily bludgeoned with the prejudices that many older people experienced almost each and every day of their lives from a young age, whether overtly or kind of tacitly. In some ways, as I look at it now, I didn't grow up in a world where I didn't think a black man couldn't be president. I just thought it hadn't happened yet. And I think that's a

profoundly different mindset and experience to have. It's a freeing thing in some ways.

Regardless of John's home socialization, his political outlook differs from his father's because their experiences have been different.

Media exposure is a fourth limit on parental socialization. I asked each Tea Partyer how they got their news, and their responses ran in two directions. Some people said news programming had solidified their conservative convictions. For example, Dale remembered a mediated conversion experience as a young teenager that introduced him to conservatism:

> I started off in 1976 when Jimmy Carter was president and I was about 12 years old. Oh, he looks friendly and he smiles and that's all I kind of expected from him. But four years later at ages 15 and 16 when Carter was running against Reagan, I could see very well that what Carter was doing wasn't working with high inflation, high interest rates, a sputtering economy, an energy crisis, a hostage crisis overseas. All kinds of things were just in shambles. Right about that time I started listening to radio commentaries on KABC talk radio. Every Monday, when I got ready for school I'd turn the radio on and there was Ronald Wilson Reagan on the radio saying here's what we should do about taxes, here's what we gotta do on spending, here's why the government doesn't do this well, here's what the Soviets are up to, here's how the Jews are treated in Russia, blah blah blah. And I thought, "Hmm, very interesting. This guy has some interesting ideas."

The next thing Dale knew, he was volunteering for Reagan's presidential campaign.

Like Dale, many Tea Partyers spoke of consuming hefty doses of conservative news and commentary, from Fox News to Breitbart News, the self-annointed "Huffington Post of the Right." But contrary to my expectations, a significant number of interviewees deliberately consume diverse news sources. Rod said the bulk of his news comes from conservative outlets, but

> I try not to limit myself to that. I subscribe to *The Nation*. I follow *Mother Jones*. I try to watch MSNBC and CNN. I'm not very good at it, but I try. It's still 80 percent conservative media, like *Bloomberg Businessweek*, but I try to get in at least 10 percent of the less-viewed news, so I won't be brainwashed by whatever Breitbart says.

Similarly, Ritchie, a political science professor, makes his students tackle a variety of news sources, a lesson he first learned at home:

> I made an interesting discovery when I went home to visit my family. They've got TVs all over the house, but the one in the kitchen is always on the news and it's always on MSNBC. Now, I don't watch network news. I have a policy about that. But if the only input they're getting is from a particular perspective,

that can be limiting. Very few people ingest news across the spectrum. I always tell students to do that because I believe it will help them to detect bias and arrive at an objective narrative.

And there was a fifth limit on socialization: personality variables. Differences in personality and temperament seem to explain why some African Americans sign up for the Tea Party and others don't. Even among siblings, not everyone seems born to be a Tea Partyer.

Case in point: Kevin, or more precisely, his older sister Joanie. Of the ten siblings in Kevin's close-knit household, Joanie, eighteen months ahead of him, is closest to him in age. That means brother and sister were probably socialized similarly as children, hearing many of the same messages from their parents about how to be in the world. To be sure, Kevin says, the two siblings have similar values, whether it's respect for family or belief in hard work. Yet their temperaments couldn't be more different. Kevin—the fellow who described himself as a chest-bumping getting-right-up-in-their-faces-so-they-can-smell-my-breath kind of guy, is an outspoken take-no-prisoners street fighter. When the Tea Party came along in 2009, he was so unconcerned about possible blowback from other African Americans that he became a Tea Party organizer in his state. Joanie, not so much. "She's not going to be leading any charges," Kevin says. African Americans who are shy or introverted would seem unlikely candidates for the rough and tumble of a controversial insurgent political movement. As former US Senator Alan K. Simpson (2006) once noted, "Politics is a contact sport."

It's the same story with Byron's sister Emma, the woman Byron feels was coddled by their parents. Emma shares her brother's values, but is reluctant to take unpopular positions and has not joined the Tea Party. Emma is a Democrat, and Byron said she didn't even want to acknowledge that her brother had decided to run for public office—until the day he decided to switch parties and run as a Democrat:

> She grew up with the same family as I did, but her skin is not as tough as mine. She kind of still wants her friends to be her friends. So even though she has conservative values, because she was raised that way—you couldn't live in a house with momma and daddy and not understand that—she's like a lot of people, afraid to speak out. So when I was a Republican, she would say, "I can't tell people you're my brother." Now I'm a Democrat and she's telling the world! [*laughs*]

Whatever personality dimension or combination of dimensions that define us—and psychologists say there are five main personality traits: openness, conscientiousness, extraversion, agreeableness, and neuroticism—a person's personality reflects a mix of genetic and environmental influences from childhood, and tends to be stable over time (Vitelli 2015). That suggests that Joanie's and Emma's reluctance to join the Tea Party is not likely to waver.

So there are lots of variables—among them personal experience, media exposure, personality traits—that might limit parental socialization and help explain an African American's gravitation—or aversion—to the Tea Party. Notice one conspicuous absence: *free will.* If a person's political ideas aren't necessarily determined by their upbringing, you'd think that would suggest the power of freedom of choice. But a new cadre of experimental philosophers—scholars who use scientific methods to illuminate philosophical questions—says that's all wrong. Our decision to take one fork in the road or the other may feel like a free choice, but it's usually either a product of past experiences (such as an accumulated predilection for right-hand or left-hand turns) or it's a totally random decision (such as mentally flipping a coin). There's no such thing as actually selecting one course or the other, no strings attached (Nichols 2011).

Marketing professor Raj Raghunathan (2012), who supports this argument, draws an analogy about deciding whether to eat something that's tasty but not so good for you. Deciding whether to bite into a triple bacon cheeseburger may seem thoroughly within your control. But if you decide to eat it, it may be because your doctor didn't warn you about fatty diets, or your health hasn't suffered from your love of outsized burgers. Similarly, if you pass on the overstuffed sandwich, it may be because you read an alarming magazine article about cholesterol, or your overweight uncle had a heart attack at age forty-five, or you know your stomach will hurt under the strain of such a heavy meal. Either way, your decision has been shaped by external inputs, whether they be social (your uncle's experience), environmental (the magazine article), or possibly genetic (your stomachache). "You had no control over these inputs, which means that you had no free will in taking the decisions you did," writes Raghunathan. For example, you had no say about who your uncle is, or what advice spilled from your doctor's mouth.

Free will may be technically illusory, but the interviews suggest that socialization always comes with some degree of self-determination. Even Tea Partyers who adore their conservative parents could have rejected their parents' politics, which some did. That means some Tea Partyers become conservatives as they are socialized into conservatism by parents who voted Republican or who modeled conservative behavior or values. Other reach the same political endpoint more self-determistically by resisting socialization. These are the African Americans who rethink their parents' liberal ideas, or observing what can happen when parents coddle their children, or realizing that conservative and liberal allies can reach common goals by pursuing different strategies.

SOCIALIZING THE NEXT GENERATION

In 1904, sociologist Max Weber proposed a new way to study social phenomena: the *ideal type*. Ideal types are representations of a phenomenon—Weber was particularly interested in bureaucracies—that embody its salient characteristics (Constas 1958). They are "ideal" in the sense that they are neither good nor bad but abstractions (Hekman 1983; Burger 1987; Callinicos 1999). If Weber were alive today he might have something to say about ideal-typical black Tea Party families. After all, these families have salient characteristics that distinguish them from other families: they are often households with engaged parents who believe that the Bible is the word of God, who teach the value of hard work and principled decisions, and who downplay racism as an impediment to African Americans. Not every black Tea Party family has these features, nor are these characteristics unique to black conservative households. But ideal types are a helpful way of thinking about how African Americans become Tea Partyers because they indicate a general tendency for certain family structures to give rise to the phenomenon we're trying to understand.

And so we see Tea Partyers like Anne talking about the order and discipline that prevailed in her house, Len stressing how prayer and empathy and giving to others were stressed in his home, and Kevin remembering how his mother had a no-excuses policy for the children's household responsibilities. In turn, these principles guide how Tea Partyers parent *their* children. For example, one of the reasons Antonio said he reached across the aisle to Democrats as a legislator was to model inner strength for his children:

> I need them to see what real courage looks like. Not this preconceived view from Hollywood, but to see it up close. For my kids to see that, and to see them doing the same thing in their classes now. Not being afraid to stand for what they believe in, but also being respectful at the same time. I teach them that you can always be somebody who is contrary, but also do it respectfully.

Charlie brings to the table a different parenting sensibility. It's not about having the courage to take a stand against racism, for example. He says he didn't experience racism when he served in the US Navy, so father/son race talks seem unnecessary. Instead, Charlie is teaching his son financial literacy, which Charlie sees as tackling racism indirectly. I questioned the impact of Charlie's individual-level approach to change:

> Charlie: I think there's a need for financial literacy. We have to understand what our money is, what it does, and how to responsibly manage it because right now we don't. Why aren't there more black-owned businesses? Part of that is stigma. Black people can't always get loans for the

fact that they're viewed as credit risks. Well, why is that? How can we stop people from viewing us this way? That's all about financial literacy.

Me: So can individuals becoming financially literate change larger institutional barriers? For example, studies show that black folks are turned away for loans more often than whites who have comparable incomes, and when they get loans they often pay higher interest rates. These problems are so widespread that they seem to be built into the very structure of our financial institutions.

Charlie: Can change happen over generations? Yes. We're not talking about change that can benefit me or maybe even my kids. But it starts with me. It goes to my kids and then by their kids' generation, some of the barriers will be dead. It's a waiting game, waiting out the people who said we couldn't. But in that waiting we need to be active. Let's go out and get this education, so when our time comes we know what to do with it.

Charlie's point is echoed by observers who credit the rise of the black middle class in the 1960s to the African Americans who were prepared to take advantage of opportunities that opened after the defeat of Jim Crow segregation. For example, as early as 1958, activist Nannie Burroughs warned her fellow Baptists that implementation of the *Brown v. Board* decision would by impeded by "open defiance, political chicanery, subtle devices, and all sorts of schemes" by whites. "But blacks had to be prepared to take full advantage of any new doors that opened," writes historian Barbara D. Savage (2008, 195), suggesting that some of the challenges faced by the African American community were wholly internal.

Unlike Charlie, whose experiences with racism have been benign, Mary's have run the gamut. She knows how it feels to be driving while black. And she knows enough about workplace discrimination to change her adopted daughter's given name. Yet when she talks with her teenage sons about race, she tells them not to have any preconceptions about white people:

> I'm no fool. But again, that value was imparted to me about treating people the way you want to be treated. I still tell my sons not to tense up around a cop because you think all cops are bad. Don't tense up around this sort of person because of what you think he or she might be like. Just be aware; don't stereotype. I tell them I'm giving them knowledge so you know how to behave, and you can make an informed decision when that time comes.

These three examples show parents socializing their children in order to model desirable behavior (Antonio) and to address a potential racial obstacle indirectly (Charlie). But it's Mary's example—helping her children internalize a principle (treat people the way you want to be treated) because "that value was imparted to me"—that Weber might have designated a core element of ideal-typical parental socialization: the direct transmission of one generation's values to the second generation and onto the third.

Weber wrote that ideal types also accentuate one or more perspectives, and one of the features of black Tea Party families—and undoubtedly all families—is the imperfect nature of socialization. In a perfect world, socializing children would be simple: parents teach, children learn. "Coercive boys have coercive mothers," write psychologists Gerald R. Patterson and Eleanor E. MacCoby (1980, 12). But reality is messy, which means the intergenerational transmission of cultural information can be uncertain, unreliable, and anything but orderly. As appealing as simple top-down models of socialization may be, research shows that parent/child socialization is actually bidirectional: when they're engaged in a noncoercive joint activity—driving to a store together, for example—parents' and childrens' "streams of behavior become interwoven, so that the smooth continuation of one person's behavior depends on the partner's performing the reciprocal portion of the action," writes psychologist Eleanor Maccoby (1992, 1014). This suggests that when people like John and his SNCC veteran father talk politics, the son may temper his father's zeal as much as his father may ignite John's activism. Of course, neither party would need to act on those impulses for son and father to be affected by each other. Eventually, the two men end up in very different political orbits—John is conservative, and his father is progressive—but not without engaging in a dialectic.

There are more surprises. You'd think that socialization during someone's formative years would be a particularly potent way to instill ideas into their mind. After all, we know from observations and experiments reaching back to the nineteenth century that some young animals pattern their lifelong behavior by watching their parents in the first few hours after birth (Spalding 1873). *Imprinting*—the bonding of a young bird or mammal with an older, larger animal—is such a powerful force in nature that baby ducklings will imprint onto a man or woman if the first large animal they see after they hatch is a person (Cardoso and Sabbatini 2001). Imprinting, an instinctive biological phenomenon, may have wholly different origins than the interactive discursive social process by which young people develop their political preferences (Lazarsfeld et al. 1944). Nevertheless, because socialization begins at birth, one could rationally assume that young children are as exquisitely open to protopolitical influences as they are to biologically mediated ones.

But as it turns out, habits learned early in life aren't any more fixed in the brain than are habits acquired later on (Maccoby 1992). This might help explain why Republicans like Anne manage to emerge from a family of Democrats; being exposed to liberal ideas for the first eighteen (or more) years of her life doesn't necessarily mean those ideas are the last word.

Perhaps most confounding of all, socialization isn't a magic bullet. Psychologists have long believed that reinforcement causes a child to internalize parental messages. For instance, the more that you remind a child to say thank you, the more politeness should come as second nature to the child. Research bears that out: one study of aggressive boys found that their parents failed to punish their aggressive behavior. No surprise there; not punishing aggressive behavior would seem to condone it. But when researchers compared the parents of aggressive boys to the parents of nonaggressive boys, they found no difference in how much the parents disciplined the boys. Parents of aggressive children didn't discipline their children any less than parents of nonaggressive children did. In other words, when it came to shaping this aspect of their children's behavior, the parents' influence simply dropped out (Maccoby 1992).

So if a parent's influence over a child is powerful but clearly limited, why do some African American children grow up to make unusual political decisions that often leave their parents and siblings—the people who presumably know them better than anyone else—utterly confounded? Well, socialization explains part of the story, but of all the other influences, personality may explain much of the rest. Socialization and personality type might do more to explain an adult's political comfort zone better than either factor alone.

That's the suggestion from a team of psychologists who conducted an ingenious study about parenting, personality, and political attitudes. Back in 1991, these researchers asked 1,364 mothers of one-month-old babies about their approach to parenting. They were trying to figure out whether the mothers took an *authoritarian* approach to parenting (e.g., "The most important thing to teach children is absolute obedience to whomever is in authority") or an *egalitarian* approach (e.g., "A child's ideas should be seriously considered in making family decisions"). Four and a half years later, each mother assessed her child's temperament using a behavior questionnaire. Then at age eighteen, the children were asked about their political attitudes.

The results were striking. Eighteen-year-olds who identified as conservatives were significantly more likely than other young adults to have been raised by authoritarian mothers. That's not particularly surprising given decades of research, dating from the postwar years, showing that conservative adults report being raised by strict parents who had little tolerance for rulebreaking (Adorno et al. 1950). But the study also showed that conservative and liberal eighteen-year-olds had received different personality scores as preschoolers. Conservative teens were more likely to have been fearful children. They were also more likely to be impulsive and to have difficulty mastering self-control. Liberals, on the other hand, were more likely to have been rated by their mothers as physically restless yet more able to focus their attention while playing or working on a task (Fraley et al. 2012). Other researchers find that adults who in nursery school were rigid when distressed, uncomfortable with uncertainty, and easily offended were likely to identify as political conservatives at age twenty-three. While conservatives tended to be overcontrolled by authority figures as youngsters, liberal adults were undercontrolled as children. Liberal girls were talkative, dominating, and unconstrained by others; liberal boys were resilient and not easily thrown off their game (Block and Block 2006).

Does this mean that black Tea Partyers were anxious, fearful children who struggled with impulse control? Of course not. The ones I spoke with are accomplished and successful professionals who seem well-balanced, socially appropriate, comfortable with others, and at ease with themselves and the world. In other words, they appear to be indistinguishable in behavior and self-presentation from any other African Americans. The research on personality isn't predictive as much as it indicates a general tendency. Like a recent finding that conservatives are happier than liberals (Schlenker, Chambers, and Le 2012), the question social scientists would like to answer is not just *whether* childhood personality traits translate into adult political choices, but *how*.

CONCLUSION

So are black Tea Partyers born or are they made? There's no question that many were socialized by their parents to be self-reliant God-fearing hard workers. They were groomed from childhood to embrace household chores and familial responsibilities. These tasks sometimes have a biblical impetus, and are occasionally referenced as being entirely consistent with thriftiness, self-discipline, personal accountability, and other longstanding African American survival tactics. Thus, generally speaking, even when parents may not have served up conservative messages deliberately, children watched, they learned from what they saw, and they frequently went on to convey their ways of thinking to their own children. And so we see Tea Partyers like Hilton, the son of a US Air Force veteran, whose father instilled in him the importance of protecting and defending the US Constitution. Today, Hilton is the walking embodiment of his father. After high school, he went on to attend the US Air Force Academy, where he promised to defend the Constitution. Hilton's behavior is thoroughly consistent with the notion that while parents and children influence each other as they interact, the parents are usually victorious. As one researcher discovered when analyzing mothers and their children ages one to ten, the parents tried to influence the children four to five times more often than the children tried to influence the parents. In the end, the kids lost out because "[t]he child submits to the parent far more often than he does not" (Hoffman 1975, 231).

Socialization is indispensible. Without it, families couldn't function. Neither would cities, nations, churches, universities, or corporations, because every person in these various groups would be on a different page. There'd be no *social cohesion*, as sociologists say—no glue to hold together the group. But African American Tea Partyers remind us that socialization isn't the only influence on a person's behavior. Socialization doesn't explain how conservative Tea Partyers grew up in liberal households where the parents and other family members were loyal Democrats, or even civil rights workers. It doesn't explain why siblings heard similar messages about values, rules, and expectations and yet became adults whose political identities span an entire spectrum—some liberal, some conservative, some centrist—despite being parented by the same two people. Socialization doesn't necessarily account for childhood personality differences that may manifest as adult political preferences. Powerful as socialization may be, it's not deterministic.

And if having conservative parents heightens the chances that a child will grow up to be a conservative, plenty of liberal parents establish household rules and set moral and behavioral boundaries as well. This is what African American historian Henry Louis Suggs (1999, 81) may have been thinking when he wrote that conservatism "is not an absolute but a state of mind . . . and is not the monopoly of any one group." More pointedly, historian Peter Eisenstadt (1999, x) says any generalization about black conservatives "will also be true of many individuals who are not black conservatives."

Chapter Three

"Personal Responsibility"—Panacea or Placebo?

> If you're not doing what it takes to bring yourself an income, and instead you're relying on the government to provide instead of relying on God, that's sinful.
> —Jake, cab driver

> I've heard it said that people in poverty want to be poor, but that doesn't make sense. Nobody wants to be hungry. Nobody wants to sleep in a cold place.
> —Anne, physician

Conservatives tend to view acquiring possessions and accumulating wealth as a measure of a person's worth. They also have an aversion to public-sector interference with private enterprise and the free market (Asumah and Perkins 2000). At the same time, in addition to materialism and limited government, they respect *individualism*, the notion that hard work and competition with others allows individuals to attain self-fulfillment. In fact, many black conservatives insist that with divine grace, African Americans can surpass all obstacles by the sheer force of raw individual effort. "They embody the conservative philosophy of looking to oneself and one's God rather than to one's government," writes political scientist Paul G. Kengor (2017). By this philosophy, accepting personal responsibility for one's actions is more than its own reward; it is foundational for personal growth, occupational success, financial stability, even moral rectitude. Indeed, conservatives see individualism as the engine that drives the American Dream; the presumption is that as long as individuals are unfettered by government interference, their efforts in pursuit of wealth and material possessions will generate the most happiness for the most number of people.

To many sociologists, that word "unfettered" in the previous sentence is a red flag. These and other critics note that Africans came to the New World in chains—unlike immigrants who were willing and enthusiastic arrivals—and the long shadow of slavery lingers today in disproportionate social problems from unemployment and undereducation to misogyny and marital instability. Given these unique historical circumstances, how could the prized trio of materialism, limited government, and individualism possibly hold the same purchase for whites as they do for people who "have not been allowed to maintain their individualism or even to sustain the family structure" (Asumah and Perkins 2000, 54–55)?

Similarly, we might question economist Glenn Loury's (1995, 66–67) endorsement of conservative icon Booker T. Washington, who felt that black self-improvement was the best way to challenge white racism:

> Washington saw two factors preventing blacks from enjoying the status in American society that was their due: actual defects of character, as manifested in patterns of behavior and ways of living among the black masses; and the racist attitudes of whites. He believed that blacks had both an opportunity and a duty to address the former difficulty [through thrift, industry, and other forms of self-help], and that in so doing they would go a long way toward overcoming the latter.

Here most social scientists would balk at Loury's collapsing societal structural problems onto individual personality defects; C. Wright Mills (1959) would certainly agree that *public issues* explain large-scale societal dysfunction much more coherently than do *personal troubles.* Historians of the Reconstruction era might also note that the industry and thrift that Washington called for could have disastrous consequences for African Americans in the South, where anxious whites who felt threatened by the slightest racial improvement reacted violently to signs that newly freed blacks refused to stay in their place. Instead of welcoming black people to full citizenship, they lynched them (Litwack 2000).

But many black Tea Partyers would probably not split hairs, because the ideology of personal responsibility—using initiative and perseverance to scale the ladder of success one rung at a time—strikes a louder chord than racism does. As one black Tea Party supporter put it, "We're supposed to be the law-and-order, self-reliance, self-accountability people. That's the backbone of what we're supposed to be espousing."

Consider, for example, how Hilton, a state legislator, explains what it takes for black students to succeed in school. He doesn't say kids need to be curious, or intellectually engaged, or respectful of their teachers. Personal fortitude is what they need, he says, and not just because they're mastering challenging subject material. They also need to resist classmates who act like crabs in a barrel:

> To do well in school takes effort. *You have to study, you have to use self-discipline, you have to sacrifice.* A lot of people don't want to do that because it's hard. So they'll go the easy route. They haven't read for class. They don't care. But when they see others who are performing well, they don't want them to, because they themselves don't want to put in the effort to do it. I wanted to do well in school, and my classmates made fun of me and said I was trying to be white. [Italics mine]

And here's James explaining why, after Hurricane Ivan struck the Gulf coast in 2004, he stressed self-reliance—not empathy or compassion—to help people get back on their feet:

> We had an enrichment program for people that were coming in for some of the public housing that we rebuilt after the hurricane. We had an opportunity where they could enroll in a program and get the skills necessary to be a competent and productive member of the workforce, to where they would no longer need the government handout. *Our motto is "The road to self-sufficiency."* [Italics mine]

Let's examine black Tea Partyers' call for personal responsibility as an answer to two problems that have vexed the African American community for generations: intergenerational poverty and mass incarceration. Both problems are prime examples of what famed sociologist C. Wright Mills would call *public issues*. In his 1959 classic, *The Sociological Imagination,* Mills proposed a thought exercise for understanding the extent to which someone's personal biography might be influenced by larger historical forces that in fact shape the lives of many people. "No social study that does not come back to the problems of biography, of history and their intersections in society has completed its intellectual journey," Mills (1959, 4) wrote. The problem is that most nonsociologists fail to appreciate how larger historical forces can make a mark on an individual's personal trajectory. When that happens, they risk mistakenly assuming that, say, someone's chronic employment is the result of laziness, insecurity, or other personality flaws (*personal troubles*) instead of properly singling out larger problems—such as dysfunctional schools that fail to equip students to enter the workplace, or a lack of available jobs—that originate within institutions (*public issues*), and that are quite beyond the ability of most individuals to control:

> When, in a city of 100,000, only one man is unemployed, that is his personal trouble, and for its relief we properly look to the character of the man, his skills, and his immediate opportunities. But when in a nation of 50 million employees, 15 million men are unemployed, that is an issue, and we may not hope to find its solution within the range of opportunities open to any one individual. The very structure of opportunities has collapsed. Both the correct statement of the problem and the range of possible solutions require us to

consider the economic and political institutions of the society, and not merely the personal situation and character of a scatter of individuals. (Mills 1959, 9)

Why use the sociological imagination? Well, if policymakers don't understand whether a social problem is caused by individual failings or institutional shortcomings, they won't know whether the problem is best addressed by trying to alter people's attitudes and behaviors or by changing laws and public policies—two vastly different types of targets. But for our purposes, the sociological imagination is important because conservatives place so much emphasis on personal responsibility. If there's good evidence that African American poverty and mass incarceration are largely *public issues*, then deconstructing black Tea Partyers' insistence that they are largely *personal troubles* may explain not just the nature of their arguments, but why the arguments can feel pretty persuasive.

CASE #1: PERSONAL RESPONSIBILITY AND POVERTY

The idea that poor people are responsible for being poor predates the Civil War. Hardship and suffering were inevitable for immigrants who fled European deprivation and for waves of pioneers who pushed westward from the eastern seaboard. Yet at the time, most Americans considered a person's economic viability to be a sign of their individual industry—or lack of it (Bremner 1956). "The prevalent attitude was that personal misfortunes were personal affairs, that poverty was an individual problem that neither could nor should be alleviated by society," write sociologists William Julius Wilson and Robert Aponte (1987, 165).

That notion changed with the onset of twentieth-century industrialization, when massive unemployment, widespread disease, wretched housing, and decrepit working conditions convinced social reformers of the need for wholesale changes in the laws governing housing, public health, and the workplace. Whereas Americans had used religious metaphors such as sloth and sinfulness to describe poverty in the early nineteenth century, documentary photography and investigative reports by early social justice advocates such as Jacob Riis (1890) and Jane Addams (1902) had transformed the conversation entirely by the turn of the century. By then, "an enormous number of statistical reports and case descriptions . . . showed the poor as so hard put that neither cleanliness nor godliness were achievable aspirations" (Suttles 1976, 6). This view of poverty as a structural dilemma—a *public issue*—would dominate debates about poverty for the next sixty years, from the creation of the New Deal antipoverty programs, such as Social Security and Aid to Families with Dependent Children, through Lyndon B. Johnson's (LBJ) War on Poverty (Wilson and Aponte 1987).

But starting in the mid-1960s, many Americans began to have second thoughts. First came the publication of Daniel Patrick Moynihan's controversial 1965 report, *The Negro Family: The Case for National Action* (Office of Policy Planning and Research 1965). Moynihan compared rates of unemployment, divorce, illegitimate births, female-headed households, absent fathers, and welfare dependency between whites and blacks, and noted that "three centuries of injustice" rooted in the trauma and forced dislocations of slavery had created a "tangle of pathology" in the black community that was best repaired with policies "to strengthen the Negro family so as to enable it to raise and support its members as do other families" (Office of Policy Planning and Research 1965, 47). Even though Moynihan identified the historical roots of these problems, including inequalities dating from slavery, conservatives interpreted the report as highlighting African Americans' deficiencies. As one conservative commentator put it, "ghetto culture" yields "ghetto outcomes" (Geary 2015).

Almost immediately, conservatives seized on a second prominent study to similar effect. In 1966, anthropologist Oscar Lewis proposed that poverty is more than simply a socioeconomic level. Building on extensive fieldwork in Puerto Rico and New York City, Lewis wrote that poverty "is a subculture with its own structure and rationale, . . . a way of life that is passed down from generation to generation along family lines" (Lewis 2009, 176; 1959). The anthropologist went on to list some seventy social, economic, and psychological traits that he observed among such families, including present-mindedness, provincialism, lack of class consciousness, and feelings of marginality, helplessness, and dependency (Lewis 1966). To be sure, the anthropologist cautioned that while many groups—including African Americans—show signs of the culture of poverty, not all poor people live this way. "There are numerous examples of poor people whose way of life I would not characterize as belonging to this subculture," he wrote (1966, 23). He also went out of his way to point out some aspects of the culture of poverty that represent positive adaptations:

> [W]e must not overlook some of the positive attributes that may flow from these traits. Living immersed in the present may develop a capacity for spontaneity, for the enjoyment of the sensual, for the enjoyment of impulse, which is too often blunted in our middle-class future-oriented man. Perhaps it is this reality of the moment that existentialist writers are trying desperately to recapture, but which the culture of poverty experiences as a natural, everyday phenomenon. (Lewis 1998, 8)

But conservatives interpreted Lewis's work as condemning poor people themselves, and they used Lewis's work to push back against LBJ's antipoverty programs. Their argument was simple, says sociologist Sudhir Vankatesh: "[C]onservatives . . . say why do we want to throw all this money down the drain if, in fact, people need to change their behavior? None of this money is going to do any good unless people change themselves" (Anon. 2009c). By the time Ronald Reagan's presidential election signaled a conservative political revolution, the culture of poverty was a cornerstone of conservative thought (Ehrenreich 2012). In fact, some conservatives raised their argument to a whole new level. Antipoverty programs weren't just ineffective, they argued; the programs actually *caused* poverty. For example, Republican House Speaker Newt Gingrich warned Bill Clinton in 1994 that antipoverty programs were a policy blight: "They ruined the poor. They created a culture of poverty and a culture of violence which is destructive of this civilization, and they have to be replaced thoroughly from the ground up." As recently as 2014, former House Speaker Paul Ryan placed the blame for poverty squarely on poor people and their "culture": "We have got this tailspin of culture, in our inner cities in particular, of men not working and just generations of men not even thinking about working or learning the value and the culture of work, and so there is a real culture problem here that has to be dealt with." Ryan was criticized for implicitly disparaging African American men, although he later said his remarks had "nothing to do whatsoever with race" (Lowery 2014).

The rise of the black-dysfunctions-as-*personal-troubles* argument began at a time of significant changes in African American media representations. Because of federal desegregation initiatives, antipoverty programs that with few complaints had served white clients, including widows and disabled Americans—the so-called "deserving" poor—during the Jim Crow era began to open their doors to persons of color. This prompted concerns among some whites about whether the government should indulge the "undeserving" poor by subsidizing the presumed immoral behavior and irresponsible decisions that brought them into poverty in the first place. After the civil rights revolution, journalists who featured disproportionate numbers of African Americans in poverty-related stories contributed to consumers' association of African Americans with poverty, in contrast to the Kennedy and Johnson administrations' focus on "desperately poor, shockingly unemployed" Appalachian whites (Gilens 2003; Moynihan 1969, 25). These darker representations of poor people joined conservatives' interpretation of Moynihan's and Lewis's research to present white America with an unflattering conclusion about African Americans: America's poverty class is black, and it's their fault that they're poor.

So from antebellum America to today, a two-hundred-year-old argument that poverty reflects moral turpitude and lack of initiative has come full circle. At the same time, a second idea about poverty and wealth has spun through popular culture: the notion that successful individuals are solely responsible for their good fortune. As but one indication of the popularity of this idea, consider the dozens of bestselling young adult books written in the second half of the nineteenth-century by novelist Horatio Alger, Jr. Intended primarily for boys and with hopeful, promising titles like *Strive and Succeed* and *Strong and Steady, or Paddle Your Own Canoe,* these books were fictional accounts of poor boys who achieved middle-class respectability through perseverance, honesty, and cheerfulness in the face of adversity (Peterson 2017). Alger's popularity coincided with the rise of American industrialization, a time when Cornelius Vanderbilt, Andrew Carnegie, John D. Rockefeller, Andrew W. Mellon, and other enterprising capitalists amassed spectacular fortunes, ostensibly through their limitless ingenuity and capacity for hard work. Ironically, it was also a time when social critics railed against robber barons and pushed successfully for the workplace, public health, and housing reforms mentioned above (Tipple 1959; Bode 1959). In other words, Americans believed in self-determination even when critics argued—successfully enough to change public policies—that "the American dream of prosperity for all was a hopeless myth" (Tipple 1959, 510). This ironclad faith in the power of the individual is one of the few positions that every black Tea Partyer I interviewed embraced with open arms.

A Dim View of Anti-Poverty Programs

When I asked Tea Partyers why so many African Americans are poor, they tended to mention personal failings. Sometimes these mistakes took the form of poor decisions, regrettable strategies, a failure to select the right fork in the road. For example, Lindsay, the firefighter's son, remembered that his family sometimes had nothing more than biscuits with butter and syrup for dinner when he was growing up. But he didn't think of his family as poor. His cousins, on the other hand, were poor, at least in his mind. Their poverty took the form of a lack of spirit, a sadness he sensed when he visited the Jefferson family. His cousins lacked basic necessities, he said, and their mother beat them:

> I basically loved my cousins and I would spend time at their house in the projects, and they went from living in a high rise to having a townhouse, but their house felt poor. Felt depressed. They had the welfare peanut butter and the welfare milk, the welfare powdered milk. Food was like a high commodity to them. In my house, when we came home from school you open up the fridge and you got something to eat until suppertime. In my cousins' house, the refrigerator was like off-limits to them. Only their mother could go in the fridge and dish out the food. And even though they had everything for free because the government was providing them everything, there was this depressed vibe. I'm like 10 or 11, but I felt it. And I felt sorry for them, too. I felt like they were jealous because I had a dad and they didn't. This was never said out loud, but you just felt that. And their mother Tricia was also violent and loud and angry. And when she beat her sons, she beat them with baseball bats

and pots and pans, and my folks would never do that to any of us. Tricia was so bad that my father threatened to report her to the authorities.

Tricia's three sons endured but did not have happy outcomes. Her oldest, Billy, worked his way through college but died of AIDS in his thirties. Her other two sons, Terrence and Michael, were chronically unemployed:

> When I was in my fifties, I spoke to Terrence. He was in his late forties and never had a job in his life. I said, "Come on Terrence, I know you at least had a paper route!" He died, too. The whole family just lived on welfare their entire lives. There is one survivor, my cousin Michael. He is in a nursing home today and I had to really crack up laughing because I hadn't heard from Michael in years. And when I finally heard from him, he sent me a list of sizes of stuff to buy for him. [*laughs*]

To cab driver Jake and many others I spoke with, Michael's middle-age desperation was not inevitable. It could have been prevented, even despite a childhood of deprivation, had Michael taken more care to build his resolve, gather his resources, and set a more hopeful course for himself. When I asked Jake why so many African Americans are poor, he reached to the Bible for inspiration:

> Bible says he who deals with a slack hand will soon become poor. I think the problem is that black people haven't been as diligent about their personal well-being as they could have. We've allowed the government to look out for us. We have allowed safety nets to look out for us. We don't need safety nets. God has placed everything that is necessary for us to prosper. We simply need to be diligent.

I asked Jake what he thought poor people would say if they were told God's plan was for them to be diligent. What if you look around you, I asked, and you don't see many success stories even among your friends and neighbors who seem perfectly conscientious? I thought of Elliot Liebow's (1967) heart-breaking ethnography of African American street corner men in Washington, DC, men who had opportunities to work but only if they were willing to accept less than they needed to support themselves and their families. These men were discouraged from applying for better-paying positions by their repeated failure to secure and maintain these more-lucrative jobs:

> Convinced of their inadequacies, not only do they not seek out those few better-paying jobs which test their resources, but they actively avoid them, gravitating in a mass to the menial, routine jobs which offer no challenge—and therefore pose no threat—to the already diminished images they have of themselves. (Liebow 1967, 34)

My question to Jake was intended to explore the emotional impact of poverty. We know, for instance, that being poor or living in a distressed neighborhood can make people depressed and hopeless, which in turn can discourage them from looking for a job (Meich and Shanahan 2000; Ross 2000; Senécal and Guay 2000; Schwarz 2018). Is it realistic to expect anyone to remain diligent in the face of hopelessness? Jake sidestepped the possible emotional effects of having few viable employment opportunities. Instead, he pointed to a success story—Dr. Ben Carson, whose mother was a domestic worker:

> Ben Carson's mom had a third-grade education. She took the initiative to discipline her sons and because she led her sons to be diligent they are both successful. Your brain has millions of connections within it and over time, if certain connections aren't used, they're removed. If you want to fill that brain with meaningless things, you can. It's better to fill that brain with things of God and things of knowledge. That's what his mother did. TV goes off. If you get your homework done, you can watch two programs. Just because you are in poverty does not mean your children have to be. You need to discipline them to do the right thing. If you do that, they'll prosper.

Lindsay's rebuke of his cousins is not far from Jake's praise of diligence. Both men suggested that poverty is caused by character flaws, whether they be the sluggishness of the Jefferson family or the inattentiveness of mothers less disciplined than Mrs. Carson. And both men decried government anti-poverty programs.

To be sure, the Tea Partyers were united in their support of some government functions. As Dean put it,

> There's some things we need the government to do; there's no question. The government needs to maintain the Federal Aviation Administration and keep our skies safe. The government needs to maintain our monetary policy and our money supply; we can't have one currency in Kansas and then you drive across the border into Nebraska and you need to exchange that for something else. National defense—we can't expect Hawaii to defend itself.

There was also broad support for a safety net of government services that citizens can rely on during desperate circumstances. Some Tea Partyers themselves had been grateful beneficiaries of public aid, so they understood first-hand the value of emergency assistance. Lindsay cited his own experience after leaving his job as a graphic artist at a television station:

> I'm not saying there should not be a safety net. Of course, there should be a safety net. I quit my job in 1983. I didn't like my new supervisor at the TV station and plus I had been there 15 years and gotten awards for my work and felt like I had done this and I'm ready to move on. I walk in and quit my job with nothing else on the table. But that took me through a rocky road for

several years. I did all kinds of jobs I didn't want to do. One time my electric was turned off and I had to go down to some local government place to get some funds. And I was amazed how the people there were being treated. When you ain't got no money, you ain't nobody! I felt this vibe of disrespect. But, I thank God that that safety net was there to help me when I needed to get my lights turned on. I didn't need them to keep my lights turned on forever. But I needed them then.

The overriding concern with welfare checks, subsidized food, public housing, and other forms of government relief isn't that they're unhelpful when a family is in crisis, Tea Partiers said. The problem was that relying on this assistance can become routine. Here's how Jimmy put it:

My parents had to be on welfare during the Great Depression. They had 12 kids. There should be safety net for people who cannot do for themselves at a point in time. But in the black community, welfare is more than a safety net; it has become a generational hammock. It's not a safety net; it's a way of life. You have in some cases families that are on multiple generations of welfare. That's not a safety net, that's dependence.

When that happens, Dave explained, low-income African Americans can start to define themselves by who they are instead of who they can become. He illustrated the point by citing his own mother's experience:

Well, I do believe many times people fall into circumstances that are not of their own making. And I believe in having compassion. In scripture, Jesus was moved by compassion. But I also believe there must be a finality, that whatever circumstance you're in, you cannot make that permanent; you cannot allow that to define who you are. My mother didn't graduate from high school. She was in her early sixties when she decided to go to night school. I remember seeing my mother get her GED. She didn't have to do that. She was a spouse of a former military veteran. She could've just been comfortable with her life. But she worked really hard. She obtained that education. So, if my mother could do that at that age, with the sacrifices she made, I do believe it's attainable for everyone.

But when people become complacent with government handouts instead of making an effort to change their station in life, Tea Partiers argued, they become wards of the state. They lose their sense of agency and feel incapable of standing on their own feet. They lack the initiative—or even the incentive—to stay in school, hit the job market, start a career, build a stable family, and find a nice home of their own. And when children learn dependency instead of self-sufficiency from their parents, the road to autonomy and full citizenship becomes blocked for each successive generation. In fact, just as Newt Gingrich claimed that antipoverty programs caused poverty, the idea that public assistance contributes to the very *personal troubles*—idleness, laziness, hopelessness—that keep African Americans in persistent poverty emerged as a common complaint. It's not the *intent* of antipoverty programs that's at issue, but their *effects*.

The Flawed Nature of Government Programs

Admittedly, some Tea Partiers said, antipoverty programs are problematic in ways that all government aid is flawed. Federal intervention costs taxpayers, and the bulky bureaucracies that administer programs are never as efficient as direct action from interested local parties. Dave, a minister's son, explained his reservations with government relief by pointing to how individuals and private groups, including a construction firm that donated $10,000, united to provide relief after Hurricane Harvey, which caused catastrophic damage after making landfall in East Texas in 2017 (Anon. 2018):

> I believe that the local church, charity organizations, civic organizations, communities, neighbors can do more than what government can. I want to clarify here: I don't want anarchy; I'm not saying we shouldn't have government at all. I do believe government should be small and limited. With that said, we look at Hurricane Harvey, the impact that it had on the state of Texas. I think about the citizens there, friends of mine personally impacted by the storm and how, you know, they said if we would've waited on the Red Cross or FEMA [the Federal Emergency Management Agency], we'd have been helpless for many, many days. I think of the power of an individual. I think about [construction company owner] J.J. White of eastern Texas, the amount of money he was able to raise. I think about how churches stepped in, how civic organizations from across the state and many other states came with items needed. I think when people come together, they're able to have a much more powerful and long-lasting impact than any government agency can.

True, the federal government is massive, with upwards of nine million employees, contractors, and grantees (Davidson 2017). And there's no question that large institutions can't turn on a dime the way smaller ones can. But it might be a mistake to assume that the private sector is inherently more efficient than the public sector. Take health care, for instance. In 2009—the year President Obama introduced the Affordable Care Act—the United States wasted an estimated $750 billion in unnecessary and inefficiently delivered medical services, excessive administrative costs and service fees, and outright fraud (Smith et al. 2013; Godrej 2015). Private hospitals and physicians' offices outspend the US government on health care, which means most of that waste, fraud, and inefficiency occurred in the private sector. Likewise, a 2015 United Nations study of global privatization initiatives found "no conclusive evidence that one model of ownership (i.e., public, private, or mixed) is intrinsically more efficient than the others, irrespective of how efficiency is defined" (Everest-Phillips 2015, 4).

Other claims of the inherent weaknesses of government programs are probably more justified. For example, Joan, a former elected state official, explained that well-intentioned government initiatives frequently lose sight of their mission over time. Instead of serving their clients, their principal aim becomes to perpetuate their own existence:

> Joan: Many government programs are not very intelligent. They have good intent when they start, but unfortunately, as I have seen personally serving in office, elected officials who control the direction of the programs tend to have knee-jerk reactions to events. When situations occur, they say, "Let's hurry up, let's get some piece of legislation out there, some piece of policy to appease the public that we've done something," and they walk away from it. It's very seldom that the programs have accountability and evaluation to make sure they're doing what they're supposed to do. For example, there has been an increase in poverty programs over the years. If these programs are doing so well, the objective should be to put themselves out of business, not to be expanding, because if they're doing their mission, people will be on the road to owning a business or advancing their income. These poverty programs, they start with a budget and the next year, they have a larger budget because they're getting more clients on the books. But the philosophy and objectives of these programs should be to wean people off of government support and get them sustainable so they can stand on their own two feet.
>
> Me: So the idea should be really to ask for smaller and smaller budgets over time, not larger and larger ones.
>
> Joan: Absolutely.

Sociologist Max Weber (1947) may have written the book—literally—on large organizations, but it took political scientist Jerry Pournelle (2010) to notice, as Joan did, that bureaucracies have a tendency to perpetuate themselves. Perhaps inspired by his experience as an employee at a large aerospace corporation, Pournelle wrote his eponymous Iron Law of Bureaucracy:

> [I]n any bureaucratic organization there will be two kinds of people: those who work to further the actual goals of the organization, and those who work for the organization itself. Examples in education would be teachers who work and sacrifice to teach children, vs. union representatives who work to protect any teacher, including the most incompetent. The Iron Law states that in all cases, the second type of person will always gain control of the organization, and will always write the rules under which the organization functions.

Regardless of the aim of government programs—whether educating the next generation or lifting them out of poverty—Pournelle would likely agree with Joan that a key obstacle is the mixed motives of the people who administer them.

The Unintended Effects of Charity

If people are poor because they can't afford basic necessities, then what's wrong with the government stepping in to provide income for people with inadequate means, food for people who are hungry, and housing for people who might otherwise be homeless? It's a simple enough proposition, liberals say. Too simple, conservatives answer. "Simple governments are fundamentally defective," wrote eighteenth-century political philosopher Edmund Burke (Kramnick 1999 x, xi), "the prophetic voice of Anglo-American conservatism," who understood the complexity of human nature and was thus skeptical of efforts to perfect society by relying on government.

When it comes to fighting poverty, black Tea Partyers endorse Burke's cynicism toward government solutions. Many of the reasons connect with the American bootstrap ideal, which Tea Partyers agree is alive and well. Byron tells this story about a neighbor who bootstrapped his way out of extraordinarily grim circumstances:

> My neighbor's a Haitian guy. I had just moved to the neighborhood, and he was already there. He came over one day. "Let's have a couple beers," I said. He owned real estate. "When did you leave Haiti?" I asked him. He had come here 15 years before. "Your family was rich in Haiti?" He said, "No, my family was dirt poor. We literally ate dirt. So, when I finally got money to get on an overloaded boat that was coming to the U.S. illegally, I came here. It was supposed to be a two-week boat ride, but we had been out there for a week when things started to go wrong. The boat was leaking. People were falling overboard. People were being eaten by sharks." They finally landed in Cuba. The Cubans fixed the boat and pushed 'em back out. A week later, they ended up on Miami Beach. He finally gets to the shore. The Coast Guard is chasing him. The border patrol is chasing him. The Miami Beach police are chasing them. He finds a cab driver, another Haitian guy, who tells him to get in the cab and lay on the floor. Takes him across the bay to a room. It costs him two dollars a day to stay in this room with 20 other people. Each morning he goes to the market and buys a basket of oranges. He puts them in bags and sells them three for a dollar. Before long, he sets up a fruit stand. He eventually buys a store. He goes on to get his immigration status and 15 years later he's my next-door neighbor. If this guy can come from Haiti and be a success, how can we say poverty is generational?

Government relief is also unfair, say Tea Partyers, because for every hard worker like Byron's Haitian neighbor, a welfare recipient is scamming the system. Lindsay recalled bumping into one of his cousins who seemed to be living the good life on the public dole. The fact that Lindsay was struggling to pay a hefty tax bill at the time felt excruciating:

> Here I am struggling to survive, and I get a $15,000 self-employment tax bill. I go up to the city and I bump into my cousin Herman and he is bragging to me about his brand new townhouse. Herman has fathered a gazillion kids all over the city. Correction—he hasn't fathered them; he's been the sperm donor. He's in his fifties, he's been a drug addict his whole life, and he goes to get his methadone every week. He gets food stamps and he lives in a brand-new home. And here I am, struggling to survive, and this guy has been totally 100 percent irresponsible, and he's being totally taken care of. He has free health care, free everything. That's not right.

People like Herman may be living the (publicly funded) good life, but taking the easy route to material success does more than cheat taxpayers, Lindsay says. When you live comfortably on someone else's dime, you don't feel invested in your future. Listen to how Dean praised the merits of economic self-determination:

> Dean: Black people aren't born with a gene that says go out on the streets and riot when you don't like things. It's economic. The only people who riot are people who are poor. These hooligans in Europe go out flipping over cars and throwing bricks through windows and all that stuff after a soccer match? They're all white. Once they climb out of the lower economic stratas, they're less likely to be involved in that. You don't see people who live in nice neighborhoods marching up and down their own streets flipping over their own cars and throwing bricks through the windows of their neighbor's houses. They're economically empowered. If you have a job, you don't throw a brick through a 7-Eleven and jump through the hole you've made and steal a couple of bags of Cheetos if you have a job and a paycheck because you can just walk in and buy some.

> Me: So from your perspective, it's economic empowerment that comes before racial uplift. One allows the other.

> Dean: There's absolutely no question. Because with economic empowerment comes ownership. No matter their skin color, most people who are at the bottom end of the economic ladder don't own the property they live on. But as you begin to pull yourself up economically, you begin to take ownership and possession of goods. And when you get to the point where you own some land and the structure you live in, now you're in a completely different place mentally because you don't want to lose what you got. In fact, you get an appetite for more.

That appetite for acquisition grows even when people make mistakes, which are inevitable, Len explained. The problem comes when the government wrecks that natural yearning to acquire by providing resources that individuals should strive to achieve on their own:

> The Declaration [of Independence] says "the pursuit of happiness." It doesn't say "the guarantee of happiness." We've got to set the conditions for people to pursue that happiness. I've heard folks make the argument that they don't want people to be trapped by a job. They can stay at home, discover themselves, and get a check from the government. If you're gonna be disincentivizing work, then who's going to be the one that makes sure the government's subsidy check comes?

I think Len had tongue in cheek when he suggested that welfare checks won't come unless someone has a work ethic, but Tea Partyers would agree with his dismissing the idea that staying at home helps people "discover themselves." In fact, said Rev. Isaac, the opposite is true: it's only through gainful employment that people achieve the full measure of who they were meant to be:

> It's never good to encourage someone to depend on the government from cradle to grave for their support. It kills a desire to explore and become the very best person you can be, to reach out and learn the world and see how your skills and your talents can be used. It discourages all of that. I'm against the welfare state.

But it's difficult to achieve your full potential when you are isolated from the American mainstream. That's what happens when you're on welfare, said Andrew. You're marginalized at arm's length: "It ghettoizes black people. It puts them in the projects, which isolates them. Drugs, out-of-wedlock births, the crime, the pathologies—it's woeful. It's wrong. It's disastrous. In Chicago, the police don't even go to black communities when people are killing each other. They just sit on the sidewalk."

Isolation can indeed cripple a community. When people are cut off from networks of friends and acquaintances, they lose chances to learn about jobs and other opportunities that may not be widely known (Raspberry 1988). Plus, they're influenced by *other* people who have become socially isolated, a condition that, when combined with the widespread loss of urban industrial jobs in the 1960s and 1970s, has been blamed for the growth of a near-permanent poor population known as the underclass. Street crime, unemployment, failing schools, out-of-wedlock pregnancies, and other signs of failing neighborhoods are not far behind (Wilson 1993). As for Andrew's comment about Chicago policing, other observers have noted the callousness of these officers, particularly toward African Americans in Chicago's public housing projects (McIntyre 1999).

When black Tea Partiers talk about the social problems that plague inner cities, the bad actor that's implicated more than any other cause is the federal government. The rise of single-headed households is a good example. Over 70 percent of African American births are to unmarried mothers, which is a risk factor for poverty (Akerlof and Yellen 1996; Hamilton et al. 2015). "I think we took away that sense of individual responsibility," Len says, a reference to couples having sex without committing to marriage. But Len says Uncle Sam kickstarted today's sky-high out-of-wedlock birth rate by denying welfare payments to families if a man was present in the household. The policy, one of many eligibility requirements that varied from state to state, was intended to prevent welfare payments from going to homes where a man could presumably provide for the family (Klos 1969). In effect, however, the policy gave men a reason to abandon their families by giving women a financial incentive to live without them. As Ritchie, the political science professor, explained:

> It's difficult to establish causation, but I don't think we [African Americans] started it. I think the government started it. Once you break up the black family—once you get the father out of the picture and the mother is taking care of us—the father doesn't have to be responsible. I think our high out-of-wedlock birth rates are largely a response to that. We're like, "Have more kids, get more money. I'm a father, but I don't have to take care of my child and no one's going to hold me accountable."

When parents pass these values to their children, the next generation of African Americans learns behaviors that elevate their risk of poverty. Charlie said it best: "Younger generations say, 'What did my father do? Well, my father didn't do much.' And that cycle just keeps going."

So the case against government antipoverty programs is as follows:

1. Like all Americans, African Americans can prosper if they're willing to sacrifice and work hard.
2. When the government gives people resources (money, food, housing, etc.), they no longer have an incentive to work to obtain them, which drains their work ethic and makes them lazy.
3. Living on charity also isolates African Americans from mainstream households and exposes them to behaviors that tend to keep them in poverty.
4. People will do whatever it takes—including breaking up their families—to get "free" money.

5. As children are surrounded by absent fathers, unwed pregnancies, street crime, school dropout, and so forth, they learn these behaviors and poverty becomes intergenerational.

Descriptions of this process were repeated with minor variations by most of the Tea Partyers I spoke with. While few interviewees offered more than anecdotes to back the argument, its explanatory power seemed to be so self-evident, so logical that it seemed unassailable.

But expert opinion may not always respect common wisdom. Take the claim that welfare makes people lazy. Not necessarily true, say researchers who tested the popular perception that people on welfare squander the money by using it to stop working or to buy alcohol or cigarettes. When scholars from MIT and Harvard conducted experimental cash-transfer programs involving some 45,000 households in Latin America, Southeast Asia, and Africa, they found "no systematic evidence that cash-transfer programs discourage work" either for men or women, and no evidence that recipients spent the cash on so-called "temptation goods" (Banerjee et al. 2017, 155). Likewise, when a team headed by University of North Carolina public policy professor Sudhanshu Handa (Handa et al. 2018) studied unconditional large-scale cash-transfer programs in sub-Saharan Africa, they knew that some policymakers and editorialists had predicted that recipients would simply spend the money for immediate needs, such as food or shelter, instead of making longer-term investments. They were also aware of concerns that the programs caused dependency. It's the same concern voiced by African American Tea Partyers like James:

> Our motto is the road of self-sufficiency. The other motto we have is "Hands up, not hands out." A hand up, sure. Everybody needs a hand up. Everybody. You, me, and everybody. But a handout goes back to the old adage: Give them a fish and they eat for a day; teach a man to fish, they'll eat forever. That's what it boils down to.

Yet the researchers' findings supported a different narrative. In six of eight countries, parents used the cash subsidies to invest in their childrens' education, achieving increases in secondary-school enrollment of anywhere from 6.5 percent in Lesotho to 15.7 percent in Malawi. Similarly, there were no signs of people growing dependent on the government cash and therefore working less. "Overall, the results do not indicate a reduction in work effort," the researchers wrote (Handa et al. 2018, 277).

But what about the United States? After all, Lesotho and Malawi are one thing; what about Los Angeles and Milwaukee? Well, Africans and Americans may not be all that different. Take the Earned Income Tax Credit. This federal initiative returns a percentage of a working family's income tax back to the family in the form of a refund. It's the largest government-run antipoverty cash assistance program, and in 2017 it returned to low- and moderate-income families cash payments of anywhere from $3,400 to $6,318, depending on the number of children in the family (Connick 2018; Simon, McInerney, and Goodell 2018). Doubters say these recipients view cash relief of this magnitude as an excuse to kick back and relax. But the tax credit has actually expanded the workforce, because the refund gets larger the more a person works (Simon, McInerney, and Goodell 2018). In fact, the Earned Income Tax Credit brought more single mothers into the workforce in the 1990s than welfare reform did (Matthews 2015). And whatever you might think of welfare reform, which was proposed by congressional Republicans and signed into law by President Clinton in 1996, it's credited with helping to bring 1.3 million single mothers into the workplace from 1993 to 2002 (Haskins 2006). Americans' experience with the Earned Income Credit suggests that when you supplement a poor person's income, it doesn't kill their desire to work. To the contrary, it might encourage them to work *harder.*

Business writer John Aziz (2014) says that if government subsidies reduced Americans' work ethic, we would have an oversupply of jobs, and businesses would be scrambling to raise wages to attract scarce workers. In fact, we have an oversupply of workers. The United States has had significant excess labor since before the economic downturn of 2008, when workers outnumbered available jobs by a margin of seven to one. This suggests that unemployed people lack jobs, not ambition. "Surely there are some people who would rather claim welfare than try to work," writes Aziz. "But with so few jobs available, these people don't make a real difference. Trying to nudge them off welfare won't expand the number of jobs. It would increase the number of people looking for a job."

What about the complaint that the government destroyed the African American family structure by offering welfare payments only to women who didn't have a man in the house? That could be an exaggeration, too. First of all, bear in mind that African American family life hasn't always been about broken marriages and out-of-wedlock births. In fact, from shortly after Reconstruction (1890) through the postwar period (1950), the marriage rate for blacks was *higher* than the marriage rate for whites (Ricketts 1989). That throws a wrench into the idea, popularized by Daniel Patrick Moynihan and others, that the trauma of slavery irrevocably disrupted African American family life (Office of Policy Planning and Research 1965). Starting in 1950, when marriage rates for whites began to exceed those of blacks, black rates plummeted, especially after 1960. So the question isn't whether welfare policies dismantled the black family. It's why has marriage been increasingly unpopular among African Americans since the 1960s.

Many black Tea Partyers blame LBJ's Great Society programs, but this apparent cause and effect could be a coincidence. Sociologist Andrew Billingsley thinks the real reason marriage rates fell was a dramatic transformation of the workplace as efficient machinery began to produce goods faster than ever before. "What happened in the mid-1950s were technological changes that abolished unskilled jobs that most black men could do and created high-tech jobs that they couldn't," Billingsley says (Gordy 2011). Then, starting in the late 1960s, deindustrialization and outsourcing relocated millions of jobs from the urban North to the low-wage nonunion South and then overseas. With less seniority than whites, black men were disproportionately laid off or fired in the wake of these seismic labor-market upheavals, and many left their families because they could not support them (Gordy 2011; Perry 1995; Leondar-White, n.d.). Ultimately, the cause of so much family disruption was a catastrophic loss of jobs. "That's what kept black families from getting and staying married, not the welfare system," says Billingsley. "To say otherwise is a misunderstanding of the data, and it's a misreading of history" (Gordy 2011).

So it's entirely probable that the federal war on poverty may have coincided with black men leaving their families, but didn't cause it to happen—which is probably why Ritchie, the political scientist, rightly began his comment about what caused black fathers to leave their families by acknowledging, "It's difficult to establish causation." After all, the "no man in the house" provisions, which were imposed not by the federal government but by nineteen mostly southern states and the District of Columbia, had been in place for only ten years on average before they were struck down by the US Supreme Court in 1968 (Piven and Cloward 1971; US Supreme Court 1968). To claim that these rescinded rules explain why African American men today abandon their families suggests that policies that existed in a minority of states for just a decade are still affecting people's behavior some fifty years later.

No doubt welfare makes some African Americans lazy, just as some black men abandon their families because they never intended to support them in the first place. But like many lay observers, black Tea Party supporters tend to blame the government for baiting a hook that was swallowed by generations of black people.

In truth, many Tea Partyers argue, if you want to get out of poverty you don't need the government. You need education, Mary says: "The message I got about that when I was growing up was really that education was the way out of poverty. It was, 'When you go to school and you do well, doors can open for you.' I never got an *if* you go to college; it was a *when* you go to college."

And you need to be tough, says Anne: "If you're born into poverty and that's the only thing you know, it can become the only thing you think you'll know. But a number of people in that situation were able to move out of it because of their intestinal fortitude."

Indeed, statistics back both Tea Partyers: education and perseverance are key to escaping poverty. In a 2012 study by the Economic Policy Institute (2012), the two most important factors that allowed Americans to leave the bottom income fifth were: (1) years of education beyond high school; and (2) working 1,000 extra hours a year. People who had an education beyond high school were 31.4 percent more likely than less-educated Americans to escape the lowest income level, and people who worked the extra hours were 12.5 percent more likely to break free of poverty compared to people who worked less. (Overall, white Americans were 8.2 percent more likely to escape poverty compared to nonwhites.)

And you need desire, Byron says. When I asked Byron to estimate how many people who are born poor escape into the middle class, he answered rhetorically, "How many want to?" People like Anne and Mary and Byron understand that poor people who have any number of helpful personality characteristics—motivation, drive, ambition—have a leg up on similarly situated African Americans who lack will power, endurance, or imagination.

There's no question that escaping poverty is impossible unless people want to (barring a hefty inheritance, of course). But surely, positive traits only go so far. In the Economic Policy Institute study, even the most potent route up the socioeconomic ladder—education beyond high school—offered only a one-in-three better chance that a person with trade-school or college credentials would escape poverty. But Tea Partyers who focus on the importance of diligence or hard work nearly always imply that *everyone* who satisfies these preconditions will be successful. For example, when Byron recounted how his father returned to his home state in the Deep South despite having few resources, he said, "I learned a lesson. Hard work leads to prosperity. Mere talk leads to poverty." Because Tea Partyers like Anne and Byron don't seem to consider that poor people can and do fail to overcome poverty even after following the rules and doing the right things, they may be among the majority of Americans who overestimate people's ability to change their social class (Kraus and Tan 2015). Americans frequently overestimate the power of agency. For example, when people assume that individual agency is the main determinant of someone's fate, they might also overestimate how much wealth the average person earns on their own versus how much wealth they inherit from their parents. I suspect this is why Tea Partyers like Mary estimated that an average of 20 percent of a person's wealth is passed down from their parents, whereas economists, including former US Secretary of the Treasury Lawrence H. Summers, say the actual amount is closer to 80 percent (Kotlikoff and Summers 1981).

There were, of course, other perspectives. When I asked Rod, the shopkeeper's son, whether his parents had ever told him that people who are, say, homeless or chronically unemployed, are poor because they don't work hard enough, he said, "I can't say my parents ever said anything like that to me. I think it's a common thing to hear, especially from those who are more successful. They tend to think people who aren't as successful just didn't work as hard as they did. But I never felt that way and I don't think my parents ever felt that way, either." Likewise, Joan flatly denied that African Americans' work habits have much to do with reaching their life destinations at all. "People talk about the value of hard work, but work isn't the total determinant of someone's trajectory. There's more to it than that. You have to look at a larger picture than the sum total of a person's individual choices."

Jimmy remembered a school friend from a respectable family that he was stunned to find was on welfare:

> One of the most shameful moments in my life. This beautiful girl I used to walk home from school every day. I was so infatuated with her. I was on one of my political rants, standing on my soapbox talking about welfare people, and she looked at me and told me her family was on welfare. I felt so small. She's a good person and I knew her parents went to church. I had no idea they were on welfare and needed help. She's a doctor now. No, I don't believe everyone on welfare is there because they don't want to work.

When I asked Ritchie about the power of individual initiative to shape a person's future, his reply was nuanced. Ritchie came from three generations of hardworking African American men. Yet he acknowledged that all Americans, African Americans and whites alike, face circumstances today that are much larger than any individual:

> Both my mom and my dad are very critical of the lack of work ethic that they see in young people. There was a huge multibillion-dollar plant going up near my parents, and employers went to black churches to recruit young people to do vocational training to get well-paid jobs as welders and the like. But they got no takers, so they had to bring in migrants. My mom says about our young people, "They don't want to work." On the other side, she's also acknowledged that so many young people didn't have that behavior modeled for them in their homes, so it's hard for them to know what it's like.

Ritchie's mother is both critical of behavior she finds maladaptive, and aware that how children are socialized can explain the origins of that behavior. Likewise, Ritchie praised the personal resolve of the three generations of hard-working African American men who were his role models at home. At the same time, he acknowledged that workers today face a new reality because the nature of work has changed. These changes suggest that personal resolve doesn't carry the same heft as before:

> My dad worked on a farm growing up. When they moved to Detroit, he decided to join the military. I've never known my dad not to be a hard worker. Even now, at his age, he still can't stay in the house; he's got a part-time job working at the local convenience store. He goes out and works in the yard. My mom's the same way. My grandfather would work at the petrochemical plant during the day and then he would buy old homes and rip them out and refurbish them. He was always working. I guess we've made a transition from the days when working with your hands was enough to support a family. Now, knowledge is more important than physical strength. I think that caught an entire generation off guard because for low-skill workers, factory work was a tangible thing you could do without having any kind of advanced education, and you could make a good living doing it. Nowadays, outsourcing and the information age have had a very negative impact on anyone with low-skill labor, and that includes the white underclass. The world's not accommodating to them. We complain about their lack of work ethic, but they may not see a chance to get ahead in work any more like they used to be able to. Now the only jobs they qualify for are positions that pay very little. If they want to make a good living, they have to retrain themselves in ways that are not practical to people in those communities or at this stage in their lives.

I asked Ritchie if, then, he views African American indifference toward jobs—the same thing his parents complained about—as representing more than a moral abdication. Personality flaws might explain why some of us fail to climb the ladder to success, but can you attribute more than a fraction of this failure to personality flaws? I asked.

> No, you can't. That's a realization I had to come to. If God gave me anything it was empathy and when I became more active in the lives of people at the church I go to, and actually started going to their homes and hearing their stories, I realized just how hard their lives have been and how hard they are now.

Harvard sociologist William Julius Wilson would agree with Ritchie. "For many years, social scientists and other observers have debated the role of social structure versus culture in determining the social outcomes of African Americans," Wilson told an audience in 2008. "Conservatives tend to emphasize cultural factors, such as attitude, worldview, and styles of behavior, whereas liberals pay more attention to structural conditions . . . such as discrimination and segregation," Wilson said. "Culture matters, but I wouldn't say it matters as much as social structure. Structure trumps culture" (Schorow 2008). As C. Wright Mills would say, *public issues* trump *personal troubles*.

Many of my interviewees would dispute this assessment. Even when they recognized that an African American's fate depends on much more than their willingness to bootstrap their way up the ladder, some inexorably returned to their faith in the notion that black people are masters of their own destiny. In other words, structural constraints, whether they be neighborhood gang violence, a horrendous job market, or terribly inferior schooling, are never determinative, because nothing can keep black people down.

For some, this faith in personal agency is simply common sense. Jake acknowledged that there are plenty of things besides people's individual decisions that help to determine their fate. "Crime. Natural disasters. Accidental tragedies. Those things are outside our control," he said. But then he explained why willpower is still more important than circumstance. "Personal work ethic is in our control and because it's within our control, we can do it. We just have to want to do it."

Others spoke from personal experience. Even Jimmy, the Tea Partyer who realized while walking with his classmate that even respectable families can need government assistance, said that taking charge of your life is still the answer even when corporate decisions and economic conditions have drained the black community of meaningful jobs. "Listen to what my daddy told me," Jimmy said. "He said, 'Son if you can't find yourself a job, make yourself a job.' He didn't say, 'Son, if you can't find a job, ask the government to give you some handouts.' Out of you making a job for yourself, you will get paid and you will grow." His father's advice served him well when Jimmy lost his job early in his career and couldn't pay his rent. He went to his landlord and proposed to work in exchange for rent money. The landlord agreed, and Jimmy became the building superintendent, cleaning the apartment building, installing carpeting, and doing maintenance work for six months until he was back on his feet.

Jimmy's happy outcome confirmed in his mind the power of African American agency. His story reminded me of a comment from Andrew, the political consultant, who said divine providence has a lot to do with a person's life trajectory. Andrew was a success story, a scrappy entrepreneur who said his parents had taught him the value of honesty and integrity. When I asked him what separated him from guys who hang out on the street corner, I expected him to mention his values but he didn't. "The grace of God," he said.

Jimmy says African Americans' control over their destiny isn't about God. "I don't believe in looking at a low-income person and saying, 'There but by the grace of God go I,'" he said. "I believe you make your own luck."

CASE #2: PERSONAL RESPONSIBILITY AND THE CRIMINAL JUSTICE SYSTEM

On May 17, 2004, the NAACP held a star-studded gala in Washington, DC, to celebrate the fiftieth anniversary of *Brown v. Board of Education*, the landmark school desegregation case that paved the way to integrated public classrooms (Associated Press 2004). By the end of the evening, the event was even more memorable for off-the-cuff remarks from one of the honorees.

Bill and Camille Cosby had been invited to acknowledge the couple's longtime support of historically black colleges and universities. But when Cosby took the microphone, higher education wasn't the only thing on his mind. "Ladies and gentlemen, the lower economic and lower middle economic people are not holding their end in this deal," he said. "Brown versus the Board of Education is no longer the white person's problem. It's not what they're doing to us. It's what we're not doing." Cosby proceeded to rail against absent fathers, teens who are unembarrassed about having children out of wedlock, "people with their hat on backwards, pants down around the crack," people with Afrocentric names. "These people . . . don't know a damned thing about Africa. With names like Shaniqua, Shaligua, Mohammed, and all that crap" (Cosby 2004).

Cosby urged a return to the old-fashioned parenting he saw as a child—a mix of attentiveness and concern where children were afraid to break the rules because "every drawn shade was an eye." If we don't do a better job of policing ourselves, he said, we can't complain when the police do it for us:

> I'm talking about these people who cry when their son is standing there in an orange suit. Where were you when he was two? Where were you when he was twelve? Where were you when he was eighteen, and how come you don't know he had a pistol? And where is his father, and why don't you know where he is? And why doesn't the father show up to talk to this boy?

Cosby then famously claimed that African Americans who focus on police misconduct are missing the point. Black people who end up behind bars aren't political criminals, he said.

> These are people going around stealing Coca Cola. People getting shot in the back of the head over a piece of pound cake! Then we all run out and are outraged: "The cops shouldn't have shot him." What the hell was he doing with the pound cake in his hand? I wanted a piece of pound cake just as bad as anybody else. And I looked at it and I had no money. And something called parenting said if you get caught with it you're going to embarrass your mother.

Cosby's venue that evening was Constitution Hall, a massive stone concert building a few blocks from the White House. But by the tone of his remarks, it could have been a Tea Party rally. His insistence that African Americans take responsibility for the black community's grievous losses through the criminal justice system would have had the entire audience, white and black alike, nodding in agreement.

Listen to how James describes the difference between law-abiding black folks and thugs:

> The left wing of the black Democrats believes that they're owed. The man always trying to keep me down. The man's always trying to lock me up. The popo [police] want to . . . No. If you were doing what you're supposed to, you wouldn't have that problem. I could go sit on the corner in a predominantly white neighborhood, 'kay? And if I'm dressed like a thug, I'm probably gonna get picked up, or at least be questioned. If I'm dressed like a normal human being, conducting myself in a manner that is civil, if you will, then you don't have these problems.

Like Cosby, James conflates dress and behavior on the assumption that teens who wear conventional clothes will also do other conventional things, like respect the law. From that perspective, anyone who sags their pants is practically flaunting his criminal bravado. That might sound suicidal given the epidemic of police shootings, but social psychologists like Tamotsu Shibutani say young people who violate societal norms aren't crazy. Like everyone, they have a reference group. It's just that their reference group is low-slung rappers like Ice-T and Too Short, quite a different reference group than Bill Cosby's (Blake 2017). As Shibutani (2017, 571–72) puts it:

> An "incorrigible" boy often has many qualities that win him respect in his primary group—courage, loyalty, personal integrity, and a sense of decency and fair play. Such boys do not necessarily suffer from personality disorders; indeed, they are quite well adjusted to their world. Their conduct is judged deviant by those who are not a part of their reference group.

Novelist and anthropologist Zora Neal Hurston once cleverly avoided a run-in with the law by using an unusual reference group—white people. She eluded a ticket for jaywalking after crossing a street against a red light. "I told the policeman that I had seen white folks cross on the green and so I assumed the red light was for me," she said (Lauter 1991, 256).

Black Tea Partyers might chuckle at Hurston's insouciance, but many would probably disapprove of her tactics. They realize how overzealous policing stacks the deck against African Americans, especially young black men. In 2016 alone, 26 percent of the 1,092 victims of deadly police force were black (Khazan 2018). That means African Americans were victimized twice as heavily as you'd expect from a 13 percent population share. "I would be naïve not to acknowledge that," Mary said. "I've experienced being pulled over by a police officer for no reason." Tea Party darling Sen. Tim Scott (R-S.C.) spoke eloquently on the floor of the US Senate about how he'd been pulled over seven times by police officers just because he was a black man driving a car. Scott's 2016 speech, in which he acknowledged he had been driving too fast on two occasions but was simply driving a new car on the remaining five, recalled even harsher police treatment endured by less prominent African Americans, such as Minnesota native Philando Castile (Black 2016). Castile had been stopped fifty-two times by police officers since 2002 before an officer shot him to death him in front of his girlfriend and her four-year-old daughter during a 2016 traffic stop (deLong and Braunger 2017). The officer said he thought Castile was reaching for a handgun Castile told him he had a permit to carry; his girlfriend said Castile was reaching for his ID. Castile was killed one day after Baton Rouge, Louisiana, police officers killed Alton Sterling, another African American, whom they incorrectly suspected had threatened someone with a gun. Videos of both deaths went viral on social media and sparked nationwide protests, but neither police officer was convicted of a crime (Yan, Berlinger, and Robinson 2016).

Black Tea Party supporters like Mary say it would be reckless not to acknowledge the possibility—if not the likelihood—that these police killings are motivated by race. At the same time, their answer to such criminal injustice is personal rectitude. As Mary explained, "I talk with black conservatives who say, 'Yes, racism is a thing, but we have to pull ourselves up by our bootstraps. We have to take initiatives. We should modify our personal traits. No one's going to hand us a blue ribbon; we have to earn it.'"

Earning a blue ribbon for justice would mean overcoming three hundred years of history. It may be hard to believe, given the salience of race today, but skin color wasn't particularly relevant in the earliest years of the US colonies. Throughout most of the 1600s, social status was measured not by skin color but by a person's wealth, nationality, or religion (Berkin 2003). Eventually, however, slavery so efficiently kick-started the fledgling economy and proved so profitable to the slave-owning class that blackness and subordination went hand in hand. Colonial statutes began to reflect the new racial order. In Virginia, for example, slaves were denied the right to trial by jury and prohibited from testifying against whites. White men who raped black women were not charged with a crime, but a slave could be castrated for even *attempting* to rape a white woman (Higginbotham and Jacobs 1992). In 1787, the US Constitution further legalized racial inequality by requiring citizens to surrender fugitive slaves to their owners and forbidding Congress from banning the slave trade for the next twenty years. As the late federal judge A. Leon Higginbotham (1978, 6) noted, "The Constitution's references to justice, welfare, and liberty were mocked by the treatment meted out daily to blacks from the seventeenth to nineteenth centuries through the courts, in legislative statutes, and in those provisions of the Constitution that sanctioned slavery for the majority of black Americans and allowed disparate treatment for those few blacks legally free."

After the Civil War, the bright and fleeting promise of emancipation gave way to a flurry of state and federal laws that returned newly freed blacks to what journalist Douglas A. Blackmon (2004) calls "slavery by another name." Starting in 1865, newly reconstituted southern legislatures passed Black Codes that regulated the lives of former slaves by legalizing black property ownership and marriages but denying them the right to vote or to serve on juries. In Mississippi, vagrancy laws allowed police to arrest black adults "for the 'crime' of being unemployed" (Russell 1998, 19). Meanwhile, children of impoverished former slaves could be sold back to their former owners as "apprentices" until age twenty-one; runaways were jailed for "desertion" (Anon n.d.a.).

These and other racially punitive laws altered the complexion of the nation's prison population. Convict populations, which for decades had been disproportionately black, soon became overwhelmingly black. By 1880, the prison populations of Georgia and South Carolina were 92 percent and 96 percent African American, respectively (Oshinsky 1996, 63). With jail cells now bursting with black and brown faces, southern states compensated for the loss of slavery by leasing convict labor to white landowners. Convict leasing was immensely profitable to the lessees and the government, but its brutality was ruinous to the convicts, who in some cases were literally worked to death. In Louisiana, where hard labor in swamps and on plantations was particularly brutal, a newspaper editor suggested that it would be more humane to give a convicted felon an immediate death sentence than to lease him to a landowner for more than six years, "because the average inmate lived no longer than that" (Sellin 1976, 147).

By the turn of the century, eugenicists' alarm over race-mixing gave way to Jim Crow segregation laws, which mandated separate—and unequal—public facilities for blacks and whites. Lunch counters and water fountains weren't the only things to hew the color line; hospitals and parks were color-coded as well, as were phone booths, textbooks, cemeteries, even brothels (Russell 1998). Of course, the Civil Rights Act of 1964, which prohibited discrimination by police departments, courts, correctional facilities, and any other institution that receives federal funds, outlawed de jure racism. By 1976, the US Supreme Court had followed suit, ruling that intentional discrimination by police officers, judges, and other public officials is unconstitutional (Baldus et al. 1998).

But there's plenty of evidence that de facto racism in the criminal justice system endures. Thanks to the development of the Implicit Association Test in 1998, scientists have hard evidence that most people hold at least subtle biases against members of out-groups, including African Americans (Greenwald, McGhee, and Schwartz 1998). Where do those biases emerge? At every step in the criminal justice process. "Compared to observably similar whites, blacks are more likely to be searched for contraband, more likely to experience police force, more likely to be charged with a serious offense, more likely to be convicted, and more likely to be incarcerated," write economists David Arnold, Will Dobbie, and Crystal S. Yang (2018, 1885). For example, in one study, police officers in Illinois, North Carolina, Connecticut, and Rhode Island—four states that carefully monitor the results of traffic stops—were more likely to stop black motorists for interrogation, even though police were more likely to find drugs, guns, and other contraband when the driver was white (LaFraniere and Lehren 2015). Once inside a courtroom, defendants who have darker skin and thicker lips are more likely to receive harsher sentences than African Americans with whiter features, according to a Cornell University study. "It's not just if you're black or white, it's how black you are," says law professor Adam Benforado, author of *Unfair: The New Science of Criminal Injustice* (Swanson 2015). As a group, blacks are at higher risk than whites of receiving the death penalty even when the nature of criminal charges and extenuating circumstances (such as prior criminal record) are taken into account (US General Accounting Office 1990).

This presents an obvious question. Make no mistake: it's perfectly possible today for African Americans to get a fair shake from police officers, judges, and corrections officials. In fact, given the frankly staggering number of reforms at the federal, state, and local levels (e.g., The Sentencing Project 2000), I would argue that at no other time in American history have there been better prospects for fairness. On the other hand, racial injustice—whether the goal of the law or in spite of it—is in the very DNA of the criminal justice system, and has been for years. As we've just seen above, courtroom discrimination is so pervasive that African American defendants are judged right down to their facial features. So at a time when 34 percent of our prison population—but only 12 percent of our general population—is African American, what does it mean to take personal responsibility for our actions (Zeng 2010)? How much can acting responsibly negate three hundred years of unsavory assumptions about African Americans' potential for deviant behavior? How does someone take personal responsibility for their facial features?

Responsibility Defined

Granted, taken to an extreme, a simple call for personal responsibility sidesteps difficult historical and contemporary realities. But when we examine what black Tea Partyers are advocating, it's clear that their perspectives on crime and the criminal justice system are anything but simple. During interviews I found five very different definitions of what it means to take responsibility for one's actions in the context of the criminal justice system: following the law; showing police officers respect; teaching children what to do during a police encounter; showing others—including police officers—that you're willing to protect yourself; and challenging cultural norms.

Following the Law

Young black men born in 2001 have a 32 percent chance of spending time in prison at some point in their lives. The corresponding rate for white men is six percent (The Sentencing Project 2000). When I asked Lindsay why the black/white imprisonment gap is so large, he was blunt. "Behavior," he said.

> I know this is going to get me in trouble with a whole bunch of black folk, but behavior. Black folks kill more people than white people. Black people commit more crimes. It's just a fact. We got to wake up the black community. Tell them to get their act together and stop doing the things that they're doing and that's what's causing these disparities.

Similarly, George told me he had seen plenty of black criminal defendants throughout his long career as a court clerk. Most were headed to prison for one reason—their own terrible decisions:

> Well, I've been in the courts over 30 years. I've seen a lot of guys go to prison. I always try to look into their background, to try to see what happened in any given case. From what I hear, 99 percent of them are guilty of the crimes they committed. A lot of people do dumb things, commit dumb crimes. They wouldn't have gone to jail if they hadn't had a gun on them when they were caught doing something. That kind of thing.

Experts agree that disproportionate numbers of black and brown faces are caught up in the criminal justice system, but it's not entirely clear that the reason is too much lawbreaking. The FBI's Uniform Crime Report (UCR) statistics, our most reliable indicator of who's breaking the law, cover violent crime (rape, murder, etc.) and property crime (theft, arson, etc.) but not embezzlement, fraud, and other white-collar crime, which tends to be committed by whites. The UCR data are also restricted to crime that comes to the attention of the police. Victimless crime like prostitution or drug trafficking, in which both parties are willing participants, often flies under the radar because neither party wants to report it. On the other hand, black crime can come to the attention of police officers simply by sweeping an African American neighborhood, in which case these statistics better reflect police activity than citizen activity (Unnever and Gabbidon 2011). These are some of the reasons critics say the UCR data are unreliable. In the words of the nonprofit advocacy group The Sentencing Project (2000, 6), "While some claim that minority overrepresentation in the justice system is solely the result of people of color committing more crime, empirical analyses do not support this claim."

Respecting the Police

Other Tea Partyers feel that acting beyond reproach is a no-brainer. To them, taking responsibility for your actions means more than simply not breaking the law. It means responding to police officers in respectful ways that minimize the likelihood of a bad outcome. Len says he's never had a problem when police officers pull him over, because he's respectful toward them:

> I don't have problems with law enforcement. When police officers stop me, the most important thing I focus on is my attitude. I learned that from my father. The reason so many African Americans run afoul of the law is that many of them have never been brought up by fathers who know how to be men, and what it means to be men. They talk back and yell at the police because they've never been taught any other way. They're only repeating what they've learned by watching other young black men. Plus, it's fear. They want people to think they're tough men, but they're really boys. They're scared.

Len's description of how young black men use bravado to conceal their fears is not altogether different from *cool pose,* a tough-guy persona that young African Americans often use to mask their anger and frustration over a racialized society that assigns them permanent second-class citizenship. "It provides a mask that suggests competence, high self-esteem, control, and inner strength," write psychologist Richard Majors and sociologist Janet Mancini Billson (1992, 5). "It also hides self-doubt, insecurity, and inner turmoil."

Len denies that American racism is widespread, so during a confrontation with a police officer it may be easy for him to remain calm. That may be more of a challenge for Wallace, a software developer, who sees racism as a clear and present danger. So when police officers pull him over, he tries to disregard the possibility that he's at special risk:

> I'm afraid of some sort of likelihood, in the back of my mind, that there's a racist cop and he's gonna do something to me when he pulls me over. So I do the same thing white people do. You grab your license and registration, you pull over to the side of the road, and you put your hands in plain view. You do exactly what the officer says and you don't get shot. I look at so many blacks that are getting shot and say, "Why didn't you just do what the policeman said?"

Teaching Children

A third approach to taking personality responsibility for one's actions recognizes that every African American has an obligation to protect the interests of the rest of the community. Of course, any one citizen has limited leverage against the 2.4 million police, courtroom, and corrections officials who represent America's sprawling federal-state-local criminal justice partnership

(Bronson 2018). But every parent can start by protecting their children, black Tea Partyers say, by explaining what to do if they're stopped by the police. In Dean's experience, that's a message white parents don't always share with their kids:

> In the city I grew up in, I was pulled over for Driving While Black on a number of occasions and I knew that's what they were doing. The police seemed especially bothered when a white woman was in the car with me. So here's something I taught my son, which my dad taught me. I've explained this to lots of white guys and none of them had ever heard of this. Their fathers never taught it to them. But I told my sons that whenever you're pulled over by an officer, turn your stereo off, turn the ignition off, roll all the windows down—I don't care what the temperature is—, open the roof if your car is a convertible, and put both your hands on top of the steering wheel at 11 and 1 o'clock. If it's dark, turn on all your interior lights. That's the posture you assume, so that officer knows as he or she is approaching your car what's going on inside.

Defending Themselves

Some Tea Partyers endorse a more aggressive form of racial autonomy, in which taking personal responsibility means showing the world that African Americans are willing to defend themselves against all threats. Jimmy said that if more African Americans carried firearms, George Zimmerman might not have killed Trayvon Martin:

> I don't know whether Trayvon was right or wrong. The boy had a 'hood past, but he did not have the right to be executed on the street. The answer is not to run around whining and moaning that nobody should have guns. You have a constitutional right to have a gun. Get strapped up! Teach your kids how to use guns properly. In Florida, where Trayvon was killed, you can carry firearms if they are concealed. So, when this little busybody comes over to you and he's strapped, you be strapped. Let's make it an equal contest!

Referring to himself as a radical, Jimmy had said he was a longtime admirer of the Black Panther Party. I knew the group's formal name included the words, "for Self-Defense." Still, I was so startled by his call to arms—literally—that I asked if he was speaking rhetorically.

> No, I'm serious. I told you I was radical, brother. I am so tired of seeing black kids killed in America. If you want to see this shit stop, you educate black children. I'm not talking about arming gangsters. I'm talking about law-abiding black people. Use their right to bear arms so they can protect themselves. The government isn't protecting black people, police aren't protecting black people, and the judicial system is not protecting black people. So you do it your damn self.

Jimmy stopped short of saying African Americans should arm themselves against overzealous police officers. In fact, a fellow black Tea Partyer does quite the opposite, using a weapon to *disarm* the police. James lives in an open-carry state, where firearms don't have to be concealed. He routinely does something that many African Americans would consider unthinkable: he approaches a police officer while carrying a loaded handgun. He isn't trying to threaten the officer. He's trying to bond with them:

> I want to talk to the cops. One, I want the cop to know what I think and two, I want to know he'll keep me safe. We live in an open-carry state, and I openly carry my firearm everywhere I go, within the regulations, of course. I've had police officers say, "That's a nice weapon! What you got there?" The officer says his own gun type. I say, "Here, let me unload it. Take a look." Okay. Now. I'm a black man carrying a firearm openly, *openly*. A Negro walking with a firearm. And not one time have I ever been harassed. Never!

James says police officers always respond to him courteously and respectfully, which goes to show that police officers don't treat all black men like thugs. One person's experience isn't definitive, he admits. But it does lend credence to a common refrain among conservatives: when it comes to attracting police scrutiny, it's not who you are—it's what you're doing.

Challenging Cultural Norms

A fifth definition of taking personal responsibility relates to challenging cultural norms relating to blacks and crime. Here are two examples. As I talked with Melvin about policing, I asked what he would say if his teenage son asked him, "Dad, is institutional racism really a thing?" He paused for a moment, then said he would deny it. Not because institutional racism doesn't exist, he said. He just doesn't want the automatic assumption of racism to influence his son's thinking were he to interact with a police officer:

> If your first thought is racism, you plunge into a conversation with yourself about preconceptions, and that's not always helpful. So assume that there isn't racism and deal with the situation that way. That would be my approach. The only control I have over prejudice is to allow people to see that stereotypes aren't necessarily accurate and hopefully, they have an open mind to see that the bad apples are not the majority. There are exceptions to any rule and I'm that exception. And hopefully, if there are enough exceptions to the rule, the rule goes away.

Clinical psychologist Lewis Aiken would probably say Melvin's idea of acting counterstereotypically to generate beneficial ripple effects is pretty reasonable. "Much can be done to reduce prejudice by removing some of the supports for it," Aiken (2002, 93) writes. "If it can be demonstrated to a prejudiced person that minority group members do not necessarily fit his or her stereotype, then the person's attitude toward that group should change." In a way, Melvin's goal of challenging stereotypes one person at a time represents a micro-level approach to tackling a larger problem. If every African American took responsibly for his or her actions, he's saying, the scaffolding for prejudicial thinking would collapse. Thus, even within the narrow confines of one interaction with a police officer, African Americans could reduce dangerous policing in the black community.

So Melvin feels that African Americans can shift popular cultural assumptions about blacks and crime by acting in ways that challenge stereotypes. Rod, on the other hand, says African Americans can reduce run-ins with the law by changing their own culture. When I asked Rod to explain the high crime rates in the black community, he said the numbers are more than simply a reflection of black people doing bad things. Here's how he explained the racial disparity in incarceration rates:

> Well, the quick answer is that more blacks are getting locked up because more blacks are committing more crimes. The longer answer would be that too many blacks are still living in inner-city environments where crime has become the norm. A lot of that has to do with African American culture, which is unfortunately more sympathetic to criminals than it should be. We tend to make heroes out of local felons and drug dealers instead of the guy who wants to go a different route. You take two teenagers, one wants to be postal carrier who could make 50K a year with all these great benefits, and another teenager who wants to be a thug, like the people who are glorified in the rap music he hears and the music videos he watches, and there's no question which teenager will be treated with more respect. A lot of our crime rate has do to with the lower incomes of blacks, and a lot of it has to do with many blacks are living in inner-city environments. But also, we've got a cultural problem.

Of course, much of the rap music that Rod mentions started as a protest against police brutality (Charity, Diaz, and Drake 2014). That means the same frustration and rage that gave rise to rap music might be a starting point for black offending (Unnever and Gabbidon 2011). So together, what Melvin and Rod are proposing has symbiotic appeal: if the prejudice-reducing acts of law-abiding black people helps to reduce police violence, then young black men might have less police injustice to protest, and thus have less reason to turn to crime.

UNIFORM PURPOSE WITHOUT UNIFORMITY

The year 1906 was painful for African Americans. In Springfield, Missouri, two black men were accused of attacking a white couple and raping the woman. Though their white employer vouched for the men's whereabouts, they were lynched by a mob as law enforcement officials stood by. "We might as well have had a jellyfish for a sheriff and a set of rag dolls for police," said one local pastor (Rehwald 2018). In Chattanooga, a black man by the name of Ed Johnson was convicted of raping a white woman. He, too, was lynched even though no one heard the woman definitively identify her attacker. Justice wasn't the goal, a local judge said years later. "The object was to bring in a black body, not necessarily the person who had committed the crime" (Yellin 2000).

Of the sixty-two African Americans who were lynched that year, a few were actually guilty of a crime (Linder 2019). That was the case in Tampa, where John Black and Will Reagin were taken from police custody by a mob a few hours after a white man was found dead. Black and Reagin confessed to the crime, perhaps hoping for mercy. The mob killed them anyway (Anon. 1906b). Booker T. Washington denounced lynching in 1904 (e.g., Anon. 1904; Washington 1904), but in August 1906 it was men like Black and Reagin—the offenders, not the victims—who were uppermost on his mind as he spoke about lynchings to the Negro Business League in Atlanta. Washington encouraged his audience "to direct their efforts toward the reform of the men who disgraced their race in such occurrences," according to the *New York Times,* which reported the story under the headline, "He Condemns Those Who Provoke Lynchings." Washington said:

> Our leaders should see to it that the criminal negro is got rid of wherever possible. Making allowances for the mistakes, injustice, and the influence of racial prejudice, I have no hesitation in saying that one of the elements in our present situation that gives me most concern is the large number of crimes that are being committed by members of our race. . . . Let us do our part and then let us call upon the whites to do their part. (Anon. 1906a)

By highlighting the actions of the African American instigators, Washington seemed to imply that whites and blacks were equally responsible for lynching, a view held by few historians today. On the other hand, when Washington highlights black criminal behavior, he sounds like plenty of black Tea Partyers. When I spoke with Lindsay, for instance, he had just visited Ferguson, Missouri, where eighteen-year-old Michael Brown was shot and killed by a white police officer in 2014. He said protesters make a mistake when they automatically side with black residents against white police officers. I asked him, "Aren't white police officers more likely than black officers to prejudge black people?" He said they weren't:

> Unless they know the person they're stopping, a black police officer will probably go through the same mental calculations that a white officer does. I went to Ferguson a month after Michael Brown was killed. I met a lot of nice white people there. They treated me well. Turns out, blacks don't want to be

police officers in Ferguson. Why is it white people's fault if no black people want to join the police? Somebody's got to be on the police force!

Lindsay went on to discuss Freddie Gray, the twenty-five-year-old black man who died in Baltimore under police custody in 2015. The case gave rise to accusations of police brutality (Anon. 2015):

> People are talking about racism in Baltimore, but there are plenty of black police officers in Baltimore. That wasn't racism that killed that man. It was a situation. If you want to see if it's racism, take color out of the scenario, then reassess it. Ask yourself if the same thing could have happened if no white people were involved. If the answer is yes, then it's probably not racism.

Lindsay, a popular speaker at Tea Party rallies, has said the Black Lives Matter movement is fraudulent ever since it emerged shortly after Michael Brown's death. The problem, he says, is that the organizers have built the movement on a false narrative:

> When Black Lives Matter first started, I went to their website, which said they started their movement because of what happened to Michael Brown and he was shot even though his hands were up in the air and he was pleading with the police officer not to shoot him. So they came up with the slogan, "Hands Up, Don't Shoot." But according to the grand jury, Michael Brown was shot as he was wrestling for the police officer's gun. He wasn't shot in the back or any of that. And yet, this lie continues to be furthered. Why are they doing that? Because it fits their narrative that white cops murder blacks. And then, to put fuel on the fire, they had Michael Brown's mom speak at the Democratic National Convention, so they're furthering this lie to millions of blacks that her son was shot with his hands up by a racist white cop. That didn't happen. I don't care how you phrase it or frame it. That's evil.

Lindsay is quite correct. According to a US Department of Justice (2015) investigation conducted by the Obama administration, Officer Darren Wilson heard a report of a young black man who had stolen some cigarillos from a nearby market. Michael Brown fit the description of the suspect and was holding cigarillos in his hand when Wilson stopped him. Brown reached inside the officer's SUV, punched him, and reached for his weapon. Wilson shot Brown twice in the ensuing scuffle. The officer ran after Brown when he fled, then shot him ten more times when he turned on Wilson. Witnesses said Brown "appeared to pose a physical threat" before Wilson downed him, after which the officer stopped firing (US Department of Justice 2015, 7). Some witnesses said Michael Brown held his hands in the air briefly before the fatal gunshots, but they said Brown then dropped his hands before "charging" at the officer. The Justice Department concluded that Officer Wilson had a legitimate fear for his safety. As such, his actions were not "objectively unreasonable . . . and therefore [the case] should be closed without prosecution" (US Department of Justice 2015, 5). "Hands up, don't shoot" may be a good metaphor for many black victims of police violence, but it doesn't fit the facts of the Brown case.

Yet for every Tea Partyer who defended the police, there were even more who criticized law enforcement officials for what they viewed as an overbearing, even threatening presence in black neighborhoods. In direct contrast to Lindsay, Mary said living in neighborhoods where guns—and dangerous encounters with the police—proliferate makes her sympathetic to the Black Lives Matter movement:

> I understand a lot of the Black Lives Matter stuff, having witnessed police interactions up close. I've seen too many examples of what guns can do and what we can do to each other. Conservatives are supposed to support a well-armed militia, but I've never been comfortable around guns. I used to go visit my mom when she was living in the projects. I would go to sleep at night, no problem. But my husband would hear gunfire and say, "Did you hear that? That was an Uzi!" and he'd fall on the floor. It was white noise to me.

Similarly, Rod doesn't mind parting with other conservatives if it means safeguarding the African American community from overzealous police officers. I asked Rod if he felt that the conservative movement was a work in progress.

> Yes, I think we just saw that with gun control. Conservatives are adamant that you should be able to walk into a convenience store and buy an AR-15 [semi-automatic rifle]. I don't share that view. Conservatives also tend to blame the victims of police shootings, which I'm not happy with. Like with Philando Castile, the one who was shot in his car, and other instances like that. I definitely have some issues with the conservative movement.

That's why Antonio, a former police officer turned state representative, said he supports police reform:

> I support the police, but they have to be accountable. I pushed a police reform bill in my state, and I took a lot of flak for wanting the police to wear body cameras so people could see what they were doing. But if we're going to give them this money, we also have to keep them accountable. We just can't have these cops running around doing whatever they want to do.

Dean, the Tea Partyer who's been pulled over for Driving While Black with a White Woman in the Passenger Seat, agrees with Antonio: greater accountability means more honest policing. He says when the police are unmonitored and something goes wrong, it forces citizens to rely on the officers' version of events, which may be self-serving. "I'm not one of those who agrees when the police say, 'The suspect was injured because he was resisting arrest,'" Dean said. "No, it can't be that the person was resisting arrest every time they end up hurt."

These African American conservatives have common aspirations for safe, crime-free neighborhoods, and they would all agree that the black community would be far better off—assault rates would fall, drug crime would drop, gang violence would plummet—if fathers did a better job of supporting their families and parents taught their children to stay in school. That is to say, every black Tea Partyer I spoke with endorses the idea that African Americans should embrace their obligations to themselves, their families, and their communities. Our natural impulse may be greed, Rep. Barbara Jordan (D-Texas) (1994) told a class of graduating law students. But "our actions have consequences. And those consequences impact and affect others. There is an interconnectedness between each of us that cannot be abolished."

But there is also a dividing line within the Tea Party faithful, and it relates to the *sufficiency* of personal responsibility. Some black Tea Partyers say acting responsibly could resolve the abundance of crime in the black community. Lindsay's one-word answer—"behavior"—to my question about why so many black and brown faces are in jail captures this idea that individual African Americans are solely responsible for the overrepresentation of African Americans in the criminal justice system. People like Lindsay see these social problems as *personal troubles.*

But even more Tea Partyers see excess incarceration as a *public issue* in which the consequences of individuals' choices are compounded by racist or otherwise unsympathetic public policies and private actions. When Mary supports Black Lives Matter, or Dean complains about police officers stopping him for no cause, they are saying that no amount of personal rectitude can protect individual African Americans from larger structural forces that can harm them. To these conservatives, taking responsibility for a person's actions is what logicians call a necessary but insufficient condition for respectful treatment by the criminal justice system. That is to say, acting respectably enhances the likelihood that an African American will be treated well, but doesn't guarantee it.

CONCLUSION

So there seems to be a disconnect between how black Tea Partyers see poverty and how they view crime. The tendency is to see poverty as within a person's ability to control, such that government antipoverty programs are unnecessary and even counterproductive. The opposite is true for the criminal justice system, which Tea Partyers tend to view more as a structural problem than a personal one.

The idea that escaping poverty is a function of sheer willpower is consistent with conservatives' tendency to rely on clear-cut answers to problems (Salvi et al. 2016). People who identify as conservatives have an aversion to uncertainty, a higher need for closure, and a preference for "decisions that are quick, firm, and final," according to one analysis of eighty-eight studies from twelve countries (Jost et al. 2003, 358). Why does that differ from Tea Partyers' ideas about criminal justice, which seem more nuanced? One explanation may be that there are different types of conservatives. Some conservatives are absolutists who believe that problems can be resolved by applying a universal standard (such as personal responsibility). Others are relativists who believe that personal values may be more salient in some contexts than others. "Conservatism is not a unitary position," writes philosopher John Kekes (1997, 352). "[I]t has different versions, and their advocates disagree with each other about what political arrangements ought to be conserved."

Chapter Four

Our First Muslim President? Black Tea Partyers Weigh In on Obama

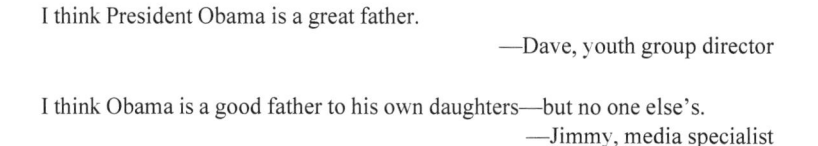

I think President Obama is a great father.

—Dave, youth group director

I think Obama is a good father to his own daughters—but no one else's.

—Jimmy, media specialist

In the summer of 2008, the BBC surveyed 22,000 adults around the world to gauge their reactions to the Democratic and Republican presidential contenders. How did the world community view the matchup between an elder statesman, a war hero whom George W. Bush called a "man of deep conviction and a patriot of the highest order" (Zaveri 2018), and a former community organizer with little foreign policy experience who had served just three brief years in the US Senate? When the votes were in, the results weren't even close. Barack Obama was the hands-down favorite in all twenty-two countries surveyed, and 46 percent of the respondents said they thought his winning the election would "fundamentally change" their view of the United States (BBC World Service 2008).

After Obama's improbable victory, buoyant African Americans felt much the same way: their view of their own country had fundamentally changed. Many were incredulous that Americans had elected a black president just a few generations after the end of slavery. Atlanta mayor Shirley Franklin called the election results "mind-boggling." Harvard professor Henry Louis Gates, Jr., told *Time*, "We jumped up, we wept, we hooped and hollered" on election night (Gray 2008).

Obama's victory even helped black Americans feel differently about themselves. The election boosted young African American men's confidence in their own success, according to research (Vaughn 2015). And the confidence boost had begun even before election day. When a nationwide sample of adults was asked to answer standardized-test questions periodically during the campaign, researchers discovered that the black-white achievement gap that usually surfaces in academic testing disappeared when Obama was performing well in opinion polls. Obama's self-assurance was contagious. Scholars dubbed this welcome outcome the "Obama Effect" (Marx, Ko, and Friedman 2009).

The president scored key legislative victories during his first months in office. A few weeks after his inauguration, he persuaded Congress to pass his $787 billion economic stimulus package, which ended the 2008 recession. A month later, Congress passed his auto industry bailout that eventually saved three million jobs, and he held a White House health care summit that laid the groundwork for the revolutionary Affordable Care Act, which reduced the number of uninsured Americans and slowed the rise in health care costs (Amadeo 2019a; Pear and Stolberg 2009). Those accomplishments begat others. "Measured in sheer legislative tonnage," wrote former presidential speechwriter Paul Glastris (2012), "what Obama got done in his first two years is stunning."

But storm clouds were gathering on Capitol Hill. Since inauguration evening, when Republican congressional leaders gathered at a Washington, DC, steakhouse to confront the grim reality of losing control of both chambers and the White House, the GOP leadership had decided on a simple counterstrategy: resist at every turn. "If you act like the minority, you're going to stay in the minority," California Rep. Kevin McCarthy steeled the group. "We've gotta challenge them on every single bill and challenge them on every single campaign" (Draper 2012, xviii). Former Ohio senator George Voinovich later explained, "If he [Obama] was for it, we had to be against it" (Grunwald 2012, 19).

Long before Senate minority leader Mitch McConnell famously declared in 2010, "The single most important thing we want to achieve is for President Obama to be a one-term president" (Barr 2010), Republicans' resistance was so resolute that they rejected their own legislative ideas when Obama proposed them. For example, in March 2011, Republicans on the Congressional Joint Economic Committee released a report urging their colleagues in both chambers to reduce the national debt by reining in expenditures and raising taxes (Brady 2011). Industrialized nations have done that successfully, Republicans argued, by reducing spending by 85 percent and increasing taxes by 15 percent. That's a far cry from the deficit-reduction package proposed by President Obama's National Commission on Fiscal Responsibility and Reform, which called for a 50 percent reduction in spending and a 50 percent hike in taxes (Biggs, Hassett, and Jensen 2010). But in June 2011, the Obama administration bit the bullet and swung over to the Republicans' side, agreeing to a whopping $2.4 trillion deficit-reduction package. The administration's proposal of 83 percent spending cuts and 17 percent tax increases was a hair away from the 85 percent/15 percent ratio the GOP had called for three months earlier. What did administration officials get for their efforts? Republicans walked out of the room. "How do you negotiate with that?" asked *Washington Post* columnist Ezra Klein (2011). By the 2014 congressional midterm elections, Obama claimed Republicans had blocked five hundred bills designed to help the middle class alone (Topaz 2014).

Political commentators were stunned by such "mindless obstruction" from conservative lawmakers (Milbank 2016). Many citizens were angry, too—angry that the federal government seemed adrift from its constitutional moorings, angry that their government had become menacingly large and intrusive and insensitive to the needs of ordinary taxpayers. But inasmuch as these protesters could have made similar accusations of government overreach during previous administrations, they reserved a special vitriol for Barack Obama.

In their "gut-level resistance to all things Obama" they questioned his policies, opposing Obamacare, the stimulus package, the Detroit bailout, and his immigration initiatives (Cassata and Regan 2016). By August 2009, conservative websites like American Thinker were accusing the president and his "czars" of "cattle-driving a legislative cramdown" after mistaking "victory against a tepid Republican presidential candidate for a mandate to reconstitute the United States of America" (Cary 2009).

They questioned his politics. "[O]ur military didn't fight and die for this country [to have] a communist in the White House," one Tea Party speaker told a rally crowd (Spellman 2009). Others called him a socialist or even a fascist. At a Canton, Ohio, Tea Party rally, a woman held a sign with images of Obama and Hitler. "Hitler made great speeches, too," read the caption (Spellman 2009).

They questioned his religion. If they didn't think Obama himself was Muslim, they seemed convinced that he was a supporter of Islam. Texas Republican Rep. Louie Gohmert went so far as to claim that the investigation into the 2013 Boston Marathon bombing was delayed because of Obama's ties to Egypt's Muslim Brotherhood. "This administration has so many Muslim Brotherhood members that have influence that they are just making wrong decisions for America," he told a conservative talk radio audience (Marzouki 2016).

Indeed, they questioned his very citizenship. So-called "birthers" contested Obama's eligibility to be president by insisting that he was born in Kenya, even after his birth certificate released by the Hawaii Department of Health showed he had been delivered in a Honolulu hospital (Zeleny 2009). Even after a researcher discovered the 1961 birth announcement Obama's parents had placed in the *Honolulu Advertiser,* the skeptics remained unconvinced (Henig 2008).

As the first putative communist, socialist, fascist Muslim Kenyan to be elected president, presumably having eluded detection by every election official in the country, Obama personified the ultimate alien—the person who doesn't belong. Moreover, he seemed to represent a president who had taken something away from the Tea Party faithful. Over time, that "something" increasingly seemed to be white racial dominance (Maxwell 2016). It wasn't just the overtly racial protest signs at Tea Party rallies that read "Save White America!" or "Obama-nomics: Monkey See, Monkey Spend" (Anon. n.d.b.; Skinner 2010). White Tea Party supporters also seemed to feel that President Obama was targeting them for harm. When pollsters asked a sample of 1,580 Americans in 2010 whether the Obama administration favored blacks over whites, 25 percent of Tea Party supporters—but only 11 percent of other Americans—said yes (Zernike and Thee-Brenan 2010). Evidently, white Tea Partyers tended to feel not only locked in a zero-sum competition with nonwhites—a perception that social scientists call *group threat* (Fossett and Kiecolt 1989)—but that Obama was upsetting the balance of power in a way that favored blacks. (The protesters may have not considered their rather explosive implicit message: if you claim that Obama is partial to African Americans simply because he's black, you're suggesting that every previous president had a finger on the scale in ways that benefited whites.)

Even more unsettling, these concerns seemed directly triggered, at least in part, by Obama's skin color. When social scientists showed hundreds of white Americans two doctored photos of Obama, those who saw an artificially darkened presidential face were nearly twice as likely to express support for the Tea Party compared to people who saw an artificially lightened portrait. "These results support our prediction that white Americans would be more likely to support the Tea Party if Barack Obama's African American heritage was made salient to them," they wrote (Willer, Feinberg, and Wetts 2016, 7).

If some white Tea Party supporters resent Obama for his African American heritage, why would an African American jump on that bandwagon? White Tea Partyers may feel anxious about the decline of white dominance, but wouldn't most African Americans see declining white dominance as a good thing? If Obama said he's a Christian, wouldn't most African Americans take him at his word? If he produced an authenticated birth certificate, wouldn't most African Americans accept that as proof of his citizenship? And even if some African Americans opposed some of Obama's policies, who would oppose them all?

This chapter explores one of the most baffling conundrums in modern politics. Namely, in a representative democracy, where we elect officials to represent our hopes and values, why would anyone go to such extreme lengths to oppose the first-ever election of someone from their group to be the leader of the free world?

NO SHORTAGE OF DOUBTERS

If Democratic strategists hoped Obama would get a pass from every African American voter, the Tea Party contingent made sure that wasn't going to happen. The discontent with Obama that rumbled through the Tea Party as a whole did not spare his black conservative critics. The issues that riled white Tea Partyers—Obama's policies, his politics, his religion, and his citizenship—also bothered their African American counterparts. Surely one of the angriest was Jake, the cab driver, who was so enraged by Obama's behavior in office that in January 2014 he tweeted, "It's time to arrest and hang him high." Jake's social media outburst came on Martin Luther King Jr. Day, an ironic juxtaposition that made international headlines—and earned him a visit from wary Secret Service agents. When I met him for lunch, he was apologetic about his timing but not about his reasoning:

> I wasn't thinking about what day it was. I was at work, okay? And unlike many people who got to take the holiday off, I was working because I have bills to pay. And in between calls I check my Twitter feed and people were talking about the things the president has done that have violated the Constitution. Everybody was so fed up. We believe the death penalty is justice for treason. Obama supplied arms to Al Qaeda and Syria, and he is responsible for the death of American citizens in the Middle East. You can't trust the words that come out of the president's mouth. The 14th Amendment says we have to go through due process before we can execute an American citizen and he did not do that with Anwar al-Awlaki or his son. That would be capital murder because it's premeditated. I would even argue that using the military against an American citizen is a national threat. I call that national war. We believe he's committed deathworthy crimes and that's why he should be hung. If a jury doesn't agree, then there's nothing we can do about it. But that's what we're going for. We're looking for justice.

Jake's claim that Obama supplied arms to Al Qaeda and Syria is technically true, but his conclusion—that Obama acted unconstitutionally by arbitrarily ordering the death of an American citizen—is misleading. The United States sent the arms to Syrian opposition forces, which subsequently lost them to ISIS and to soldiers loyal to Syrian President Bashar al-Assad (O'Connor 2017). Anwar al-Awlaki was an American citizen who had fled to Yemen and joined Al Qaeda. He and his teenage son were killed in Pakistan in 2015 by a US drone strike after the US Justice Department determined he was planning to attack American targets and he could not easily be captured.

These deaths brought the number of Americans killed by drone strikes during the Obama presidency to seven (Mazzetti 2015).

At the other end of the spectrum were black Tea Partyers who questioned the legitimacy of the Obama presidency for reasons that had little to do with Obama himself. Melvin said he doubted the authenticity of Obama's birth certificate because it was hard to know whom to trust:

> My big issue these days is I can't find any true media. When I was growing up, everyone talked about reading the newspaper. You read the first few paragraphs of a story and you have the facts. But nowadays what's in the paper isn't necessarily true. There's so much spin. Where's the truth? Obama finally presents his birth certificate and all you see on social media is that it was a fake, it was fudged. You can't even believe a PDF document these days. Where has this world gone to? Nothing is true.

Melvin, a sort of African American Diogenes, appears to have been stymied by the so-called netroots movement, an aggressive effort begun in 2002 to use the internet as a political tool. Progressives used social media and other internet platforms to oppose George W. Bush, only to see conservatives turn the tables and use the internet as an alternative information source against Obama (Boehlert 2009). The mutual proliferation of mainstream media facts and "alternative facts," as White House counselor Kellyanne Conway later famously termed them (Blake 2017), from less-reliable internet sources, sowed confusion and doubt among news consumers. As one *Forbes* contributor noted, "News may be information, but information doesn't necessarily produce informed citizens" (Butterworth 2010).

Even people who trusted the authenticity of Obama's birth certificate were suspicious that the White House took two and a half years to produce it. When I asked Rev. Isaac if he believed Obama was an American citizen, he hesitated to say no:

> All I can say is I have my doubts. Can I prove he is not a citizen? No, I cannot. One thing that really concerned me is the birth certificate issue. Why is it that a sitting president had to wait until he was in office nearly three years to produce his birth certificate? That I didn't understand. And I can't understand why to this very day his college transcripts are sealed. I mean, if you want to see my college transcripts I'll show them to you right now.

President Obama himself attributed the delay in producing his birth certificate to his "bemusement . . . at the degree to which this thing [the false citizenship rumors] just kept on going" (Office of the Press Secretary 2011). The claim that his college transcripts are sealed is "a falsehood" proliferated by "countless anti-Obama websites," according to the Annenberg Public Policy Center (Jackson 2009).

Regarding Obama's religious convictions, some black Tea Partyers are convinced that the president is either a Muslim or an apostate who has renounced Islam. University of Michigan political scientist Brendan Nyhan thinks these rumors are a proxy for uncertainty and wariness and shouldn't be taken literally. "Part of it may just be people being down on Obama and attaching themselves to any label they perceive as negative," he told the Poynter Institute (Holan 2010). But Kevin, a former member of the Nation of Islam, took the rumors seriously. He said Obama had revealed his allegiance to Islam through a subtle linguistic tell:

> I absolutely *know* he's a Muslim. I've heard the president describe his relationship to Christianity. I heard his couched language. That's the language I used evolving back to Christianity after seven years of being in the Nation. If you want to know the truth about whether Barack Obama is or is not a Muslim, go to a press conference and ask, "Is Jesus Christ your Lord?" Put him on the spot, publicly. I guarantee he'll say Jesus was the prophet. When you hear somebody say that, that means they're a Muslim. They won't acknowledge Jesus as Lord.

Because Obama had said he is a Christian and Tea Partyers had little direct evidence to the contrary, their claims were by necessity circumstantial. Byron's reasoning was particularly elaborate:

> In his two books, Obama talks about his mother, his father, his grandparents, and he talks about them being socialists. His father came from Kenya. His mother—and Lord knows I don't like to talk about nobody's mama—but his mama met his father and the reason that she met was because of a socialist meeting they attended. They made little Barack. The father went to Harvard on a scholarship, and then on to Kenya. Barack Obama was basically raised by his mother, who was a socialist. Now, Barack Obama's father was a Muslim. He was raised over in Indonesia and that's the largest Muslim country in the world, population-wise. The people who know him say, and he has said, that the most beautiful sound in the world is the call to evening prayer. And some people who know him well say if you want to hear the call to evening prayers chanted well, ask Barack to do it. Everybody around him is a Muslim. It's hard for me to believe that that influence did not affect him. He has brought other Muslims into the cabinet, like [John] Brennan.

Obama does discuss his family members in both *The Audacity of Hope* and *Dreams from My Father*. But aside from wondering how his mother's parents ever consented to his pearly-skinned mother marrying his dark-skinned Kenyan father at a time when miscegenation was a felony across much of the country ("There was nothing in their background to predict such a response, no . . . wild-eyed socialists in their family tree" [Obama 2004, 12]), he writes very little about his family members' political or religious affiliations. Obama's father was indeed a Muslim, Obama did attend elementary schools in

Indonesia, and Indonesia is indeed home to more Muslims than any other nation (Jacobs 2011; Schamberg and Barker 2007; Pew Research Center 2015). But Obama's father and mother met at a Russian language class (not a socialist gathering) at the University of Hawaii (The Editors of Life 2008). And Byron's comments about Obama singing the evening call to prayer are reminiscent of a widely circulated YouTube video, "Obama Admits He Is a Muslim," which "edits Obama's words to create a false impression" that he is a Muslim, according to the Annenberg Public Policy Center (Jackson 2009). The claim that former CIA Director John Brennan is Muslim seems to be based on the hearsay of former FBI agent John Guandolo, who claimed that two unnamed colleagues heard Brennan recite the *shahada,* a one-sentence acceptance of Allah and the Prophet Muhammad that converts the speaker to Islam, while Brennan was stationed in Saudi Arabia in the 1990s. The investigative reporting website Snopes.com, which looked into Guandolo's claim, found it "unproven" (Snopes Staff 2015).

As for political ideology, some black Tea Party supporters felt that Obama's praise for capitalism as "the greatest driver of prosperity and opportunity the world has ever seen" (Blake 2016) rang hollow in the face of his rhetoric about corporate excesses and redistribution of wealth, which sounded too un-American for comfort. Whitney, bemoaning Obama's "wholesale government regulation" and "takeovers of entire industries," said the president's behavior reminded him of a lesson he learned in his high school economics class. "We would say that's socialism," he said. Byron agreed, critiquing what he called Obama's "socialistic" programs and noting correctly that journalist Vernon Jarrett, Obama advisor Valerie Jarrett's father-in-law, had endorsed the Communist Party in the 1940s. "I want to believe it's not him [Obama], that it's the people around him, but I really believe it's him," Byron said. "He has been brought up on this idea of socialism to an extent that it's in his DNA nature."

Wallace said he was concerned that Obama's admiration for Scandinavian leaders—"If only everyone could be like the Scandinavians, this would all be easy," Obama once told an interviewer (Goldberg 2016)—signaled a creeping socialism that threatened to gradually shifts the government's balance of power:

> We've all heard what happens when you throw a frog in water and start heating it up. The frog hardly notices the temperature change until it ends up being boiled alive. The thing is, what Obama's introducing are more and more socialist constructs into our government, right? So, to me what I'm saying is that, first off, Denmark is, what, five million people? What would make him think that what necessarily works for Denmark, necessarily works for America, number one? Number two, as you work toward government getting more and more involved in people's lives, the thing is, we have a federalist system. All the things he's imposing, he's imposing from the federal level. In our

system of government, powers that are not given to the federal government are given to the states. What he is advocating for are things that give more and more power to the federal government and that is why what he's doing is unconstitutional. You're talking wealth redistribution, universal health care, universal college, all these things. Who are you giving the power to? Him.

Len offered an even more detailed indictment of Obama's presumed socialist tendencies:

There are four components of socialism. Number one is the nationalization of production. When you have automobile industry bailouts and the health care industry is dominated by the government and the financial sector is controlled by [the] Dodd-Frank [Wall Street Reform and Consumer Protection Act], you're having government control over production. The second thing about socialism is the expansion of the welfare state. You can look at the statistics and they speak for themselves: from 2009 until now [2014], you look at what has happened with the growth of poverty, the growth of food stamps. The third thing is this idea of creating some type of social utopia and when you hear people talk about income inequality, you hear people talk about shared prosperity, economic equality, fairness, fair share, and so forth. I'm sorry, but I'm five-foot-eight, and there are only certain things I can do. I don't hate LeBron James for being six-foot-six and making millions of dollars. That's his talent. I have my own talents and you can't create some psychosocial utopia where everyone is egalitarian. And the last part is a move toward a secular society. The Declaration [of Independence] talks about inalienable rights that come from the Creator. If all of a sudden you move the Creator out of the way, then inalienable rights are given and taken away by man. That's not who we are as a people. America has a Judeo-Christian faith heritage. It's not about promoting it, but allowing [it] to thrive.

For Wallace, a tech executive, Barack Obama personifies everything he loathes. It's not just Obama's politics. It's about an entire approach to life that violates everything Wallace learned from his parents:

I just felt like when Obama got in, this man does not stand for a single thing that I am for. I am just 180 degrees diametrically opposed to anything this man thinks. Because to me, Obama is about Marxism, he's about socialism, and he's one of these black people who, I don't know, for some reason, has bought into the idea that the only thing that's workable for black people—I don't say African American, I say black—that our only solution is that we have to depend on the government. I mean, I just don't know how people can think that way. My parents just didn't teach me to think that way.

Opposition as "Issue Animosity"

While questions about Obama's religious convictions, citizenship status, and political ideology were prominent, black Tea Partyers were most likely to critique his policies. "I can't think of one good thing he's done for this nation," Hilton told me. Here's Anne's take on what it is about the Obama presidency that most often rubs Tea Partyers the wrong way:

> I think the criticism from what I've read is issue animosity. Come on, he went to Harvard! So he's a very liberal guy. I don't know why anyone would expect differently from him. That's what he is. I didn't vote for him because he's very liberal. And the policies he was talking about were not ones that I wanted to support.

Similarly, Len ticked off a list of policies that he said were fundamentally misguided:

> The problem is the president's understanding of what works best for us is wrong. His disdain for the business class is wrong. His wanting to take from us to take care of them is wrong. They need to take care of themselves to a certain extent. And then we can help the rest. He's overregulating the markets. He's saying, "We didn't build this." Has Obama been misled by his advisors? I don't know. I think he's very intelligent but his policies are wrong.

In July 2012, the president had emphasized the importance of government investments in infrastructure by saying to business leaders, "If you were successful, somebody along the line gave you some help. . . . Somebody invested in roads and bridges. If you've got a business—you didn't build that. Somebody else made that happen." Critics said Obama's statement constituted an attack on free enterprise (Walter, Hartfield, and Good 2012).

Lindsay pointed to objectionable policies at home and abroad:

> This thing of him telling folks, telling young blacks that he believes cops are out to harass them and murder them, that's despicable and that's done solely to continue the narrative that blacks are victims and that the only way that we can get these mean racist white folks off of your backs is to vote for Democrats. I don't like the way that Barack Obama gave the Iranians $150 billion to fund terrorism. He does so many things against this country. He went around the world apologizing for America. It's like having a father who does not think you're great and he goes around apologizing for you. This is the guy running our country but he hates America. I can't think of all the other reasons I find deplorable at the moment. I'll be happy when he's gone and I'm hoping and praying that Donald Trump beats Hillary.

An analysis by the *Washington Post* found that Obama's critiques of racially discriminatory police treatment, and his frequent assertions that most police officers are conscientious public servants who treat citizens fairly, are supported by academic studies (Ehrenfreund 2012). The $150 billion figure refers to Iranian assets that were frozen under a July 2015 agreement by six nations, including the United States, to deter Iran from developing nuclear weapons. Secretary of State John Kerry released the assets in 2016 after confirming that the International Atomic Energy Commission had determined that Iran's nuclear program was for peaceful uses only (US Department of State 2016). Because $150 billion, a figure reported by conservative websites, was such a high dollar amount—the official US government estimate was $56 billion—and because the assets had belonged to Iran to begin with, the idea that the United States was involved in a scandalous giveaway is "dodgy," according to the Poynter Institute (Greenberg 2018).

Some Tea Partyers centered their objections to Obama around one or two key issues that were important to them. For Rev. Isaac, the issue was same-sex marriage:

> When Mr. Obama came up in favor of same-sex unions—I do not use the term "marriage" because marriage is between a man and a woman—I was one of the first ones that said, "No, that is wrong because it goes against the Bible and anyone who claims to be a Christian cannot possibly endorse marriage between two men as being right and normal." Should I then change the Bible because Mr. Obama is the first black president? I don't think so.

On the spectrum of religious thinkers, Rev. Isaac is a *moral absolutist*, someone for whom biblical texts that some Christians might contextualize as emerging from a certain time and place "are instead elevated to the status of overriding and ideologically governing absolutes" (Pratt 2018, 9). Of course, using the Bible to oppose Obama's support of LGBTQ rights presupposes that the Bible condemns homosexuality in the first place, a point disputed by some religion scholars (Steinmetz 2015; Seow 1996).

Mary, a parent who lost confidence in her local public schools ("Teachers were just teaching to the test," she said) and was home-schooling her three children, was particularly concerned about the Obama administration's reluctance to support school choice. She pointed to the D.C. Opportunity Scholarship Program, an initiative that allowed low-income parents to use federal vouchers to send their children to private schools in the nation's capital:

> Look at the D.C. Opportunity Program. It was enacted by a Republican Congress in 2004 and it was signed into law by George W. Bush. This was a school voucher program where mostly minority students were given vouchers and did extremely well. They were outperforming their public school peers by leaps and bounds—I've got the data somewhere—not only their black public school peers, but all public school peers, because it was mostly charter schools. And Barack Obama pulled the plug on that. I think the teachers' unions had a lot to do with it, too. And that's my position—that teachers' unions act in favor of what's best for teachers and not necessarily for students.

The backstory here is that President Obama had feared the program would divert resources from already struggling public schools, but he said he was willing to give vouchers a chance (Gibbs 2009). "Let's see if the experiment works," he told *The Milwaukee Journal Sentinel* in 2008. "If it does, whatever my preconception, you do what's best for kids" (Hess 2015). But his patience was short-lived, and his 2010 decision to reduce funding by 25 percent for the popular voucher program while sending his own daughters to the exclusive Sidwell Friends School in Washington, DC, did not escape critics. "There's one America for the elites, like members of Congress and President and Mrs. Obama, who send their kids to private schools, and there's one for everyone else," wrote *U.S. News and World Report* columnist Peter Roff (2009), who, like Tea Partyer Mary, praised the voucher program for boosting students' academic proficiency. "According to the department's [US Department of Education (DOE)] evaluation of the three-year-old program, 'those offered a scholarship were performing at statistically higher levels in reading—equivalent to 3.1 months of additional learning,'" Roff wrote.

But DOE's assessments of the vouchers actually showed mixed results. After the first year of the voucher scholarships, evaluators found "no significant impacts of the Program on reading or math achievement" (Wolf et al. 2007, 44). After three years, the program had a positive impact on reading scores—as Roff noted—but not on math scores (Wolf, Gutmann, Puma, et al. 2009). By the next assessment, voucher students had *lower* reading and math scores compared to their peers in public schools (Dynarski et al. 2018). In their final report, evaluators acknowledged that voucher students enjoyed higher graduation rates than non-voucher students did, but there was "no conclusive evidence" that the program did the one thing it was designed to do: boost student achievement (Wolf et al. 2010).

For that reason, Democrats blasted the voucher program as ineffective and Obama scrapped it in 2012 (Burke 2012; Severns 2015). Republicans protested, blaming the death of the program on Obama's "slavish devotion to teachers' unions" (Miller 2010). It's not unreasonable to wonder if these unions may have influenced Obama's decision; upwards of 97 percent of their campaign contributions from 2000 to 2016 went to Democrats (Center for Responsive Politics 2019). And teachers' unions historically have opposed school choice, says Stanford University political scientist Terry Moe. "To the teachers unions . . . any expansion of [school] choice is deeply threatening," Moe (2012, 25) writes. "When families are given new options, the regular public schools lose children, and thus money and jobs, and this is the last thing the unions want to allow."

By far the one policy issue that generated the most pushback was Obamacare. Mary had a personal reason to have reservations about the Affordable Care Act. It involved her late mother, a cancer patient:

> I do not like single-payer health care. I do not like socialized medicine. I saw my mom die as an indigent person with stage-four cancer in a public hospital. I saw her wait for hours in adult diapers for doctors' appointments. So, my view of Obamacare is informed by not only knowing what both sides are saying about the issue, but by personal experience.

Waiting times for medical care are generally lower in the United States than in Canada and other OECD nations, but an industry-funded study found that average waits for doctors' appointments for new patients in fifteen large US cities had increased by 30 percent from 2014 to 2017 under Obamacare, partly because more patients were insured and were coming to doctors' offices for care (Japson 2017; Merritt Hawkins 2017; Siciliani and Hurst 2003; Barua and Hasan 2018; Pipes 2018). Dr. Christopher Hughes of Doctors for America, a patient advocacy group, would probably empathize with Mary's experience. "The bottom line is that we aren't really any great shakes with our waiting times," he writes (Hughes 2011).

Other objections to Obamacare were more philosophical than experiential. They corresponded with conservatives' embrace of limited government power and traditional Christian beliefs. Antonio said he feels strongarmed by the health law:

> I mean, look at this monstrosity. Look at how it's laid out. A lot of the things I said when the law was being debated have played out. I knew then that you couldn't keep your doctor. I was up in arms about that. I think about a lot of my friends who are entrepreneurs. They don't have insurance, but if something was to happen to them, if they had gone to a hospital for an emergency, they would've just paid the bill. But with the Affordable Care Act, it forced them to buy insurance and if they don't do it then they get fined and penalized. I just have a problem with government saying, "Let's ban something or penalize the people if they break the rules." I have a huge problem with government forcing its way onto people. I don't care who's in power. Whether it's Democrats or Republicans, I don't like it.

Milton, the state representative, feels the same way. He said government-mandated health care constitutes federal overreach that bends the US Constitution to the breaking point. He likened the Tea Party to campaigns for women's rights and even the civil rights movement: to him, these three social movements all represent resistance to tyranny:

> With Obamacare, you've got a situation to where people are forced to buy a product from a private company, or even from the government exchanges, whether they want to or not. And if they don't, then they are fined and can actually face jail time. That is tyranny, and nothing in our Constitution gives our executive branch or legislative branch the authority to do that, and nothing gives the Supreme Court the authority to uphold it. It's a clear abuse of power. If you protest that by not paying your taxes, you will be thrown in jail. The Tea

Party is responding to Obamacare just like other cases where Americans refused to bow down to tyranny and risk going to jail. So I would say The Tea Party movement is equivalent to the women's suffrage movement, the civil rights movement, and even the Civil War itself, which was fought to free slaves.

Other Tea Partiers objected to the *effects* of Obamacare. Dale was disturbed that health insurance premiums were increasing:

> They're going up 25 percent nationally, on average. In Arizona, they're going up 116 percent. One one six. So now you're paying $100 a month and next year you pay $216. There are a lot of people, 116 bucks per month, who can't, they don't have that. Then it's okay, let's just skip a couple months. Let's wash our clothes once a month instead of twice a month. This is not good.

Dale's numbers were spot on. When I interviewed him in 2016, the average price of the second-least expensive "silver plan" on HealthCare.gov, the federal portal for Obamacare coverage, had increased 25 percent from the year before, and Arizona was indeed projected to face a 116 percent spike in premiums (Robertson 2017; Bice 2017). The fine print—the detail that Dale didn't mention—is that the 25 percent premium increase was for individual health care plans, which are more costly than group plans, and that insure only 7 percent of the market. Over the same period, premiums for employer-sponsored family coverage, which are carried by 49 percent of Americans, increased by only 3 percent. And much of that increase came because the Affordable Care Act required insurers to provide more benefits, such as providing preventive care without copays or deductibles, and covering children without regard for preexisting conditions. "Added benefits, added costs," is how one analyst summed it (Robertson 2017).

Dale also worried that the Affordable Care Act didn't do much to increase the supply of physicians needed to care for newly insured patients:

> Now you got this whole thing imploding. You've got doctors leaving the system. One of the scariest things about Obamacare is it's 2,801 pages, and not one syllable on increasing the supply of doctors out there. So, you have these new people coming into the system who don't have new doctors for treatment and we make life difficult for doctors, with electronic medical records and stuff. Guess what? They go play golf, they go blow off steam, they go play with their grandkids.

It's true that not all physicians are happy with the Affordable Care Act—nearly half of the doctors in one 2016 survey gave the law a D or F—but as a rule, they're not hanging up their stethoscopes and jumping ship. In fact, the retirement age recently rose by two years, according to the Association of

American Medical Colleges. Meanwhile, the number of physicians has increased 8 percent under Obamacare (Gore 2017).

Interestingly, even a reduction in the supply of physicians wouldn't necessarily have translated to worse access to care, because utilization rates vary widely across the country. Visits per doctor are lowest in the Northeast (where there are many practicing physicians) and highest in the Midwest (where people are highly reliant on primary care doctors) (Glied and Ma 2015). So the health legislation may not address increasing the physician supply, as Dale charges. But in retrospect, the issue doesn't seem to have needed congressional attention.

Wallace objected to Obamacare for religious reasons. For him, the issue was birth control:

> I'll tell you the one thing that really bothered me probably more than anything was the Obamacare mandate that said if you are a private employer you must provide birth control for free. How can the federal government tell a private business they have to give something to someone for free? And he [Obama] included religious institutions. A Catholic charity, a Catholic hospital. Things that are clearly against their teaching, you have to give free birth control, something that's already cheap, already readily available. How sick do you have to be?

Antonio, the Republican state representative who reached out to Democrats, didn't like Obamacare because he felt it was a partisan power play:

> I was speaking out against the Affordable Care Act because I didn't like how basically one party was trying to pass it. I think when you're gonna do something as monumental as that, you can't take nothing from the other side of the aisle. I've experienced that. I went through that for three years in our legislature, and when you have one-party rule, they dictate everything.

Of course, the inference is that congressional Democrats excluded Republicans from these deliberations. We now know that Republican lawmakers had little interest in bipartisan cooperation, having vowed to do everything they could to block Obama's legislative agenda. As noted earlier, Republicans rejected their own proposals when Obama supported them, so strong was their urge to derail the administration. One of the best-known examples of this political self-immolation is the so-called individual mandate, the Obamacare requirement that all Americans purchase health insurance or face a cash penalty. This provision, widely panned by conservatives during the Obama era, was actually devised by two conservative think tanks, the Heritage Foundation and the American Enterprise Institute, in 1993. It was supported by Senate Republicans as an alternative to Hillary Clinton's single-payer plan (Cooper 2012).

Yet conservatives accused Obama of failing to advance his liberal agenda without acknowledging these and other political headwinds they had created for the president. "He didn't accomplish much, and some of what he did accomplish proved problematic," wrote one columnist in *The American Conservative* (Merry 2017). I wondered whether African American Tea Partyers who criticized Obama for not accomplishing more in office were willing to acknowledge that Republican resistance was partly responsible. The answer for the great majority of interviewees—all but two, in fact—was no.

For example, Lindsay entirely disputed the idea that Republicans had been obstructionists. To the contrary, he said, Obama had his way with Congress:

> Barack Obama hasn't gotten a rough reception from the Republicans at all. In fact, he has gotten everything he wants. Think about all of these executive orders he's written. The Republicans have funded everything he's wanted funded, despite the fact that they [Democrats] have the power of the purse. They could have fought him on executive amnesty, but they have just given him a full ride because they are petrified of being called racist against the president.

Likewise, Jimmy denied that Republicans had reneged on their earlier support for the health care mandate. In fact, he denied that the mandate was even a Republican idea. His claim came as we bantered about Obama's personal qualities:

> Me: A lot of conservatives tell me, "We don't hate Obama because he's black. We hate him because of his policies."
>
> Jimmy: I don't hate him.
>
> Me: Oppose him.
>
> Jimmy: I oppose him because of his policies. I think Obama is a great father to his daughters—but not to anyone else's.
>
> Me: Personally you have no qualms with the man?
>
> Jimmy: Personally, even though he throws like a girl, I'd probably like to hang out with him.
>
> Me: Lots of members of Congress reject him even when he comes to the table with a Republican idea.
>
> Jimmy: When has he ever done that?

Me: Well, the health care mandate was a Republican idea.

Jimmy: No, that was a Romney idea. When Mitt Romney implemented Romneycare in Massachusetts, I felt one day that's going to come back and bite us. That's a moderate Republican idea, not a conservative Republican idea. You can't mandate Americans to buy anything. That's not a Republican idea. When has Obama come to the table with Republican ideas? He's a hoodlum. He talks like a hoodlum even though he throws like a girl.

Me: Girls can be hoodlums, too, you know.

Jimmy: Oh, I know.

Contrary to Jimmy's characterization, the *New York Times* reported that the health care mandate was supported by conservative Republicans, not moderates (Cooper 2012). Whether former Massachusetts governor Mitt Romney is a conservative or a moderate is debatable; more than one observer has bristled at his chameleon-like flexibility (Boyack 2010; Shafer 2019; Page 2012). Gendered references to Obama's throwing competency appeared after the president began to toss ceremonial first pitches at baseball games (e.g., Editor 2009; Cressey 2010).

Ritchie, one of the only Tea Partyers to acknowledge Republicans' role in blunting Obama's legislative inertia, explained that being a black president came with narrow rhetorical and political restrictions:

> I think Republican roadblocks played a significant part in getting in Obama's way, which is why he had to resort to executive orders to get a lot of things done. Whether that opposition was motivated by opposition to his policies in general or anything else like racism, that's a question that's gonna be debated for some time. I believe there's probably a little bit of both there. But I think ultimately, he was also not a man who was going to pursue a revolutionary path, if you will. I really do believe he took seriously the idea that as president of the United States, he was truly the president of all people. If he had been radical—I mean, look at Jessie Jackson, who ran on a number of occasions. He had his coalitions and all that, but he would never become president. When people talk about Obama's failures, I really do believe that to call them his failures is to presume that there was a lot he could do to begin with. I think those who want to put that weight of failure on him, either they're opponents who have never approved of anything he did anyway or they're people who had greater expectations of him, which might've been unrealistic given that he was trying to be president of all the people.

Ritchie is one of the few interviewees who would agree with *Washington Post* columnist Jonathan Capehart's (2012) assessment that "Republicans are complicit in the failures they rail against."

Race Traitors?

I wondered if it was difficult for these African Americans to challenge Obama. Even though they weren't racial turncoats, did opposing the president make them feel twinges of disloyalty? Were they concerned that history—or for that matter, their neighbors—might judge them harshly?

Far from it. Len said it made no sense to go easy on an underperforming black president just because he's black. He raised an analogy from his military experience. "Say a battalion has five company commanders, two black and three white. I'm not going to look at the black commanders any differently than I do the white commanders. We all have a job to do," he said. Mary said people who call African Americans racist for opposing Obama don't really understand racism. "If you lived in the 1950s or 1960s, you understand what that word means," she said. Ritchie added, accurately, "Even President Obama has said that opposing him doesn't necessarily constitute a racial grievance" (Cottom 2016; Kamisar 2017). In short, these Tea Partiers felt comfortable challenging President Obama not because they're disloyal but because they're civic-minded. For them, *failing* to criticize any president for poor job performance is much more worrisome than a complaint from individual citizens, regardless of the president's skin color or theirs.

In fact, they argued, Obama's blackness doesn't make him more vulnerable to criticism. It actually makes him tougher to criticize, not because black critics are afraid of being called insulting names, but because Obama is a sort of modern-day Ronald Reagan. Just as Reagan was smilingly impervious to circumstances that would roil less-resilient presidencies, Obama's supporters seem willing to forgive shortcomings they would disparage in other commanders-in-chief (Kornacki 2009). To his black critics, that "Teflon" quality gives Obama an edge that makes laughable any claim that their criticism is somehow inappropriate. John said African Americans have treated Obama with kid gloves since day one of his presidency. As proof, he said, look what happened when Harvard philosopher Cornel West and media personality Tavis Smiley attacked Obama for what they said were the president's policy failures (and personal snubs) (Granderson 2013). West complained that Obama wasn't doing enough to lift black people out of poverty (Granderson 2013). Smiley said Obama's theory that a rising tide lifts all boats doesn't work for African Americans, whose disproportionate suffering "requires a disproportionate response" (Harris 2010). West "sacrificed friendships and cut ties with former comrades" over his scorched-earth fusillades against

Obama (Dyson 2015). After being pilloried by black listeners, Smiley left a nationally syndicated radio show because he couldn't "take the hate he's been getting on the Barack issue," according to host Tom Joyner (Farhi 2008). Given these outcomes, my interviewee John asked rhetorically:

> What happens when you have an African American president who is the face of authority in a nation, and you don't hold him accountable, and then you simultaneously muzzle the voices of those individuals who would otherwise be giving a full rebuke of that policy, who would otherwise be giving a full endorsement of what needs to be happening in a community? That criticism did not happen because people didn't want to hurt the brother.

John might not agree with far-right political commentator Dinesh D'Souza (2012, 109), who accused the forty-fourth president of "a certain kind of low cunning" for saying one thing and doing another. But he would certainly agree with D'Souza that Obama's presidency "muted effective criticism and sustained for him a level of political loyalty that would be unthinkable in any other president."

John then asked me to imagine the reaction from African Americans if the tragic racial incidents that occurred on Barack Obama's watch had instead played out under George W. Bush:

> Can you imagine what would've happened if, under George W. Bush, Eric Garner had died, Trayvon Martin had died, and Tamir Rice had died after getting shot holding a toy gun in two seconds? Can you imagine John Crawford III walking into a Walmart in Ohio, an open-carry state, picks up a toy gun in aisle 11 and gets shot dead in aisle nine without any warning? Can you imagine if all these things happened under George W. Bush? America would be on fire right now.

Garner was choked to death by a police officer on a Staten Island sidewalk after police accosted him for selling untaxed cigarettes (Baker, Goodman, and Mueller 2015). Crawford was shot while holding a BB gun for sale at a Walmart store; Rice, a twelve-year-old boy, was holding a toy gun when he was shot two seconds after officers arrived at a Cleveland park to answer a 911 call about someone pointing a gun at people (Gnau 2014; Izadi and Holley 2014). John's point, of course, is that however considerably African Americans protested these disturbing deaths—tens of thousands of angry residents took to the streets when a grand jury decided not to indict the police officer who choked Eric Garner—the outpouring of frustration and disappointment would have been even more spectacular had a white man occupied the Oval Office (Fuller et al. 2014). Given Obama's place in history, most African Americans were unwilling to taint his legacy with indications of dissatisfaction from his own community. That's another way of saying it doesn't make sense to portray African American Tea Party critics as victimizing Obama, John said.

Jake went still further. Tea Partyers aren't the race traitors, he said. The real race traitor is Obama himself:

> They can't call me a racist, because I'm black, but they do call me an Uncle Tom, or a self-hating black man, or a token. And then I pose the question to them: you know, Barack Obama pushes this Common Core thing. He doesn't help blacks; he doesn't help schools. He does help Bill Gates, who is white, because his company is responsible for the programming. He does help the owners of the major computer companies, because they're selling computers to the schools. Those guys are white. And it helps Jeb Bush; Jeb Bush is white. So doesn't that make our first black president an Uncle Tom?

Common Core, an education reform initiative designed to teach schoolchildren problem-solving and critical-thinking skills, emerged in 2009 after Bill Gates paid $200 million to help develop learning benchmarks for children that would do more than require rote memorization. The Obama administration liked the idea. Tech companies like Apple did, too, profiting handsomely when schools in Los Angeles alone spent $1 billion for iPads used in Common Core testing. And Florida Governor Jeb Bush supported the new standards before parents across the country rebelled against them, turning Common Core into "the biggest conservative bogeyman since Obamacare" (Murphy 2014; Killough 2015; Catanese 2015). (Ironically, Common Core was a state-level initiative, not a federal one; Gates developed it in concert with the National Governor's Association [Murphy 2014].) By 2017, even Gates (2017) admitted that "the overall impact" of Common Core "was limited," and eleven states had either rewritten their Common Core standards or replaced them with different standards (Ujifusa 2017). Common Core may have been the product of good intentions, but Jake's argument—that the initiative benefited a few wealthy white Americans more than it did black schoolkids—is hard to refute.

Jake wasn't the only black Tea Partyer to criticize the president for not doing enough to help black people. Like Tavis Smiley and Cornel West, John said that while the Obama presidency brought "some good things as far as equality goes, there were bitter, bitter, bitter disappointments." Byron agreed:

> We love him dearly, but we're probably worse off now than before he was president. Detroit? Come on. Chicago? That place is a war zone. Is he saying anything about how we need to go into black communities and stop this crime and stop this killing and stop this drug use? Has he said anything about that? Never. He doesn't even mention it. And because we love him, we ignore it. We ignore the fact that he's ignoring us.

Setting aside the question of whether Obama may have betrayed African Americans' trust in him, criticism of his presidency was by no means confined to African American conservatives. Indeed, some of the harshest commentary on Obama came from the left, particularly as the euphoria over the 2008 election results quieted over time. Detroit-based Solidarity, "a socialist, feminist, anti-racist organization," wondered how the first African American president made it through his first State of the Union speech without mentioning African Americans or the disproportionate impact of the 2009 economic crisis on the black community (Miah 2009). In 2011, California Rep. Maxine Waters told reporters that she and other members of the Congressional Black Caucus were "getting tired" of excusing Obama's lackluster job-creation record, adding that she didn't understand why a three-day bus tour by the president stopped in no black communities (Miller 2011). In 2016, Princeton professor Eddie Glaude, Jr., author of *Democracy in Black: How Race Enslaves The American Soul*, blasted Obama for creating over the span of eight years only a single high-profile program—My Brother's Keeper—dedicated to improving the life chances of young black men. Given the profound challenges facing African American men and boys, Glaude called the program "a Band-Aid for a gunshot wound" (Bacon 2016).

In this way, the Obama presidency may have done more than break with complexional tradition. It may have challenged discursive tradition, too, by helping to change the way black people talk about problems within the African American community. For years, black Americans have internalized a cardinal rule of safeguarding the community's reputation by not exacerbating prevailing ideas about African American dysfunction. Thus *The Philadelphia Tribune*, the nation's oldest continuously published black newspaper, reminded readers, "There was a time when Black people, even if they were at each other's throats, would never let those outside of the African-American family know that there was dissent or discord within the ranks," an editorialist wrote in 2011, stressing the longtime practice of not airing dirty laundry. "Family disputes must be private" (Anon 2011). But the Obama presidency helped bury that discursive practice, aided in no small measure by African American Tea Partyers who refused to be silenced when they disagreed with a popular black president.

NO SHORTAGE OF SUPPORTERS

And yet the short answer to why black Tea Partyers rejected President Obama is: they didn't, at least not entirely. Len said he was full of respect for the president. During Obama's presidential campaign, he didn't want his concerns about Obama's alleged socialist tendencies to deny the young senator a place in history. "I voted for him in 2008. I wish him well; I want him to succeed. I think there are a lot of ignorant people out there who think he cannot do this because he's black. That's racism. They marginalize the man because of where they say he was born. That's outrageous." Len's comment seemed to take three unlikely turns: respecting the president, calling out racism, and critiquing birthers. It was not the response I expected from a diehard Republican conservative.

Even Tea Partyers who didn't vote for Obama recognized the momentous nature of his victory. Dale remembers the electricity in the air on inauguration day:

> When he arrived in Washington in January '09, I remember walking to the apartments right across the street for lunch. It was about a 10-minute walk. I walked up the street about 10 minutes to noon. Every bar, every restaurant was filled up with people. It was like the World Series. Everybody's watching the TV. I was sitting there very solemnly waiting to see America's first black president sworn in. It was a very touching experience, very moving. I didn't vote for him, but this was a huge milestone for us as a people, as a nation, and we all can share in this very special moment. Almost all of us who didn't vote for him still recognized this is still a red-letter day in American history.

Presidential Personality

Quite a few interviewees spoke glowingly of the president's personality. John liked Obama's compassion for communities that policymakers frequently overlook:

> I like to separate Barack Obama the president from Barack Obama the man. Because there is no doubt in my mind that Barack Obama the man cares deeply and passionately about what happens in black and brown communities. You don't leave Harvard Law School and start organizing the South side of Chicago because you don't care about people. I mean, even the most—even an individual with the most delusions of grandeur, who somehow believes he's going to be president of the United States doesn't go that far with it. By every account, this is a man who cares deeply about people, who cares deeply about the needs of individuals. I have no doubt that he will leave the presidency and in many ways reshape what it means to have a post-presidential life.

Obama's life after leaving the White House has been pretty conventional. Leading the charge against the opposition party while giving pricey speeches "is not shattering norms," according to politics scholar Nicholas F. Jacobs (2018), who has studied presidential life after the Oval Office. But John's point about Obama's appealing personality was echoed by Byron, who recounted hearing an admiring remark about Obama from an unusual source—a fellow Republican activist. Byron was a state delegate to the 2008 Republican National Convention when he fell into a conversation with a friend and fellow delegate who confessed an unexpected affinity for the Democratic nominee:

> Everybody in the delegation is staying in the same hotel. They put you on a bus and they take you through security so you can get to the convention site. So we're driving down the road, and one of our good friends, a white lady, says, "Byron, I know I shouldn't tell you this, but you know that Barack Obama? The more I listen to him, the more I like him." I leaned over to her. I said, "Darling, let me remind you, we're on our way to the Republican convention and you're a delegate. You're not supposed to be liking the Democrat." She said, "I don't care. The more he talks, the more I like him."

Indeed, Obama's decency as a human being won praise from many black Tea Partyers who distinguished between his policy decisions and his personal qualities. "I think he's a great father," Dave noted. Rod agreed: "I think he raised black culture a level. I think the Obama presidency shows that you can be bookish and intellectual and still be kind of cool. I think he and his family are very dignified and intelligent. The things I would say positive about Obama are more personal than political." As they compartmentalized their policy concerns, Tea Partyers like Ritchie broke from the pack by dismissing some of the more flagrant allegations about the president:

> I don't agree with all of his policies, but I didn't think of him as the anti-Christ or anything like that. I thought he was a skilled politician, he was a great orator, and as a person, he set a fine example for young black men everywhere by being a devoted husband and father. And I do believe that his instincts were to try and be a conciliator. So no, I didn't vote for him, but that doesn't mean I hated him or thought he was somebody that would convert America into a socialist Muslim state. Some of my dear black conservative friends say these things and I just shake my head and think, "Oh boy, who got to you?"

Charlie, the young military veteran who said he was attracted to the Tea Party because of his concern over the national debt, agreed with Ritchie that some of the conservative backlash against Obama is senseless. When I asked Charlie if he thought the government threatens individuals' rights and freedoms, a unifying premise of the Tea Party, he implied that black conservatives who peddle Obama conspiracy theories are ill-informed:

> I don't believe it threatens our rights and freedoms as much as some other people do. They look at things like what the NSA [National Security Agency] is doing and they're immediately freaked out. And I guess maybe because I was in the military and I worked in Washington, DC, before Obama got to town, I always knew that we had a sophisticated spying capability. So to me it's okay; this is nothing new. You guys [Tea Partyers] are outraged about something that did not start with Barack Obama. It doesn't bother me and that's not to say the people who are against it are doing anything wrong, but

the outrage, I think that's probably more ideological than anything else. Would we be complaining about the government's ability to listen in on people's phone conversations if a Republican was in charge? The question is moot because we didn't. Yes, the government is threatening in the sense that it's been threatening for a long time. But on most security issues that the Tea Party and even some Republicans are complaining about, I don't see it.

The phrasing of Charlie's last sentence, in which he separated Tea Partyers from the Republican mainstream, underscores political scientist Christopher Parker's (2013) characterization of Tea Party loyalists as conservative extremists—people outside of the Republican mainstream.

Religion, Citizenship, and Race

Thanks to the Tea Party's "freewheeling anti-Obama paranoia" (Skocpol and Williamson 2012, 78), many of its supporters have expressed grave doubts about Obama's citizenship and religion. These doubts resonate with some African American Tea Partyers, as we've seen above. But just as Ritchie dismissed concerns that Obama would convert America into a Muslim state, and Charlie rolled his eyes at the idea that the NSA is an Obama-inspired spy cabal, most of the Tea Partyers seemed to push back *en masse* against the many of the fanciful conspiratorial claims about the president.

Wallace was blunt. "Of course, he's an American citizen. His mom was an American citizen. I thought that was a pretty stupid argument. Those are the crazy people of the Tea Party." Ritchie, the political science professor, agreed. "I never bought the birther thing," he said. "I know a lot of people that do, but frankly, it's just so ridiculous to think something like that could be covered up." Charlie's faith in Obama's citizenship rested on his military experience, which required security clearances. "For me, working in government, knowing that Senator Obama was on the Senate Foreign Intelligence Committee, I know the background check he went through. If he was born in Kenya, we'd know. If he was a Muslim, we'd know. That stuff has been settled. I hear stuff like that and say, 'Yeah, move on.'" Government insiders like Charlie dismissed Tea Partyers who speculated about Obama's bona fides without understanding how implausible their claims are. Len had little patience with these arguments:

Me: You say this controversy over the president's birth certificate is bogus.

Len: Bogus. Non-issue.

Me: What about the question of whether he's a Muslim.

Len: Ridiculous.

Me: And some people say he's not an American.

Len: He's just as American as you or I. Bogus. Non-issue.

In 1957, psychologist Leon Festinger suggested that people strive to be internally consistent on any given topic so that their attitudes line up with their opinions. "Certainly one may find exceptions," Festinger wrote. "A person may think Negroes are just as good as whites but would not want any living in his neighborhood." But on the whole, he said, "It is still overwhelmingly true that related attitudes or opinions are consistent with one another" (Festinger 1957, 1). Following Festinger's thinking, we would expect African Americans who support the Tea Party to accept most if not all of its core principles. But the black Tea Partyers who never doubted Obama's American Christian bona fides scoff at some of those principles, and certainly at some of their fellow Tea Partyers' more creative conspiracy claims. This suggests that two Australian psychologists may have more currency than Festinger. Matthew J. Hornsey and Jolanda Jetten (2005) say that in individualist western cultures, group norms are typically seen as irrational influences that limit individual potential. Thus the heroes in our films and literature are solitary figures who challenge norms, not obedient conformists who follow them. Hornsey and Jetten, among others, suggest that by joining a group that permits distinctions between group members, people in individualist cultures find a middle ground that provides both belonging and differentiation.

That might help explain why African Americans like Charlie and Len who disagree with other Tea Partyers still feel comfortable being a part of the Tea Party collective. It might also explain why they're Tea Party loyalists despite the possibility of being stigmatized by other African Americans: as black contrarians they can simultaneously stand out from the black crowd and be part of the black group.

One thing these black contrarians agree on was how race played out during Obama's presidency. Unlike those who say Obama was privileged because of his race, these Tea Partyers said he was slammed for it. Whitney, a state official with a doctoral degree who represents a mostly white constituency, said that anyone who tries to claim race doesn't factor into how people evaluate African American public officials is a Pollyanna:

> I will tell you, based on my academic experience, that race always trumps everything. Voters may feel a lot of things about a black candidate, some good, some bad. But race is always part of the calculus. I mean, there's no doubt that President Obama's race was an elephant in the room, just like there's no doubt that my race was an elephant in the room when I was running for office.

Anne, the physician, agrees that race was an inescapable drag on the Obama presidency:

> I am sure, absolutely sure, that some conservatives and some Tea Partyers reject him just because he's black. I'm absolutely sure of that. What the percentage is, I don't know. There may be some true conservative patriots out there who say they only care about the issues. I suppose it's possible that they could have rejected a white president who wanted to advance the same policies as what Obama stands for, but it didn't happen that way.

Both Len and Wallace felt that white Tea Partyers' concerns about the issues are more germane than their concerns about Obama's race. "If there's someone who lines up with their values, they love them," Wallace said. "If they hated Obama because he's black, why are they falling all over themselves over Herman Cain or Ben Carson?" Yet both Tea Partyers acknowledged unfriending white Tea Partyers on Facebook for spewing racist anti-Obama vitriol. If these online relationships were tense, one can only imagine face-to-face encounters between white and black Tea Party loyalists who oppose President Obama, though perhaps for different reasons. This potentially volatile prospect is explored in the next chapter.

CONCLUSION

If black Tea Partyers feel good about being black and want to advance the interests of the black community, why not support our first black president? In truth, they did celebrate Obama's historic *victory*. Even today, they praise the president for his values, particularly his devotion to family. Their qualms aren't over whether Obama is black enough, an early charge from Dr. Ben Carson on the right and Cornel West on the left (Capehart 2016). Nor is it about his political style, which liberal critics say is too accommodating to Republicans, and conservatives say is too timid against America's enemies.

For some, the burning issue is the legitimacy of Obama's presidency. But unlike Tea Party protesters who object to Obama's fundamental differentness, not all African American Tea Partyers agreed that Obama personifies an alien essence. On basic questions of whether he is an American citizen or a pretender, Christian or Muslim, crusader for capitalism or supporter of socialism, we see as full a range of black Tea Party opinion as on any other issue.

The common denominator among every African American Tea Partyer I spoke with was concern over the president's policies. Even those who believed Obama's presidency was legitimate—and most of them did—suggested that his policies were misdirected. Whether it be gay marriage, school choice, policing, the health insurance mandate, or Obama's "disdain for the business class," as Len put it, black Tea Partyers feel that the president's policy decisions undercut the rights of individuals, upset the balance of power between the federal government and the states, disrespected the US Constitution, or otherwise undermined the interests of citizens generally and African Americans in particular. And there was no apparent irony in their critique of our first black president; as black people they seemed motivated by patriotism and civic duty, not betrayal or disloyalty. Racial animosity may have motivated some white Tea Partyers to go after Obama, but racial pride united his black Tea Party critics in celebration of the president's election and in respect for Obama as a person. Black Tea Partyers who blamed Obama for not doing enough to help the black community didn't always acknowledge how resistance from conservative Republicans blunted the president's initiatives, but neither did they suggest that African Americans aren't capable of achieving and maintaining the highest professional and intellectual standards. In other words, the notion that their opposition to Obama signaled self-loathing, unconcern for other African Americans, or anything more than disagreement with his policies seems unsupported by evidence.

Of course, their reasons for opposing Obama bear scrutiny as well, because people's rationales varied widely. I found it easy to accept objections that rested on simple differences in political philosophy, as when Len said Obama is "overregulating the markets" and Wallace said Obama is "advocating for . . . things that give more and more power to the federal government . . . and that is why what he's doing is unconstitutional." Likewise, I felt sympathy for objections grounded in religious beliefs; it made sense to me that Rev. Isaac, like many Christians, might object to Obama's support for same-sex marriage. And there were Tea Partyers whose policy objections were strenuous but rational. For example, Dale objected to the Affordable Care Act for its lack of measures for increasing the nation's supply of doctors, even though, as it turns out, the number of physicians has actually increased under Obamacare (Gore 2017).

Then there were critics like Kevin, who was convinced that Obama is a Muslim; and Rev. Isaac, who thought he might not be an American citizen. These Tea Partyers, who felt that Obama's presidency rested on fabrications, joined policy critics whose objections were as counterfactual as the idea that Obama is a socialist communist. For example, Lindsay claimed that Obama "gave the Iranians $150 billion to fund terrorism" when the assets, which were surrendered to Iran under the terms of an international nuclear nonproliferation agreement, likely totaled $56 billion, and they belonged to Iran in the first place (Greenberg 2018). Whitney claimed Obama had "supplied arms to Al Qaeda and Syria" when in reality the arms were sent to Syrian opposition forces, which subsequently lost them to ISIS and Syrian president Bashar al-Assad (O'Connor 2017). And Lindsay said, "Republicans have funded everything he's wanted" without acknowledging Republicans' attempts to block every Obama initiative, even ones they championed before he took office (Cassata and Regan 2016). Social psychologist Jonathan Haidt says however much westerners may prize rationality and logic, our emotions frequently crowd out reason. "[W]hen a group of people make something sacred, the members of the cult lose the ability to think clearly about it" (Haidt 2013, 34). Whether the sacred is Barack Obama or his illegitimacy as a president, people across all political spectrums surely run this risk if they remain wedded to groupthink.

Recall that I had asked interviewees to identify their favorite news sources, on the assumption that steady exposure to Fox News, Breitbart News, and other conservative broadcasts and websites would expose Tea Partyers to partisan critiques that are not always reliable (Stroud 2011; Levendusky 2013). Sure enough, people who turned to liberal or progressive information sources—Huffington Post, MSNBC, *The Nation*—in addition to conservative ones were more measured in their assessment of President Obama. But diversifying one's news sources isn't a cure-all. Mary, who mischaracterized schoolchildren in the D.C. Opportunity Scholarship Program as "outperforming their public-school peers" said she deliberately exposes herself to news from across the political spectrum, from left-leaning Salon.com and Jezebel.com to more centrist Apple News (a daily news digest for iPhone users) to Breitbart News and The Daily Signal. Otherwise, her intent—civil engagement with conservatives and nonconservatives alike—is wholly admirable. "You can't really have a nuanced discussion with someone if you don't now where they're coming from," she told me.

One unexpected revelation that emerged during these conversations was the deeply personal nature of some of the opposition to President Obama. Consider Mary, whose cancer-ridden mother endured a disastrous stay at a public hospital. People who didn't know Mary's story might assume that she is: (a) a racial naif who doesn't realize the once-in-a-lifetime (thus far) significance of having a black president; or even (b) a self-hating African-American who is acting on internalized racism. The truth is she is: (c) a person for whom the mention of Obamacare brings traumatic memories. "I can't help but think of my own experience with government-financed health care every time I hear about Obamacare," Mary said. "I would never want anyone else to go through that."

Similar experiences from other black Tea Partyers humanize their opposition to Obama. For example, in 2015, President Obama gave what some critics called a long overdue speech on the need for criminal justice reform. Speaking before the NAACP, he said, "Mass incarceration makes our country worse off, and we need to do something about it" (Lartey 2016). In the months that followed, Obama became the first sitting president to visit a federal prison. He launched an initiative to reduce unnecessary police arrests at the local level and granted clemency to one thousand inmates. He also directed Attorney General Eric Holder to begin a comprehensive review of the nation's policing, prosecuting, and sentencing procedures. The idea was to scour our criminal justice juggernaut for evidence of systemic racial bias and other injustices, and repair a broken system (Lartey 2016).

Because the criminal justice system weighs heavily on the black community, you'd think every African American would celebrate the president's actions. But Melvin didn't. A black Tea Partyer and armed forces veteran, Melvin had qualms about the Obama plan after he talked with his brother, a career criminal. "When young black guys go to jail, all they talk about is how they could have gotten away with the crime if they had just handled some detail differently," Melvin's brother told him. "When they get early release, they're back on the streets, they're back to crime, and before you know it, they're back in jail." Forget about investigating a racist system, Melvin says. We need to keep black men behind bars *longer*, to force them to rethink the ill-advised decisions that landed them in jail.

In 1969, feminist activist Carol Hanisch helped to popularize a catchphrase that quickly spread through the women's movement and into popular culture. Noting that the problems women faced in their private lives were almost always rooted in women's relative powerlessness, Hanisch (1969) wrote that when she and other women gather in meetings, "One of the first things we discover in these groups is that personal problems are political problems." Hanisch's essay helped give rise to the saying, *the personal is political.* Tea Partyers like Mary and Melvin may or may not consider themselves feminists, but their wariness of the Obama administration's health care and criminal justice initiatives drew a straight line between their personal experiences and their Tea Party activism.

Chapter Five

Is This a Real Invitation? African Americans Come to the Tea Party

There's bigotry against the Tea Party.

—Kevin, Realtor

There are people in the Tea Party who are just mad that Obama is black.

—Charlie, US Navy veteran

In 1897, William Edward Burghardt Du Bois, the first African American to earn a PhD at Harvard and a founder of the NAACP, published an article in *The Atlantic Monthly* in which he addressed a question that he said white people were too polite to ask him. In their attempts to show their good intentions, they would decry "these southern outrages" or say they knew "an excellent colored man in my town." What they really wanted to know, he imagined, was: *How does it feel to be a problem?* Du Bois's answer to that question speaks to the dilemma of every African American who straddles two worlds—one white, one black; worlds whose contrary inclinations can be difficult to reconcile. "He does not wish to Africanize America, for America has too much to teach the world and Africa," Du Bois (1897) wrote. But neither does he "wish to bleach his Negro blood in a flood of white Americanism, for he believes—foolishly, perhaps, but fervently—that Negro blood has yet a message for the world."

Unlike African Americans who lived in segregated enclaves, removed from regular interactions with whites, Du Bois's position at the intersection of both worlds meant he had daily opportunities to study whites closely. "Of them I am singularly clairvoyant," he wrote. "I see in and through them" (Du Bois [1920] 1999, 17). After all, Du Bois practically invented the practice of making careful street-level observations that we now know as sociological fieldwork, a method that was unheard of at the time among his fellow social scientists, whom he derisively labeled "car window sociologists" (Du Bois [1903] 1994, 94). What Du Bois saw in his field observations was chilling:

> I have seen a man—an educated gentleman—grow livid with anger because a little, silent, black woman was sitting by herself in a Pullman car. He was a white man. In Central Park I have seen the upper lip of a quiet, peaceful man curl back in a tigerish snarl of rage, because black folk rode by in a motorcar. He was a white man. (Du Bois [1920] 1999, 19)

In the facial expressions of white people Du Bois saw contempt peeking through a veneer of civility. It didn't take much for white folks' true feelings to emerge, particularly about African Americans who defied their station by owning an automobile or sitting in what was considered to be a luxury railroad car (Khederian 2018). And Du Bois knew how dangerous that white rage could be: "We have seen,—merciful God! in these wild days and in the name of Civilization, Justice, and Motherhood,—what we have not seen, right here in America, of orgy, cruelty, barbarism, and murder done to men and women of Negro descent" (Du Bois [1920] 1999, 19).

In 2009, these concerns resonated for many African Americans just as clearly as they did a century earlier for Du Bois. Like Du Bois, the black conservatives who flocked to the Tea Party occupied a racial middle ground. They didn't want to transform the taxation protests into a black political movement; there was no intent to make it something it wasn't. On the other hand, they didn't want to lose their blackness in a sea of white, thereby surrendering their concerns as persons of color just so they could be a part of the Tea Party insurgency. Not wanting to change the protest movement, yet not wanting to be changed by it, they arrived at meetings and rallies where mostly white crowds protested a black president using rhetoric that over time grew increasingly racially charged.

Like Du Bois, the Tea Partyers had reason to be wary of whites. As an indication of African Americans' unease around white people, consider residential patterns. As African Americans' net worth increases over time, they live in different types of neighborhoods than do other ethnic groups. Chinese American or Mexican American families typically leave their ethnic enclaves as they become more affluent; African American families don't. "Wealthy African Americans live in neighborhoods that are nearly as black as the poorest African American neighborhoods," says sociologist Gregory Smithsimon (2018). It's not that African Americans simply like to live with other African Americans; surveys consistently find that African Americans actually prefer to live in neighborhoods that are half white, half black, though such neighborhoods are rare. The fact is, African Americans live in black neighborhoods because they're wary of living anywhere else. "Anyone who lives in a black neighborhood can name nearby white neighborhoods with reputations for intolerance, prejudice, and violence where they would rather not go," writes Smithsimon (2018). And the dangers aren't confined to one's would-be neighbors. In the decade before Obama's election, police officers shot and killed twenty-one unarmed persons of color, usually with few legal consequences (Juzwiak and Chan 2014). "When you're black in America, there are certain things you must consider whenever you're out and about," says writer Jill Robi (2018). "The mundane is never mundane; there's always mental preparation involved."

Moreover, despite the joy around Obama's victory, the 2008 election results also had potentially ominous racial repercussions because, just as in Du Bois's day, the perception that African Americans are out of place heightens the likelihood that some whites will feel emboldened to act on their racial resentments. The 2008 election was a klaxon for a subgroup of whites who don't feel motivated to portray themselves as unprejudiced, says psychologist Allison Skinner. In experiments at Northwestern University, Skinner and a colleague found that simply reading excerpts from a newspaper article on the Obama election was enough to make these whites score higher on implicit bias tests, which measure subconscious racial prejudice, compared to a control group that read no excerpts (Skinner and Cheadle 2016). "These findings are consistent with a concept known as group threat theory, which is the idea that when minority groups grow in size or power, the majority group feels threatened," Skinner (2017) wrote. "But group threat doesn't just increase intergroup bias. It also seems to make people more politically conservative." So beyond its stated concerns about taxes and federal overreach, the Tea Party may have emerged at precisely the right time to capitalize on a surge of racially inspired conservatism. No wonder a nation that's becoming more diverse is also experiencing, oddly enough, an upswing in white nationalism, says Skinner (2017).

Indications of that hybrid nationalist racial intolerance appeared at Tea Party gatherings, where posters grouping Barack Obama with Adolf Hitler and Vladimir Lenin commingled with bumper stickers advising "Don't Re-Nig in 2012" and T-shirts with the rallying cry, PUT THE WHITE BACK IN THE WHITE HOUSE (Shepherd 2012). The historical references didn't always hit the mark, notes *New York Times* art director Stephen Heller:

> The transposition of Obama as a Soviet/Red . . . and the smearing of the Democratic Party as Marxist . . . shows a decided lack of . . . historical knowledge. First, socialism as a practice (i.e., Sweden) and Soviet Communism (remember the breakup of the Soviet Union) are quite different political beasts. Representing the Obama administration with the hammer and sickle is as stupid as smearing it with a swastika. . . . Just as George W. Bush was not a Nazi for starting the Iraqi War, President Barack Obama is not a "commie-

fascist" for advocating a government-subsidized health care plan. (Seidman 2009)

And sometimes the spelling was approximate. At a Houston rally a blogger who said he was the founder of the Tea Party held a sign that read CONGRESS=SLAVE OWNER, TAXPAYER=NIGGAR. Halfway across the country, a Florida man posted a yard sign calling Obama a HALF-BREED MUSLIN (Ponder 2010; Edwards 2008).

But the hostility and racial overtones were clear enough to the NAACP, which passed a 2010 resolution condemning the Tea Party's "continued tolerance for bigotry." NAACP president Ben Jealous told CNN that the nation's oldest civil rights organization believed in freedom of speech and freedom of assembly, but the Bill of Rights doesn't protect the freedom to spew racist rhetoric. Tea Party Express national spokesman Mark Williams, who is white, fired back. "I am disinclined to take lectures on racial sensitivity from a group that insists on calling black people 'colored,'" Williams said (Travis 2010). Williams later posted a satirical letter from African Americans to Abraham Lincoln asking that slavery be reinstated because black people couldn't tolerate adult responsibilities: "Freedom means having to work for real, think for ourselves, and take consequences along with the rewards," the letter read. "That is just too much to ask of us Colored People and we demand that it stop!" Williams removed the letter after igniting a firestorm of protest, including objections from The National Tea Party Federation, which expelled Williams's group (Coates 2010; McEwen 2017).

Given this maelstrom of racial charges, countercharges, accusations, and self-indictments, I wondered what would possess an African American Tea Partier to join a group of angry white people whose stated purpose was political but whose undeniable subtext was racial hostility. What calculus would fuel such a decision? Did black Tea Partiers consider in advance how to respond to an untoward remark or unwelcome glance? Should they brush it off, to try to fit in as a Tea Partier? Or should they challenge it, to assert their dignity as an African American? How were they treated at meetings and rallies? Did their sympathy for the Tea Party make them insiders, or did their blackness make them outsiders? Did they find that white patriots welcomed all comers, or were they shunned as loathsome embodiments of Barack Obama? And if black Tea Partiers were shunned, why did they remain faithful to the Tea Party?

This chapter addresses the most explosive concern of people who understand that American racial confrontations can have catastrophic consequences. Given this backdrop, what the interviewees said about their experiences at Tea Party gatherings was eye-opening. The twenty-six people who had attended a Tea Party gathering reported three types of experiences. A few experienced overt racial hostility; to their credit, they intervened to put a stop to it. Others acknowledged that racial hostility is a Tea Party problem but said they had never experienced it personally. Astonishingly, the largest faction concluded that racial hostility in the movement simply doesn't exist.

EXPERIENCED RACIAL HOSTILITY

Sparks flew at some gatherings. Antonio was a police officer when he brought his wife and three children to an otherwise all-white Tea Party rally. As he was leaving the event, a white man followed him and asked him a question:

> I catch this guy following us. He comes out and says to me, right in front of my wife and kids, "Where you headed, you leaving?" I said, "Yeah, I'm leaving." He said, "It's a good day to hang somebody up on a clean rope, don't you think?" I said, "What'd you say?" I looked at him, I said, "You better be glad you're not picking up your teeth right now." I showed him my gun and badge and I said, "What I want to do right now, I won't because my kids are here." So, when I got in the car, my son broke my heart. He said, "Daddy, why would he want to hang us up? Is it because we're black?" Imagine having to explain that.

Rev. Isaac never attended a Tea Party gathering, but he said he didn't need to have an experience like Antonio's to be suspicious of white people's intentions. I asked him if he thought many African Americans see the racially loaded signs and posters at rallies and decide that they can't stomach being a part of the Tea Party:

> This is very true. Yes. I don't want to be naïve. There are perhaps some in the Tea Party who use the movement as a cover for their inherent bigotry and racism. That is very, very plausible and I believe that that is true. There are some in the movement that are not only opposed to big government but they are also opposed to the fact that there is a black man who is president and that irritates them to no end. The Tea Party gives those people a legitimate cover for feelings that are not socially acceptable.

Charlie, who organized a Tea Party event in 2009, agreed that some Tea Party animosity is about Obama's skin color:

> There are people in the Tea Party who are just concerned about policy, and I'd like to say that that makes up about half of it. There are people in the Tea Party who are mad at President Obama for strictly political reasons. Of the other half of the Tea Party, that's about half of that group. The rest of them are just mad because he's black, and it exists. I've seen it, so I can't say it's not there.

I asked Charlie how he knew that people were motivated by racism. He recounted a conversation with a white Tea Party supporter that made him uncomfortable:

> I think for me it's when people are talking to me. I can usually tell where you're going when you start talking. If you're talking to me about policy I know you're going to stay there. If you're talking to me about politics I know you're going to stay there. You're not going to veer off. But if you come to me and say, "Let me tell you something about that boy in the White House . . . " Okay, I already know where this is going; I know where it's going to end up. I have to kind of stand there and absorb it, but I've seen the signs with Obama made up to be a witch doctor. I've seen stuff like that at other rallies. I've heard about stuff happening and I've heard it from people I trust, and I know, okay, you're really not making this up. It really did happen. It's there.

This particular unenlightened patriot must have seen Charlie solely as a fellow Tea Partyer. How else can we explain why, without a hint of malice toward Charlie, a white person would use a demeaning reference to black men ("boy") in conversation with a black man? As Charlie the Tea Partyer patiently waited the man out, Charlie the African American was taking body blows. It was a classic W. E. B. Du Bois moment, a moment where "[o]ne ever feels his twoness—an American, a Negro; two souls, two thoughts, two unreconciled strivings, two warring ideals in one dark body, whose dogged strength alone keeps it from being torn asunder" (Du Bois [1903] 1994, 3).

Several people were stunned to find racially offensive emails or social media posts from friends or acquaintances. Opening a demeaning email from a friend was even more off-putting than seeing an offensive message at a rally, because it was so unexpected. Sally, a Realtor, was livid when her neighbor, a white Tea Party supporter, sent her a racist caricature of President Obama. "I think she thought I would find it as amusing as she did. I couldn't believe she would send me something so insulting," Sally said. "I deleted it immediately, and I haven't spoken to her since." Like the white man who approached Charlie at a Tea Party rally, Sally's neighbor seemed oblivious to how offensive her email would be to an African American. However, there is added potential for injury when the white offender is a friend, because it's not uncommon for a white friend to deny they are prejudiced against black people by saying, "I don't think of you as being black." When a white friend of Naomi Tutu, daughter of South African archbishop Desmond Tutu, gave Tutu that "compliment," the daughter took serious offense. "I love being a Black woman," she wrote. "[Saying you don't think of me as black] tells me I am OK as a person if you can ignore this one fact about me. And it is not a little fact" (Tutu and Bator 2006–2008).

Unlike people who feel conflicted or ambivalent about their blackness, these Tea Partyers' response to offending posts was unequivocal. Wallace was clear that he didn't want to be associated with racists: "I've seen some of these things on Facebook. There were definitely some racists that I thought were my Tea Party friends. They made some racist comments and I unfriended them in a heartbeat." Whitney felt the same way. "If something ever popped up on my screen like 'Can't wait 'til that monkey comes out,' I'd just say 'Seriously dude, monkey?' and I'd expeditiously get it off my page."

NO PERSONAL EXPERIENCE, BUT CONCERN

More numerous than the few people who attested to overt racism were those who acknowledged its possible existence but hadn't personally experienced it. They agreed that racial hostility could be a problem, though they disagreed over its nature and extent.

The group ran a spectrum by degree of certainty. On the one hand were people who were certain that any given gathering likely contained Tea Party patriots who opposed President Obama for reasons that had more to do with pigmentation than policy positions. Rod characterized these Tea Party supporters as outliers who give the movement a bad name. But he said the Tea Party—like all groups—has bad seeds:

> When I went to rallies, I never felt I was treated differently for being black. I think the examples of racism in the Tea Party that people talk about are exaggerated, and on occasion, suspicious. I'm not sure that all of the people who've given the group a bad name are sincerely Tea Partyers, but I know some of them are. It's just a reflection of the thing that when you get a large group of people, some of them are going to be bad people, whether they be Tea Partyers, whether they be NAACP supporters or NRA people or Planned Parenthood people or even just Yankees fans. If you get a large enough group of people, you're going to find some very bad people within that group. It's just an unfortunate part of being human, I guess.

Those "very bad people" have been portrayed unfairly by inflammatory news reports as typical of the group as a whole, several Tea Partyers said. As Wallace put it, "Anything that's bad about the Tea Party movement gets shown as proof that we're up to no good, and that stings because the movement is not those people."

Some interviewees' only exposure to Tea Party gatherings came through media images. But the sight of white people making overt racial appeals was enough to give them serious pause. Elton, the college student, said he was drawn to the Tea Party for its emphasis on lower taxes and personal responsibility, but news images of Tea Party rallies disturbed him:

> The Tea Party movement, at least when I was in middle school, had a lot of white protesters saying a lot of racist remarks. Some of them were bigots.

They just had this ignorant mindset, if you understand. The way they would talk about black people, the way they would talk about Obama. You know, calling him a Muslim, saying he wasn't born here. I never for one second thought he was a Muslim. I don't know, a lot of that is rooted in bigotry. They see a black man with the last name Obama, and they can't believe he's just a Christian, regular American citizen. They just can't believe that.

Media depictions of Tea Party rallies were a tough nut for Charlie to crack, too. In fact, he credits one scene as a turning point that made him rethink his affiliation with the Tea Party. On March 20, 2010, Tea Party protesters were rallying on Capitol Hill as members of Congress walked from their offices to the Capitol building to vote on the Affordable Care Act. The protesters surrounded the congressmen, shouting "nigger!" at Rep. John Lewis (D-Georgia), spitting on Rep. Emanuel Cleaver (D-Missouri), and calling Rep. Barney Frank (D-Massachusetts), the only openly gay member of Congress, a "homo" (Douglas 2010). Republican leaders such as Rep. Michelle Bachmann (R-Minnesota), head of the House Tea Party Caucus, denied that anyone had proof of these events, which were witnessed by reporters and captured on video (redarrowguy 2010). Charlie was stunned by the images:

> I think when you go back to spitting on the congressman, that was a point where I said, "Okay, this ain't good. As long as it doesn't get any worse, I can stick around." Even that August, I said, "Okay, this is going in a way I don't like, but maybe it's not going to be this way forever. Maybe after we get done with the politics of it all in 2010 and 2011 it will normalize itself back out." That really didn't happen. In 2009 the Tea Party was an accountability movement. By 2010 it went from accountability to trying to become a political movement, and by 2012 it was a political movement that wanted to actually to have power within the Republican Party. At that point, I was fully in the Republican Party structure, so I saw it from that standpoint—the absolutism, the litmus tests, people saying "If you don't believe A, B, C, and D, you're not a Republican." I think that was the final part of my decision not to associate with the group any more. It had gone in a completely different direction than I thought it would when it first started.

At the other end of the certainty spectrum were black conservatives who acknowledged that racist behavior at Tea Party gatherings might conceivably be a problem, but because they had never experienced it they were reluctant to say it exists. Hilton, the Tea Partyer who compared movement loyalists to suffragettes and civil rights activists in their objections to state tyranny, said he had faith that if racism ever emerged in the Tea Party movement, "the spirit of the nation" would resolve it:

> I have been to several rallies and I never saw anything offensive. I've even organized rallies, probably close to six rallies. Each time between 300 and 400 people would show up and I never saw anything offensive. About twice a year,

one group asks me to come and speak to them. It's a group that's all white, in a rural part of the state. That's where a bunch of rednecks live. They ask me to come and speak because what I speak about is America and our values and individualism and my love for this country. I do love this country. This is a great nation. And of course, there are faults. There are problems. They're everywhere, in every nation. In this nation, when there are legitimate concerns, the spirit of the nation will try to correct it.

In one particularly nuanced response, Ritchie said he'd been treated with uncommon kindness by white people when he'd spoken at a rally, though their motivations weren't entirely clear:

I'll give you a story about one Tea Party event where I was received very warmly. I spent the evening talking to them about a variety of things. They allowed me to speak and they even took up what they called a love offering because they knew I had driven down there in my own vehicle on my own time and the love offering was supposed to pay for my gas. Anything I had left over was mine. A white couple that was there offered to let me stay at their house for the evening. And then when I got up in the morning, they wouldn't let me leave until they fed me breakfast. So, here I am, clearly a person of color and at least by their actions they're showing me that's not as important to them as the fact that I'm aligned with them in belief. And that's why I say the Tea Party movement isn't racist. That was my recollection, is that a lot of these people treated me very kindly and even in some cases, with a great deal of love. They're friends to this day and are generally concerned about me. It's hard for me on a personal level to just dismiss them as somehow being this caricature of evil that people paint them as.

I asked Ritchie if, despite their personal kindness, some Tea Partyers might be motivated by racial antagonism to oppose welfare programs on the (incorrect) assumption that most welfare recipients are black. He said the thought had crossed his mind:

I wonder about that sometimes, to be honest with you. In my church we have a lot of ethnicities. Some of the people I counsel are white people on welfare and government assistance. I was talking to a white single mother a couple of weeks ago, who was complaining about the stigma people attach to receiving this type of assistance. And I know this person—she's working on her education, working hard to better herself, but for right now, she needs that assistance if she's going to survive and her kids are going to survive. And I think people who oppose welfare reflexively have to understand something. I'm not comfortable with them assuming that getting rid of welfare will hurt just black people. It's going to hurt white people, too. It was fascinating to read in *Hillbilly Elegy* that the white underclass would always rail about the welfare state while at the same time collecting welfare checks. What they were really railing against wasn't necessarily the welfare state; they somehow thought they were worthy of the aid and others weren't. That's why I can't say with any kind of certainty that their opposition to welfare would strictly be policy-based because I don't know that I understand or trust the emotional motivations behind it.

The racial antagonism of the working-class whites in *Hillbilly Elegy* by J. D. Vance reminds us of the power of mediated images of "undeserving" African American welfare recipients, as noted in chapter 3 (Gilens 2003). Ritchie's comments speak to the racial tensions that may underlie otherwise genial interactions between whites and blacks at Tea Party events.

RACIAL HOSTILITY DOESN'T EXIST

In contrast to Hilton, who viewed Tea Party racism as hypothetical, and Ritchie, who agreed that it's difficult to know what agreeable white people are actually thinking, over a dozen African Americans argued that there is no racial hostility in the Tea Party. They arrived at this position via one of three paths. Some seemed charmed by how graciously they had been treated at Tea Party gatherings. Unlike Ritchie, who was grateful for white Tea Partyers' generosity but wasn't sure how much to trust it, these African Americans were convinced by their kind treatment that Tea Partyers weren't racist. A second group claimed that images of Obama as a witch doctor or of the First Family as apes were the work of Democratic operatives and left-wing dirty tricksters who had infiltrated the Tea Party with the aim of giving the movement a bad name. Rod's above-mentioned skepticism about the bona fides of some Tea Party protesters ("I'm not sure that all of the people who've given the group a bad name are sincerely Tea Partyers") represents this second group of racism deniers. A third group claimed—most astonishingly, in my opinion—that the many anti-Obama signs and posters, with their demeaning images and overt racial appeals, which had been seen by hundreds of thousands of people at Tea Party rallies and across the internet, simply didn't exist.

The Appeal of a Gracious Welcome

Upon arriving at Tea Party events, one of the first things that struck many African Americans was a sense of order and calm. Byron, who had spoken at several Tea Party rallies, called it "a family environment. There was no violence. Everybody cleaned up after themselves." Lindsay contrasted the peaceable crowds at Tea Party events with the raucous behavior at the 2011 Occupy Wall Street protests:

> Tea Partyers have been the nicest, salt of the earth, easygoing folks. I've never seen any kind of disruptive behavior at a Tea Party rally. When we had 1.7

million people in D.C., several of the news stories talked about how people left the place neater than when they got there. At Occupy Wall Street, people are getting raped and robbed, people are doing drugs, and they dump a bucket of feces in a bank lobby.

Contemporaneous news reports did, in fact, praise gatherings of "well into the tens of thousands" of Tea Partyers as "orderly, with no arrests made" (Isenstadt 2009) while describing the Occupy Wall Street protests as raucous and unruly, with all-night drumming, dozens of misdemeanor and felony arrests, at least one sexual assault (thus a women-only tent), and several protesters who dumped "a mixture of human waste" in a Chase Bank ATM lobby (Lupez and Johnson 2011; Anon 2012b). None of that lamentable behavior occurred at the Tea Party events Melvin attended:

> The rallies I've gone to were always upstanding. There have been "Stop Obama Now" posters, but there weren't any effigies of him or any of these disrespectful types of things. I've said a lot of things about the Obama administration, but I've always respected the president as the president of the country and I've felt, yeah, you don't have to like him, but you don't have to call him names. And no one in the Tea Party does that, in my experience.

Of course, the best indication of white people's racial attitudes is not how orderly the events were, or whether people saw Obama effigies, but how black attendees were treated. I asked Jimmy if he had ever been made to feel conspicuous or unwelcome at a Tea Party event. Perish the thought, he said. "I've never been targeted. I've been embraced. I've been hugged. I've been prayed for," he said. Similarly, when I asked Ashley, a forty-two-year-old chaplain, if she ever felt that white Tea Partyers seemed uncomfortable with her presence, she denied it:

> Umm, I didn't really get that sense. They were always happy to see any kind of black or brown face instead of it just being a group of old white people. So, I got more that than anything else. It was uncomfortable, but not because it wasn't welcoming; it might've been *too* welcoming. I felt like saying, like, "Guys, I know that I might be the only black one here, but I'm really not that special. It's not like I'm the only one who buys into what you're selling; it's just that I'm the only one willing to come out and talk."

Accordingly, Dean called Tea Partyers

> the most racially agnostic group I've ever encountered. I've attended events all over the country, and I've never once encountered anything that resembled racism or bigotry or anything like that ever. I encounter racially offensive material from liberals every day of my life! So, the Tea Partyers have consistently embraced me with open arms. I mean, they invite me to come speak. Why would a group of racists do that? The narrative is the exactly the opposite

of how Tea Party people are portrayed, at least what I've seen. They are the most welcoming, opening, and embracing group of people I've ever been around and that's consistent from state to state, anywhere I've ever been.

Like Hilton, who had been invited to speaking engagements by people he characterized as rednecks, black Tea Partyers felt comfortable even in the presence of whites who have a reputation for racial hostility. Kevin recounted being the only African American in a group of white southerners, a theoretically combustible moment that in practice resulted in no palpable racial tension at all. In fact, he said he felt like an "honorary redneck":

> When I'm with Tea Party people I feel at home. I've gone to Tea Party meetings where I'm the only black there. Matter of fact, I went to a memorial service for a friend's dad. His father was a veteran, so they've got the American flag and they're outside sitting around a bonfire and I'm walking up to the group. Now, most black folks would not walk up to a group of white folks sitting around a bonfire. You go in the opposite direction! But the point is, the Tea Party is a group of people who just love the values, love the Constitution, and they're American-bred. I call them Christian patriots and rednecks. They overlap with the Tea Party. The Tea Party can be anyone and a redneck can be anyone. In that case, I'm two out of three—I'm Christian and I'm a patriot. And an honorary redneck, too.

People like Kevin said shared values unite Tea Partyers across racial lines, turning rallies and meetings into islands of calm rather than flashpoints for racial tension. Anne said it didn't matter that she was one of the few African Americans at the rallies where she spoke as a political candidate; she didn't feel outnumbered or threatened in any way. "I think the only bond for the people was the issues," she said. "If you were for their issue, hey, they were for you." Melvin said he couldn't agree more. In his experience, ideological common ground trumped any insider-outsider distinctions:

> I've been welcomed at the Tea Party. They're glad to see me. I get strange looks on occasion because they don't expect me there, but once they come up and talk to me and we have discussions, they find we have the same ideas about where we need to go for the good of the country, the way the Constitution was written, and God's in control. We shouldn't ever feel like we're more powerful than God.

Melvin's reference to the power of God and Kevin's characterization of Tea Partyers as "Christian patriots" were typical among the interviewees who reported positive experiences at Tea Party gatherings, and suggest that a shared Christian identity helped these African Americans feel a part of the larger group. Inasmuch as a gracious reception can help any outsider feel comfortable in a new setting, the experience of being welcomed to events by white Tea Partyers—a group that's flush with conservative Christians (Clement and Green 2011)—may have resonated with "countless examples from both the Old and the New Testament" (Roberts and Roberts 2018) of biblical injunctions that instruct Christians to welcome strangers.

But above all, these testimonies forced me to rethink my expectation that any African American would feel reflexively anxious in a crowd of white conservatives, a group not particularly known for racial tolerance. In fact, I wondered if the presence of African Americans at these events might actually *decrease* any anti-black attitudes at these events. In 1954, social psychologist Gordon Allport hypothesized that face-to-face contact could reduce tension between members of different groups. In *The Nature of Prejudice*, Allport (1954, 281) explained that the contact must satisfy several conditions to be effective:

> Prejudice (unless deeply rooted in the character structure of the individual) may be reduced by equal status contact between majority and minority groups in the pursuit of common goals. The effect is greatly enhanced if this contact is sanctioned by institutional supports (i.e., by law, custom or local atmosphere), and provided it is of a sort that leads to the perception of common interests and common humanity between members of the two groups.

Allport's thesis has been confirmed by a recent meta-analysis of 515 studies, 94 percent of which found that interpersonal contact leads to a statistically significant reduction in intergroup prejudice (Pettigrew and Tropp 2006). If the formula for reducing prejudice is, as Allport suggests: (1) institutionally sanctioned contact; (2) between two equal-status groups; and (3) who have shared interests and common goals, then it's likely that: (1) Tea Party-sanctioned contact; (2) between blacks and whites as co-equals; and (3) who share conservative values in pursuit of likeminded public policies could reduce any anti-black prejudice at these gatherings.

Infiltrators, Frauds, and Democrats

On a bright sunny day in Len's hometown, I sat down with the former federal official at a Starbucks and asked him what he thought of the demeaning racial images of President Obama that had been spotted at Tea Party rallies. He hadn't seen them at the rallies he had attended, he replied. Then he warned me of the possibility of deception:

> The other thing you have to be careful of is this. I'm a pretty smart military guy, and one of the forms of maneuver is infiltration. So it is very simple for someone to show up at a rally and hold up something and somehow that one little sign seems to be the one sign that gets promulgated all across the internet and everything. I've seen instances where people have been sent to come in and ask certain questions, do certain things.

Len wasn't the only person to suggest that the Tea Party had been infiltrated by pretenders whose sole goal was to stain the protesters' reputation. Jimmy, who also likened political movements to military campaigns, said politics is a gloves-off blood sport where only the toughest survive. That is to say, the likelihood of enemy infiltrators is a no-brainer. I asked Jimmy what he thought about the anti-Obama rally signs.

> Number one, I don't believe most of them are Tea Party. If I'm opposition and I do dirty tricks, I'll show up to a Tea Party place with signs that are abhorrent. We live in a dirty world, and people play dirty tricks. All the time. Genuine Tea Party people don't want to be associated with racist messaging. But when I go to rallies and I see signs that say "Impeach Obama"? Now, that's fair game. I say stop whining and take it like a man. You want to be equal in America? Get used to be targeted by the opposition in America. I don't think it's right to call any president a mongrel, but they called Bush every name in the book. It's politics.

Andrew Breitbart agreed that Tea Party rallies were being ambushed by liberal "[gate]crashers out to discredit the movement." The prominent conservative publisher told *The Daily Beast* in 2010, "If I believed there was a strain of racism [in the Tea Party], I wouldn't put myself within a city mile of this" (Sarlin 2010). In retrospect, news stories don't seem to show that any campaign by outsiders to disrupt these gatherings was very effective. An Oregon schoolteacher who founded a group called Crash the Tea Party threatened to infiltrate Tax Day rallies on April 15, 2010, and there were reports of individuals carrying mock protest signs on that day at rallies in Boston, New York, St. Louis, Washington, DC, and other major cities (McMorris-Santoro 2010; Zombie 2010). But the gatecrashers seem to have been harmless, having been quickly sussed out by the crowds and escorted away by police officers or volunteer security teams. According to the conservative website PJ Media, these "fizzled crashings" fooled "exactly nobody" (Zombie 2010).

Still, some Tea Partyers find energy in conspiracy theories. Jonathan Kay, author of *Among the Truthers: A Journey Through America's Growing Conspiracist Underground*, says the Tea Party's "modern-day prophets" include radio host Alex Jones, who claims that the Obama campaign represents a plot by leaders of the New World Order to "con the American people into accepting global slavery" and the propagators of the 9/11 Truth movement, who predicted that "a false prophet such as Barack Obama will upend American sovereignty and render the country into a godless, one-world socialist dictatorship run by the United Nations from its offices in Manhattan" (Kay 2010). It makes sense that people who traffic in such conspiracy theories—not to mention suspicions about the president's citizenship or religious preference—might also believe that the Tea Party movement is being victimized by gate-crashing conspirators, an assumption that would allow them to attribute to outsiders embarrassing behavior for which they would otherwise have to blame their own group.

But in fairness to the Tea Party, conspiracy theories serve a useful function in groups that have lost power or are trying to understand complex societal events. By restoring a sense of meaning and control, they help people cope with feeling marginalized and distrustful (Newheiser, Farias, and Tausch 2011). To the extent that Tea Partiers experienced these feelings before or after the 2008 election, their gravitation to conspiracy theories is consistent with the psychological literature. The fact that African Americans frequently endorse conspiracy theories (cf. Goertzel 1994; Thorburn and Bogart 2005) suggests that black Tea Partiers could be particularly likely to embrace outsized ideas about movement infiltrators.

A Little Help From Photoshop

But while it's one thing to blame questionable acts on outsiders, it's quite another to claim that those acts don't exist. That's precisely what more than a few interviewees argued when I asked about indications of racial hostility at Tea Party rallies.

Their denials took several forms, all of which stretched credulity. Lindsay dismissed the offensive rally signs by saying they allegedly had been seen by only a single person:

> Ben Jealous of the NAACP said, "I saw sign that said 'Lynch Barack Obama.'" That was a baldfaced lie. He was lying. If those signs existed, they would have gone viral big time. The Dems would have loved to have signs like that to say, "See, see, see?" But to this very day, no one has ever seen those signs except for Ben Jealous of the NAACP. The fact that he's Ben Jealous and he said this is supposed to mean it had to be true.

Lindsay's point was clear: the alarm wasn't credible because the messenger was a political enemy. But of course, there were additional reports of disturbing messages (cf. Anon. n.d.b.; Shepherd 2012), including, you might recall, some from Lindsay's fellow black Tea Partiers—his political friends.

Kevin took that argument a step further. Even if the signs existed, he said, they wouldn't be racist:

> Kevin: Those signs were either Photoshopped or carried in by infiltrators. I have never been to a Party event where I've seen signs like that. There's cameras all over, everyone's carrying phones. It would be on YouTube. These people are liars. There were no signs and I challenge anyone to produce those signs.

> Me: Are you saying that an image of President Obama hanging from a noose doesn't send a racial message?
>
> Kevin: Well, why would it? If the president was white, you could have the same image. Why does it all of a sudden become racism if the president is black? President Obama is being treated like every other president. But he and his supporters want special dispensation. They want him to be put into a different category. But he's a failure on any topic. It's not the color of his skin that's the problem; it's the color of his ideas. He's an embarrassment, and it has nothing to do with skin color.

Kevin's comments deserve some unpacking. First, he denies the existence of the signs solely on the basis of his personal experience, unlike black Tea Partyers like Hilton and Ritchie, who hadn't seen the signs personally but acknowledged that they might exist. Hilton's and Ritchie's more nuanced approach of using personal experience as one of many possible data points instead of the sole reference point is more defensible given the inherent evidentiary weakness of anecdotes, which can be unrepresentative. "There is nothing wrong with accumulating evidence to support a theory; even anecdotal examples . . . are not automatically disqualified," write social psychologists Carrie A. Goodwin and C. James Goodwin (2017, 19). "The problem occurs when one relies too heavily on anecdotes or makes too much of them than is warranted." Second, anyone who's aware of the gruesome public lynchings that claimed 4,742 black lives between 1882 and 1968 appreciates the unmistakable significance of a hangman's noose in black history (Litwack 2000). For African Americans, the noose is the visual equivalent of the swastika to Jews (ADL n.d.). That means Kevin might as well have made the unlikely claim that a swastika carried in protest of a Jewish leader means no more than a swastika that protests a Hindu or Muslim leader.

The most stunning form of claim rejection was flat denial with no explanation. In the aftermath of the March 20, 2010, incident where angry white Tea Party protesters shouted a racial slur and spat on black members of Congress—an event witnessed by journalists and documented on videotape (Kane 2010; redarrowguy 2010; Cawthorne 2016)—Len said the name-calling and spitting didn't happen.

> Len: We looked for the n-word on placards at rallies, and we never found any. We never found the story to be true with members of the Congressional Black Caucus being spit at. We could never confirm that story. We interviewed staffers. There's nothing to make me believe that story ever happened. And we hounded that story. We bird-dogged it.
>
> Me: Did you get to the people who claimed they had been spat on?

Len: Yes.

Me: And they said . . .

Len: They did not confirm it. And don't you know if you've been spat on, you would confirm it.

Len's denial, which suggests that Rep. Emanuel Cleaver actually recanted his claim of being assaulted by insults and spit, fits with a narrative promoted by Andrew Breitbart and other conservatives. After the spitting incident, Breitbart posted a forty-eight-second YouTube video of the members and their staffers leaving the Capitol building to booing crowds, but no racial epithets or spitting. But the video showed the members as they *left* the Capitol, whereas the assaults happened as they *entered* the building an hour before. "I'm not saying the video was conclusive proof," Breitbart said when questioned about his video (Washington 2010).

But Breitbart and others had an incentive to fabricate a narrative, because people begin to believe lies if they're repeated enough times. This phenomenon, called *illusory truth,* was first documented in 1977 by a team of psychologists who asked a group of college students to judge the veracity of sixty plausible statements, some true and some false, drawn from history, biology, current affairs, and other fields. Every other week for one month, the students were given another sixty-item list and again asked which statements were true and which were false. Each successive list was a mix of new assertions and repeated assertions from the previous list. The students did a good job of differentiating between true statements (e.g., "Kentucky was the first state west of the Alleghenies to be settled by pioneers") and false statements (e.g., "The People's Republic of China was founded in 1947"). But as the experiment continued and students encountered some of the false statements a second or third time, they tended to judge them as true. "Frequency, then, must have served as a criterion of certitude," the scholars wrote. "Indeed, the present experiment tends to lend empirical support to the idea that 'if people are told something often enough, they'll believe it'" (Hasher, Goldstein, and Toppino 1977, 112). This tendency for lies to sound credible with repetition suggests the value of exposure to diverse news sources instead of relying on a single outlet like Fox News or even MSNBC. Fully 60 percent of the claims by hosts and pundits on Fox News—and 44 percent of those on MSNBC—were false or mostly false, according to one Poynter Institute study (Sharockman 2015).

There's another reason black Tea Partyers might reject worrisome assessments of their fellow white patriots: the potential consequences if the assessments are accurate. Nobody wants to borrow trouble. Beyond the possibility that a random white patriot could assault them physically or verbally, African

Americans who have many Tea Party interactions over time could run the risk of chronic exposure to so-called *microaggressions*—everyday insults, slurs, or incivilities, which can be unintentional. Regardless of intent, long-term exposure to microaggressions are a risk factor for medical conditions (e.g., hypertension, increased heart rate), emotional problems (e.g., depression, anxiety), behavioral effects (e.g., rage, hypervigilance), and cognitive disruption (e.g., diminished learning and problem-solving) (Sue 2010). Rather than feel vulnerable to these or other problems, it makes sense that African Americans would downplay the risks of mixing with white Tea Partyers by dismissing movement racism out of hand. I suspect that this response likely represents psychological *denial*, "a protective defense in the face of unbearable news" (Carey 2007)—the same normal reaction we might have on hearing that a spouse has an ominous medical diagnosis, or that a beloved uncle has died. For black Tea Partyers, denying racism is easier than acknowledging they may have placed themselves in harm's way.

Finally, anthropological and psychological research suggests that the ability to overlook disturbing evidence functions to foster close relationships. Here's how *New York Times* reporter Benedict Carey (2007) puts it:

> The psychological tricks that people use to ignore a festering problem in their own households are the same ones that they need to live with everyday human dishonesty and betrayal, their own and others'. And it is these highly evolved abilities, research suggests, that provide the foundation for that most disarming of all human invitations, forgiveness.

Conceivably, then, denying racism within the movement likely serves two psychological functions for black Tea Partyers: it protects them from imagining the disconcerting possibility that they, too, could be targets of a racist confrontation from their white counterparts. And it might foster closer relationships between black and white Tea Party supporters whom outsiders assume are the most unlikely bedfellows. Psychologically, for black Tea Partyers, that's a win-win.

CONCLUSION

If W. E. B. Du Bois were alive today, what would he have to say about African American Tea Party supporters? Would he view them with resigned empathy, knowing that people who have their feet in both worlds—one white, one black—have no choice but to navigate majority-white institutions as well as majority-black ones? Would he warn them not to trust the *Glad to meet you!*s and the *We're so glad you're here!*s at Tea Party events, because behind the polite smiles and the handshakes, white Tea Partyers are still wondering *How does it feel to be a problem?*, still viewing African Americans with contempt wrapped in civility?

Before he came to any conclusions, the father of sociological fieldwork would probably pick up his notebook and hit the field. He would go to Tea Party meetings and watch people interact. He would assess for himself whether Tea Party rallies are simple celebrations of American values or a more complicated mix of Christian patriotism and xenophobic unease. He would seek out people who bring offensive signs to rallies to discern whether they're Tea Party regulars with pent-up racial hostility or pretenders who are trying to give the movement a bad name. He would ask people to explain why a man with a foreign-sounding name can't in fact be an American Christian. Compared to the richness of fieldwork-driven data, he would probably say that merely interviewing black Tea Partyers is pretty close to car-window sociology.

However, the interview data alone are instructive, because they help explain both African Americans' wariness about Tea Party gatherings and their enthusiasm for them. Wariness is easy to explain: it's intuitively reasonable to think that a black person who has experienced overt racism at a Tea Party rally, or who has seen indications of racism at movement gatherings but hasn't experienced them personally, would feel that racism is alive and well at these events. That also means that outside observers who scorn the African Americans in Tea Party crowds because they assume that all black conservatives are racial unsophisticates should realize that some black conservatives are quite critical of white people, and as a result may be reluctant to congregate with them. The televised images of Tea Party rallies show only the African American conservatives who attend the rallies, not the ones who stay away.

On the other hand, the interviews also suggest that even in the face of dubious posters and racist slurs, not all African Americans subscribe to essentialist assumptions about white treachery. This willingness to approach white people with a clean slate as individuals, rather than as members of a group that is guilty of unspeakable racial offenses, likely opens the door at Tea Party meetings and rallies to interracial alliances forged by ideological congruence and untroubled by racial tension. African Americans who universalize their positive or benign personal experiences with white Tea Partyers are likely to show this willingness to approach subsequent whites nonjudgmentally. Similarly, those who dismiss Tea Party racism capitalize on the psychological effects of denial, with its ability to reduce racial anxiety and build interracial relationships. Even African Americans who are alert for racism at these events can find comfort in the inevitability of a few bad apples.

Epilogue

I began this book with three hypothetical explanations for why African Americans would align with white conservative extremists who sometimes harbor troublesome racial ideas, instead of with 99 percent of the African American community in celebration of America's first African American president. I surmised that African Americans might support the Tea Party because they have mixed feelings about being black, which might make them feel ambivalent about President Obama; because they downplay racism, which leads them to doubt the need for Obama-era race-related policies, such as criminal justice reform, and minimize the potential for racial tensions at Tea Party events; or because they were socialized to be self-reliant hard workers, which inclines them to presume both that poor people are lazy and that government entitlement programs are unnecessary and counterproductive. My findings suggest that all three hypotheses are problematic.

First, African Americans who support the Tea Party don't seem at all ambivalent about being black. To the contrary, they seem perfectly happy with their brown skin and they are passionate about finding ways to help other African Americans thrive. Contrary to critics' presumptions about the racial loyalty of black Tea Partyers, there's no question that the reference group for these African American conservatives is the black community. Any suggestion to the contrary is simply not supported by the evidence.

Second, while some black Tea Party supporters downplay racism and dismiss its effects, others situate racism as a grievous challenge both throughout society at large and within the protest movement. This mixed reaction to racism resembles their disparate reactions to attending Tea Party rallies and the willingness of some interviewees to acknowledge the troubling racial overtones at Tea Party events.

Finally, while socialization is an imperfect, incomplete, nondeterministic social mechanism, many black Tea Partyers were indeed socialized to be self-sufficient. And most of the interviewees said African Americans could greatly diminish chronic poverty, excess incarceration, and other gnawing social problems if more children simply listened to their elders. Yet some Tea Partyers acknowledged that parents aren't always present in their childrens' lives, which means the younger generation loses opportunities to learn from their elders. Upwards of one-third of the interviewees understood poverty as a *public issue* that results from structural defects such as inadequate schools and insufficient numbers of jobs that pay a living wage. Moreover, most of the interviewees agreed that simply acting responsibly is not enough to protect African Americans from a criminal justice system that tilts against them. And virtually everyone supported government relief, albeit as a temporary bridge from precarious circumstances to something more stable. Thus, these Tea Partyers were critical of conservatives' typical claim that black-community dysfunction is simply a reflection of individuals' inherent character defects.

So if you're an African American who supports the Tea Party, what's your take on President Obama? It depends on what aspect of the Obama presidency is on the table. Reviews of Obama's policies and political perspectives were uniformly and unapologetically negative. However, while a few doubters had reservations about his bona fides as an American citizen or as a Christian, most accepted the legitimacy of his presidency and didn't question his faith. And everyone appreciated the enormous significance of Obama's electoral victory and his admirable qualities as a father.

Indeed, if there is a consistent theme to the narratives in this book, it is their inconsistency. *African American Tea Partyers are a study in diversity despite apparent uniformity.* To their critics who roll their eyes (or worse) and assume that these wayward political anomalies have somehow lost their inner racial compasses, black Tea Party supporters may seem cut from the same self-loathing cloth. But a closer look reveals a vast range of perspectives, as reflected in the divergent epigraphs that begin each chapter. On any given topic, whether it's the relevance of racism, the wisdom of government entitlements, or the meaning of Tea Party events, any two black Tea Party supporters might have polar-opposite perspectives on the core questions that fuel this study.

These Tea Party stalwarts differ in upbringing and temperament as well. During the course of their interviews, some quoted biblical passages as their inspiration to join the protest movement. Jake, for example, mentioned God or Bible verses an average of once every seventeen minutes during a nearly three-hour conversation. At the other extreme, Jimmy spoke for over three hours and hardly referenced religion at all.

Some black Tea Partyers tend to be politically doctrinaire, infusing their remarks with Republican talking points. These are frequently ideological purists who deny racism, dispute the legitimacy of the Obama presidency, and feel that crime, unemployment, and other problems in the black community are caused by a combination of poor individual decisions, corrupt black leaders, and failed Democratic initiatives. For example, Byron's wife Claudia, a Tea Party fan who sat in on my 2014 conversation with her husband, said President Obama's desire to provide Americans with so-called positive economic rights, such as protection from poverty and unemployment (Gregory 2012), "puts us one step closer to totalitarianism." Well into Obama's second term, Claudia, an African American woman, had not softened her alarm that our first African American president was fundamentally un-American. However, more-practical interviewees accepted the Obama presidency; acknowledged the role of both individual and structural factors (including systemic racism) in determining a person's life chances; and sometimes even supported like-minded Democrats. Anne, who recognized racism within the conservative community, said she supports Democrats and Republicans alike for elected office "as long as I agree with them on the issues."

Some people said the reason they place so much value on hard work and self-sufficiency is their strict conservative upbringing. Len mentioned his mother and father ten times in our seventy-minute interview. It was a surprising number of parental references for a fifty-four-year-old man, but Len wasn't the only middle-aged Tea Partyer who repeatedly credited parental socialization for teaching them everything from how to manage their finances to how to behave during a police traffic stop. Others hardly mentioned their parents at all.

These findings suggest considerable variation in a population that we frequently assume is monolithic. Historian Michael Ondaatje (2010, 156) got it right when he wrote that black conservatives are united "more by the contingencies of circumstance" than by "a single, coherent system of ideas." Moreover, by exploring cases where liberal-leaning black Tea Partyers have pushed back against the movement by calling out Tea Party racism and praising government protections, my research adds nuance to what political scientist Tasha Philpot (2017, 21) calls the "multidimensionality of the liberal-conservative continuum" for black Americans.

This diversity also helps explain African Americans' gravitation to the Tea Party, because not all African American Tea Partyers support the protest movement to the same extent, nor for the same reasons. Consider Charlie, the Navy veteran who was attracted by the Tea Party's message of fiscal responsibility because he didn't want his son's generation to inherit a massive federal debt, but was repulsed by the racism he saw at Tea Party protests. Or Len, who dismissed all signs of Tea Party racism and supported the protest movement for its uncompromising opposition to socialism. Or Jake, who never claimed that President Obama is a socialist but, like many Tea Partyers, expressed grave doubts about the president's citizenship.

In this hodgepodge of interests and motivations, we find different voter archetypes. For example, some African Americans seem to have been drawn to the Tea Party by the political ideas of their conservative parents. In their influential work *The American Voter,* political scientists Angus Campbell and colleagues (1960) wrote extensively about partisans who are socialized by their parents to support one party or another. People like Andrew, a conservative Republican whose father supported conservative Republican Sen. Strom Thurmond, follow this general model. Hilton, a conservative Republican who hails from a family of liberal Democrats, does not.

Alternatively, I also found people who make political decisions more intuitively than by a precise weighing of each candidates' pros and cons. This approach, which political scientists Richard R. Lau and David P. Redlawsk (2006, 8, 13) compare to "low information rationality," allows voters to decide whom to support by using "cognitive shortcuts." Consider Kevin, who said, "I know absolutely he's a Muslim" because, he predicted, Obama would refuse to say Jesus Christ is his Lord. Or Rev. Isaac, who had doubts about Obama's citizenship because it took so long to produce his birth certificate.

Not every black Tea Partyer is as well-informed as Mary, who makes it a practice to consume news from across the political spectrum and to seek out diverse conversation partners. With the help of reputable fact-checking websites, it's easy to distinguish between Tea Party claims based on empirical facts and those driven by opinionated punditry, but not every African American Tea Party loyalist questions movement orthodoxy. Nor is everyone as critical a thinker as Anne, who as a candidate refused to be silenced by GOP officials who felt she hadn't paid her dues. That's a far cry from dutifully respecting one's elders, as conservative traditionalists might advise.

In the end, few black Tea Party supporters struck me as irrational. Their reasons for coming to the Tea Party make sense, particularly once we understand that everyone I spoke with celebrated Obama's election victory; everyone embraces their African American identity and feels devoted to the black community; many (but not all) acknowledge racism; and while they caution against making welfare subsidies a way of life, everyone supports them *in extremis.* These convictions make black Tea Partyers look a lot like other African Americans. Where they represent ideological outliers compared to the rest of the black community, they usually have a coherent rationale, rooted in family history or their own experiences, for their unusual perspectives, whether that means denying racism or opposing Obamacare. And while it's true that some of these iconoclastic positions, such as doubting Obama's citizenship, originate in sketchy internet rumors, it's not necessarily illogical to make political decisions based on hearsay. Political rumors may be groundless but they "often consist of plausible explanations . . . about important phenomena and are offered without an explicit claim of truthfulness or a secure standard of evidence" (Weeks and Garrett 2014, 402).

Despite the diversity that emerged in this study, there were also elements of commonality. In addition to broad agreement on the value of hard work, the avoidance of government relief, and other conservative principles, most of the interviewees had a history of not following the crowd. I had expected to find unconventional thinkers who followed their own minds even if their decisions were unusual or unpopular, and black Tea Partyers didn't disappoint. Jake wrote a blog post so critical of the President Obama that it earned him a visit from cautious Secret Service agents. He didn't realize that his message posted on King Day, but it's not clear that the irony would have troubled him if he had. Jimmy, who spoke admiringly of his father being booed at a PTA meeting for taking an unpopular stand; went on to admire the Black Panther Party, a group that remains highly controversial even within the black community (e.g., Anon. 2019; Anon. 1970). Several interviewees had launched improbable political campaigns: Anne raised $1 million as an upstart candidate for the House of Representatives, and Whitney represents a virtually all-white district of conservative southern whites.

Not all black conservatives are comfortable playing the gadfly, they said. Byron explained that while he and his sister share the same conservative beliefs, she is afraid to go public with them. Thus, most agreed that being a political anomaly requires fortitude. "It's vicious out there," said Len, the former federal official. "It takes a certain strength of character to stand up to this criticism." Interestingly, interviewees spoke of hearing support for their iconoclastic positions, albeit privately, from other African Americans. Kevin explained that while most African Americans are left-of-center politically, they also understand the importance of working hard, staying in school, and having a strong moral compass. "Most African-Americans are politically liberal but socially conservative. As a result, many more blacks support Tea Party principles than will acknowledge publically," Kevin said. "When black folks see me in public, they come up to me and they whisper, 'Keep sayin' it, man.'"

But most Tea Partyers didn't seem to need community affirmation, because they were bedrock certain about their convictions. This armor of élan suggests that while black Tea Party supporters are criticized as being insecure—ostensibly the reason they're branded as sellouts—they feel self-assured about following their minds, even if few people agree with them. For example, Tea Party supporter and author Deneen Borelli (2012) seems to revel in her role as iconoclast; her book *Blacklash* mentions the words "liberty" thirty-two times and "individual" thirty-six times, as if to celebrate the freedom to march to her drummer.

When I asked interviewees where they find the courage to defy the crowd, their responses brimmed with confidence. Dean said that when people call him a sellout, he winces—not because his feelings are hurt, but because the taunt is so banal. "Is that the best you got?" he fires back. Elton said his Republican sensibilities make him a bit of a pariah at his HBCU, so he challenges his progressive classmates to consider the value of two political parties—not just one—addressing civil rights legislation, criminal justice reform, and other issues of broad appeal. He doesn't win over every critic, he admits, but sometimes the conversation can be a game changer. "They're telling me, like, 'You're not as bad as most Republicans, because I can actually talk to you about politics.'" When I asked Mary where she finds the strength to stand up to doubters, she said it was an easy question. "Because I think I'm right," she said without hesitation. Anne went a step further. She'd been influenced as a young girl by her carefree grandmother who taught her to "wear the worries of the world like a loose jacket." That was a daring proposition in the 1950s, and as we sat at Anne's kitchen table discussing her life in the sometimes bruising world of contemporary politics, she explained how she handles brickbats today. "When somebody criticizes me, I wonder what's wrong with them!" she said with a smile.

Sociologist C. Wright Mills wrote that thinking sociologically—viewing people's actions in the context of their personal biographies and the historical events that shape their lives—has a way of subverting our expectations. As Mills put it, thinking sociologically makes the familiar strange. It's the same with African American Tea Partyers: the closer we look, the less they are who we thought they were. This presents lessons for scholars and nonscholars alike, lessons about tolerance and open-mindedness, and resisting the urge to judge until we have the facts. It's also a reminder to *reach out* for the facts in the first place. After all, over half of all Americans—even adults over fifty—now say they get their news from Twitter, Facebook, and other social media (Reuters 2017). That means it has never been easier to find a news source that resonates with what we already think. But to really understand, we need to remember to reach beyond what we think we know.

Appendix

Interview Questions

1. BIOGRAPHY

Let's begin with some biographical questions.

In what year were you born?

Where did you grow up?

How many siblings did you grow up with? How old are they compared to you?

How many people lived in the house where you grew up? (*Clarify relationship to interviewee.*)

Tell me about your parents/guardians.
> Are they alive?
> What do/did they do for a living?
> What kind of parents were they? What was it like to grow up in your household?

When you think about the messages that you received as a child from your parent(s) about life lessons and the kind of person they wanted you to grow up to be, what messages and ideas seemed to be repeated the most?

Did your siblings seem to get the same messages, or did your parents talk with them about other concerns?

Do you remember hearing much about the value of hard work?

Did your parent(s) ever talk about people who couldn't seem to get a job, or keep one, or who never seemed to have enough money? Why were people in this situation, according to what you were told?

As you look back on your childhood, were there other adults who were especially influential on your development as a person? Can you talk about them and some of the life lessons you picked up from them?

Where did you graduate from high school?

Tell me about your education after high school.

What's your occupation?

What social class do you consider yourself to be a part of?

May I ask you about your income range? Would you say you make less than $50,000 a year, $50,000–75,000, or over $75,000?

Here's a related question about wealth that's general, not about you specifically. Most people benefit from some sort of inheritance when their parents die. On average, how much of a person's wealth would you say is passed down from their parents?

2. POLITICS

I have some questions for you about politics.

What political party are you affiliated with?

Do you consider yourself a conservative?

What does the Tea Party mean to you? If you were to describe the group to someone who had never heard of it, what would you say?

Do you think of yourself as a member of the Tea Party?
    If no: Why not?

If they have siblings:

You mentioned your siblings.

How do they feel about the Tea Party?

If any siblings don't like the Tea Party:

How do you explain how someone who grew up in the same home as you did and heard many of the same messages from your parents turned out to be so different politically?

How does it feel to march to a different drummer?

I'd like to ask you about your news sources. On any given day, where are you likely to go for news about national and international affairs?

What's your opinion of other news sources? *Ask open-ended question first, then specify in order of political ideology from center to left:*

    Do you ever watch CNN?
    Do you read the *New York Times* or the *Washington Post?*
    Do you read [the closest major newspaper to the interviewee's city]?
    Do you listen to National Public Radio?
    Do you ever watch MSNBC?

Are you familiar with publications like *The Nation* or *Mother Jones*? Do you read them?

What are some of the most important issues that you think need to be addressed regarding our government?

Do you think the government threatens our rights and freedoms?

Do you think federal programs should be cut back to reduce the power of the government?

Do you think the government imposes too may regulations on business and interferes with the free-market system?

Do you think the government interferes too much in people's daily lives?

How do you feel about the job Barack Obama is doing as president?

Do you think he's moving the country toward socialism?

How do you feel about the Affordable Care Act (Obamacare)?

3. THE RADICALIZATION PROCESS

I'd like to ask how you became interested in the Tea Party.

People find lots of ways to get involved in politics. Some may send money to a candidate's campaign, or join a political action committee. When you first learned about the Tea Party, had you been considering lots of different ways to get involved in politics?

If yes: What other options were you considering?

The first time you heard about the Tea Party, what was it about this movement that appealed to you?

How long did it take you to decide that the Tea Party was right for you?

Can you talk about the process you used over this time to narrow these options to the one(s) you selected?

The Tea Party has been described as a grassroots movement. How did you become affiliated with local Tea Party members? Can you describe that process?

Did you ever feel that this might not be the group for you? Do you ever vacillate in your support for the Tea Party?

If yes: Why do you return to the Tea Party?

Sometimes after people are in a group, they have moments when they reflect on their decision to join the group. They might feel good about the decision or have regrets about it. Have you had moments like this with the Tea Party?

If yes: Can you explain?

Have you been to local Tea Party gatherings?

If yes: Tell me about the first one you attended.
What were your impressions?
Statistics say about 80 percent of Tea Party members are white. Were you the only [black] person there?
How did you feel about that?
Did you feel welcome? What did people do to make you feel that way?

Did you feel that people responded to you any differently than anyone else?

Have you ever been to a large Tea Party rally involving hundreds or thousands of people?

If yes: How was that experience different than the local gathering?

You've probably seen the photos of Tea Party members holding posters that play on stereotypes of black people. I'm thinking of images of President Obama as a witch doctor, or of the White House with a watermelon patch on the grounds. When you see those images, what goes through your head?

How much do you think the criticism President Obama has received is because of his race?

4. RACE

Now I have some questions for you about race.

People of African ancestry have been referred to in lots of different ways over the years, from Negroes to blacks to African Americans.

What do you call yourself?

(If anything other than *black* or *African American*):

Is there a reason you don't call yourself black or African American?
Does it bother you that most people of African descent refer to themselves differently than you do?
Generally speaking, are you the kind of person who is comfortable going against the grain?

If yes: Can you share an example from your life where most people did one thing, and you did something else entirely?

How close do you feel to the following groups of African Americans (very close, close, not close, not very close at all):

Poor blacks
Religious and churchgoing blacks
Middle-class blacks
Older blacks

Do you think racism against blacks is or is not widespread in the United States? Why or why not?

Do you think that you are personally affected by racism?

Do you feel that racial minorities in this country have equal job opportunities as whites, or not? Why or why not? Black unemployment is typically twice as high as white unemployment. What's the best way to explain that discrepancy?

So in general, who do you think has a better chance of getting ahead in today's society—white people, black people, or do white people and black people have about an equal chance of getting ahead? Why do you feel this way?

Do you think the American justice system is—or is not—biased against blacks? Why or why not?

Black people are jailed at a rate six times higher than whites. How do you explain that?

Do you think racial discrimination against blacks is a major factor, a minor factor, or not a factor in: (*mention in random order*)

>   Lower average education levels for blacks in the United States. Why or why not?
>   Lower average income levels for blacks in the United States. Why or why not?
>   Lower average life expectancies for blacks. Why or why not?
>   A higher percentage of blacks in US prisons. Why or why not?

All in all, do you feel that too much has been made of the problems facing black people, too little has been made, or that it is just about right?

References

Addams, Jane. 1902. "The Housing Problem in Chicago." *Annals of the American Academy of Political and Social Science* 20: 99–107.
ADL [Anti-Defamation League]. n.d. "Noose." Accessed March 4, 2019. https://www.adl.org/education/references/hate-symbols/noose.
Adorno, T. W., Else Frenkel-Brunswik, Daniel J. Levinson, and R. Nevitt Sanford. 1950. *The Authoritarian Personality.* New York: Norton.
Aiken, Lewis R. 2002. *Attitudes and Related Psychosocial Constructs: Theories, Assessment, and Research.* Thousand Oaks, London, and New Delhi: Sage.
Akerlof, George A. and Janet L. Yellen. 1996. "An Analysis of Out-of-Wedlock Births in the United States." *Brookings Policy Brief Series*, August 1, 1996. https://www.brookings.edu/research/an-analysis-of-out-of-wedlock-births-in-the-united-states/.
Alexander, Michelle. 2012. *The New Jim Crow: Mass Incarceration in the Age of Colorblindness.* New York: The New Press.
Allen, Richard L. 2001. *The Concept of Self: A Study of Black Identity and Self-Esteem.* Detroit: Wayne State University Press.
Allport, Gordon. 1954. *The Nature of Prejudice.* New York: Perseus Books.
Amadeo, Kimberly. 2019a. "What Has Obama Done? 14 Major Accomplishments." The Balance, February 19, 2019. https://www.thebalance.com/what-has-obama-done-11-major-accomplishments-3306158.
———. 2019b. "Racial Wealth Gap in the United States." The Balance, March 28, 2019. https://www.thebalance.com/racial-wealth-gap-in-united-states-4169678.
Anon. n.d.a. "History is a Weapon: Mississippi Black Codes." Accessed March 3, 2019. https://www.historyisaweapon.com/defcon1/mississippiblackcode.html.
———. n.d.b. "Party Racist Signs White Slavery." https://sendirikan.blogspot.com/2012/11/party-racist-signs-white-slavery.html.
———. 1904. "Negro Leader on Lynching." *New York Times,* February 9, 1904. https://www.nytimes.com/1904/02/29/archives/negro-leader-on-lynching-booker-t-washington-denounces-mob-violence.html.
———. 1906a. "Spread of Negro Crime Alarms Mr. Washington." *New York Times,* August 30, 1906. https://www.nytimes.com/1906/08/30/archives/spread-of-negro-crime-alarms-mr-washington-he-condemns-those-who.html.
———. 1906b. "Two Negroes Lynched." *New York Times,* July 29, 1906. https://www.nytimes.com/1906/07/28/archives/two-negroes-lynched-seized-by-a-florida-mob-they-admit-they-killed.html.
———. 1970. "Attacks on Black Panthers." *The Oakland Post,* January 1, 1970.

References

———. 2009a. "Houston Tea Party, February 27, 2009." Video. February 27, 2009. https://www.youtube.com/watch?v=DgdWL8pjo6I.

———. 2009b. "File: Protest Sign During Tea Party Protests.jpg." Wikimedia, April 15, 2009. https://commons.wikimedia.org/wiki/File:Protest_sign_during_tea_party_protests_2009.jpg.

———. 2009c. "The Culture of Poverty." National Public Radio, Talk of the Nation, March 23, 2009. https://www.npr.org/templates/story/story.php?storyId=102246990.

———. 2011. "Family Disputes Must Be Private." *The Philadelphia Tribune*, October 1, 2011. https://www.phillytrib.com/commentary/family-disputes-must-be-private/article_e4b15e4c-e016-50b5-bfce-ce12f386b47a.html.

———. 2012a. "Black Officials More Likely Probed for Corruption?" National Public Radio, July 15, 2012. https://www.npr.org/2012/07/13/156724059/black-officials-more-likely-probed-for-corruption#.

———. 2012b. "Occupy Wall Street Protester Arrested for Dumping Feces in Chase Bank." Huffpost, March 22, 2012. https://www.huffingtonpost.com/2012/03/22/occupy-wall-street-feces_n_1372293.html.

———. 2013. "Apostle Claver Kamau-Imani, President and CEO, Broadcast Activist." August 22, 2013. http://www.ragingelephantsradio.com/broadcast-schedule-host-bios/apostle-claver-kamau-imani-president-ceo/.

———. 2014. "Teaching the Children: Sharp Ideological Differences, Some Common Ground." Pew Research Center, September 18, 2014. http://www.people-press.org/2014/09/18/teaching-the-children-sharp-ideological-differences-some-common-ground/.

———. 2015. "Policing Baltimore's Police." *The Baltimore Sun*, May 4, 2015. https://www.baltimoresun.com/news/opinion/editorial/bs-ed-freddie-gray-police-brutality-20150503-story.html.

———. 2018. "JJ White Inc. Contributes $10,000 to Hurricane Harvey Relief Efforts." https://www.jjwhiteinc.com/2017/08/31/jj-white-inc-donates-10000-hurricane-harvey-relief-efforts/.

———. 2019. "Nation of Islam." Southern Poverty Law Center. https://www.splcenter.org/fighting-hate/extremist-files/group/nation-islam.

Arnold, David, Will Dobbie, and Crystal S. Yang. 2018. "Racial Bias in Bail Decisions." *The Quarterly Journal of Economics* 133, no. 4: 1885–932.

Associated Press. 1963. "Riots Erupt in Birmingham; JFK Sends Troops to State." *Pittsburgh Post Gazette*, May 13, 1963. https://news.google.com/newspapers?id=axoNAAAAIBAJ&sjid=KWwDAAAAIBAJ&dq=birmingham-crisis&pg=5844%2C1871492.

———. 2004. "NAACP Gala Toasts Brown Pioneers." NBCNews.com, May 17, 2004. http://www.nbcnews.com/id/5000624/ns/us_news-life/t/naacp-gala-toasts-brown-v-board-pioneers/.

———. 2009. "Mayor Hits Rough Patch over Watermelon Pic." CBS News, February 25, 2009. https://www.cbsnews.com/news/mayor-hits-rough-patch-over-watermelon-pic/.

Asumah, Seth N. and Valencia C. Perkins. 2000. "Black Conservatism and the Social Problems in Black America." *Journal of Black Studies* 31, no. 1: 51–73.

Atieh, Jennifer M., Arthur P. Brief, and David A. Vollrath. 1987. "The Protestant Work Ethic-Conservatism Paradox: Beliefs and Values in Work and Life." *Personality and Individual Differences* 8, no. 4: 577–80.

Aziz, John. 2014. "Does Welfare Make People Lazy?" *The Week*, March 18, 2014. https://theweek.com/articles/449215/does-welfare-make-people-lazy.

Bacon, Perry Jr. 2016. "The Professors vs. the President: Has Obama Done Enough for African-Americans?" NBC News, February 28, 2016. https://www.nbcnews.com/news/nbcblk/professors-vs-president-has-obama-done-enough-african-americans-n523811.

Bader, Michael. 2010. "We Need to Have Empathy for Tea Partiers." *Psychology Today*, March 5, 2010. https://www.psychologytoday.com/us/blog/what-is-he-thinking/201003/we-need-have-empathy-tea-partiers.

Baker, Al, J. David Goodman, and Benjamin Mueller. 2015. "Beyond the Chokehold: The Path to Eric Garner's Death." *New York Times*, June 13, 2015. https://www.nytimes.com/2015/

06/14/nyregion/eric-garner-police-chokehold-staten-island.html?login=email&auth=login-email.

Baldus, David C., George Woodworth, David Zuckerman, Neil Alan Weiner, and Barbara Broffitt. 1998. "Racial Discrimination and the Death Penalty in the Post-*Furman* Era: An Empirical and Legal Overview, With Recent Findings from Philadelphia." *Cornell Law Review* 83: 1638–770.

Banerjee, Abhijit V., Rema Hanna, Gabriel E. Kreindler, and Benjamin A. Olken. 2017. "Debunking the Stereotype of the Lazy Welfare Recipient: Evidence from Cash Transfer Programs." *The World Bank Observer* 32, no. 2: 155–84.

Barr, Andy. 2010. "The GOP's No-Compromise Pledge." Politico, October 28, 2010. https://www.politico.com/story/2010/10/the-gops-no-compromise-pledge-044311.

Barua, Baccus and Sazid Hasan. 2018. "The Private Cost of Public Queues for Medically Necessary Care, 2018." Fraser Institute, May 23, 2018. https://www.fraserinstitute.org/studies/private-cost-of-public-queues-for-medically-necessary-care-2018.

Bauman, Zygmunt. 1991. "The Social Manipulation of Morality: Moralizing Actors, Adiaphorizing Action." *Theory, Culture & Society* 8: 137–51.

Baumrind, Diana. 1971. "Current Patterns of Parental Authority." *Developmental Psychology Monograph* 4(1, pt. 2): 1–103.

BBC World Service. 2008. "All Countries in BBC Poll Prefer Obama to McCain." September 10, 2008. http://news.bbc.co.uk/2/shared/bsp/hi/pdfs/10_09_08_ws_us_poll.pdf.

Berger, Judson. 2009. "Modern-Day Tea Parties Give Taxpayers Chance to Scream for Better Representation." http://www.foxnews.com/politics/2009/04/09/modern-day-tea-parties-taxpayers-chance-scream-better-representation.html.

Berkin, Carol. 2003. "Ethnicity in Seventeenth-Century English America, 1600–1700." In *Race and Ethnicity in America*, edited by Ronald Bayor, 1–20. New York: Columbia University Press.

Berman, Russell. 2018. "The Democratic Party Apologizes to Black Voters." *The Atlantic*, July 20, 2018. https://www.theatlantic.com/politics/archive/2018/07/the-democratic-party-apologizes-to-black-voters/565697/.

Bertrand, Marianne and Sendhil Mullainathan. 2004. "Are Emily and Greg More Employable than Lakisha and Jamal? A Field Experiment on Labor Market Discrimination." *American Economic Review* 94, no. 4: 991–1013.

Bice, Allie. 2017. "Did Arizonans See 116 Percent Increase in 'Obamacare' Premiums?" azcentral.com, November 27, 2017. https://www.azcentral.com/story/news/politics/fact-check/2017/11/27/did-arizonans-see-116-percent-increase-obamacare-premiums/842108001.

Bifulco, Robert. 2005. "District-Level Black-White Funding Disparities in the United States, 1987–2002." *Journal of Education Finance* 31(2): 172–94.

Biggs, Andrew G., Kevin A. Hassett, and Matthew Jensen. 2010. American Enterprise Institute for Public Policy Research. AEI Economic Policy Working Paper 1020–04, December 27, 2010. http://www.aei.org/wp-content/uploads/2011/10/20101227-Econ-WP-2010-04.pdf.

Black, Eric. 2016. "Driving While Black: GOP Sen. Tim Scott Tells of His Experiences." Minnpost, July 14, 2016. https://www.minnpost.com/eric-black-ink/2016/07/driving-while-black-gop-sen-tim-scott-tells-his-experiences/.

Black, William R. 2014. "How Watermelon Became a Racist Trope." *The Atlantic*, December 8, 2014. https://www.theatlantic.com/national/archive/2014/12/how-watermelons-became-a-racist-trope/383529/.

Blackmon, Douglas A. 2004. *Slavery by Another Name: The Re-Enslavement of Black Americans from the Civil War to World War II*. New York: Anchor Books.

Blake, Aaron. 2017. "Kellyanne Conway Says Trump's Team Has 'Alternative Facts.' Which Pretty Much Says It All." *Washington Post*, January 22, 2017. https://www.washingtonpost.com/news/the-fix/wp/2017/01/22/kellyanne-conway-says-donald-trumps-team-has-alternate-facts-which-pretty-much-says-it-all/?noredirect=on&utm_term=.8c3db8d636de.

Blake, John. 2017. "The Fall of the Sagging Pants Era Is Upon Us." CNN, October 20, 2017. https://www.cnn.com/2017/10/20/us/sagging-pants-era-over/index.html.

Blake, Paul. 2016. "Obama Defends Capitalism and International Free Trade in 'Economist' Essay." ABC News, October 6, 2016. https://abcnews.go.com/Business/obama-defends-capitalism-international-free-trade-economist-essay/story?id=42614080.
Block, Jack and Jeanne H. Block. 2006. "Nursery School Personality and Political Orientation Two Decades Later." *Journal of Research in Personality* 40: 734–49.
Bode, Carl, ed. 1959. Front matter in Horatio Alger, Jr., *Ragged Dick and Struggling Upward*. New York: Penguin Books USA.
Boehlert, Eric. 2009. *Bloggers on the Bus: How the Internet Changed Politics and the Press*. New York: Free Press.
Bolce, Louis, Gerald DeMaio, and Douglas Muzzio. 1992. "Blacks and the Republican Party: The 20 Percent Solution." *Political Science Quarterly* 107, no. 1: 63–79.
Bonilla-Silva, Eduardo. 2003. *Racism without Racists: Color-Blind Racism and the Persistence of Racial Inequality in America*. Lanham, MD: Rowman & Littlefield.
Borelli, Deneen. 2012. *Blacklash: How Obama and the Left Are Driving African Americans to the Government Plantation*. New York: Threshhold Editions.
Borjas, George, Jeffrey Grogger, and Gordon H. Hanson. 2010. "Immigration and the Economic Status of African-American Men." *Economica* 77, no. 306: 255–82.
Boyack, Connor. 2010. "The Chameleon-Like Qualities of Romney's Conservatism." Connor's Conundrums, March 20, 2010. http://www.connorboyack.com/blog/the-chameleon-like-qualities-of-mitt-romneys-conservatism.
Bracey, Christopher A. 2008. *Saviors or Sellouts: The Promise and Peril of Black Conservativism, from Booker T. Washington to Condoleeza Rice*. Boston: Beacon Press.
Brady, Kevin. 2011. "Spend Less, Owe Less, Grow the Economy." Joint Economic Committee Republicans. Republican Staff Commentary. https://www.jec.senate.gov/public/_cache/files/c4eb04a7-48b5-4e4c-b9d8-1622432f0b4b/commentary---spend-less-owe-less-grow-the-economy.pdf.
Bremner, Robert H. 1956. *From the Depths: The Discovery of Poverty in the United States*. New York: New York University Press.
Broman, Clifford L., Harold W. Neighbors, and James S. Jackson. 1988. "Racial Group Identification among Black Adults." *Social Forces* 67, no. 1: 146–58.
Bronson, Jennifer. 2018. Data Collection: Justice Expenditure and Employment Extracts Series, Table 2, Percent distribution of employment and payrolls for the justice system by level of government. https://www.bjs.gov/index.cfm?ty=dcdetail&iid=286.
Brown, Michael K., Martin Carnoy, Elliott Currie, Troy Duster, David B. Oppenheimer, Marjorie M. Shultz, and David Wellman. 2003. *Whitewashing Race: The Myth of a Color-Blind Society*. Berkeley, Los Angeles, and London: University of California Press.
Bump, Philip. 2015. "When Did Black Americans Start Voting So Heavily Democratic?" *Washington Post*, July 7, 2015. https://www.washingtonpost.com/news/the-fix/wp/2015/07/07/when-did-black-americans-start-voting-so-heavily-democratic/?utm_term=.9c854c45d0c5.
Burger, Thomas. 1987. *Weber's Theory of Concept Formation: History, Laws, and Ideal Types*. Durham, NC: Duke University Press.
Burghart, Devin and Leonard Zeskind. 2010. "Tea Party Nationalism: A Critical Assessment of the Tea Party Movement and the Size, Scope, and Focus of its National Factions." Kansas City, MO: Institute for Research and Education on Human Rights.
Burke, Lindsay. 2012. "Obama's Budget Ends Funding for DC Opportunity Scholarship Program." The Daily Signal, February 13, 2012. https://www.dailysignal.com/2012/02/13/presidents-budget-eliminates-funding-for-d-c-opportunity-scholarship-program/.
Butterworth, Trevor. 2010. "The Tea Party and the Return of Media Bias." *Forbes*, September 30. https://www.forbes.com/sites/trevorbutterworth/2010/09/30/the-tea-party-and-the-return-of-media-bias/#67ae6b4e27db.
Cain, Molly. 2016. "Conservatives Say Raising the Minimum Wage Kills Jobs. New Research Says They Are Wrong." Common Dreams, October 28, 2016. https://www.commondreams.org/views/2016/10/28/conservatives-say-raising-minimum-wage-kills-jobs-new-research-says-theyre-wrong.

References

Callinicos, Alex. 1999. *Social Theory: A Historical Introduction.* New York, NY: New York University Press.
Campbell, Angus, Philip E. Converse, Warren E. Miller, and Donald E. Stokes. 1960. *The American Voter.* Hoboken, NJ: John Wiley & Sons.
Campbell, B. J. 2018, August 26. "The Two Confusing Definitions of Racism." medium.com. https://medium.com/handwaving-freakoutery/the-two-confusing-definitions-of-racism-2d685d3af845.
Campo-Flores, Arien. 2010. "Are Tea Partiers Racist?" *Newsweek,* April 25, 2010. http://www.newsweek.com/are-tea-partiers-racist-70695.
Capehart, Jonathan. 2012. "Republicans Had It in for Obama before Day 1." *Washington Post,* August 10, 2012. https://www.washingtonpost.com/blogs/post-partisan/post/republicans-had-it-in-for-obama-before-day-1/2012/08/10/0c96c7c8-e31f-11e1-ae7f-d2a13e249eb2_blog.html?utm_term=.6d23cd207031.
———. 2016. "Ben Carson and Cornel West Actually Agree: Obama's Not 'Black Enough.'" *Washington Post,* February 23, 2016. https://www.washingtonpost.com/blogs/post-partisan/wp/2016/02/23/ben-carson-and-cornel-west-actually-agree-obamas-not-black-enough/?noredirect=on&utm_term=.8e24441003f3.
Cardoso, Silvia Helena and Renato M. W. Sabbatini. 2001. "Learning Who Is Your Mother: The Science of Imprinting." November 4, 2001. http://www.cerebromente.org.br/n14/experimento/lorenz/index-lorenz.html
Carey, Benedict. 2007. "Denial Makes the World Go Round." *New York Times,* November 20, 2007. https://www.nytimes.com/2007/11/20/health/research/20deni.html.
Cary, Lee. 2009. "The Obama Resistance Grows." American Thinker, August 5, 2009. https://www.americanthinker.com/articles/2009/08/the_obama_resistance_grows.html.
Cassata, Donna and Michael D. Regan. 2016. "GOP Breaks May Stem From Party Resistance to All Things Obama." PBS News Hour, March 5, 2016. https://www.pbs.org/newshour/politics/gop-breaks-may-stem-from-party-resistance-to-all-things-obama.
Catanese, David. 2015. "Bush: 'Common Core' Is 'Poisonous.'" *U.S. News and World Report,* August 14, 2015. https://www.usnews.com/news/blogs/run-2016/2015/08/14/jeb-bush-common-core-is-poisonous.
Cawthorne, Cameron. 2016. "CNN Anchor Claims She Say Tea Party Members Spit on Members of Congress." *The Washington Free Beacon,* November 14, 2016. https://freebeacon.com/politics/cnn-anchor-claims-saw-tea-party-spit-members-congress/.
CBS News. 2012. "Tea Party Supporters: Who They Are and What They Believe." CBS News, December 14, 2012. http://www.cbsnews.com/news/tea-party-supporters-who-they-are-and-what-they-believe/.
Center for Responsive Politics. 2019. "Teachers Unions: Long-Term Contribution Terms." OpenSecrets.org. https://www.opensecrets.org/industries/totals.php?cycle=2018&ind=L1300.
Charity, Justin, Angel Diaz, and David Drake. 2014. "A History of Rap Songs Protesting Police Brutality." COMPLEX, August 18, 2014. https://www.complex.com/music/2014/08/rap-songs-police-brutality/.
Chater, Nick. 1997. "Simplicity and the Mind." *The Psychologist* (November): 495–98.
Chemerinsky, Erwin. 2002–2003. "Separate and Unequal: American Public Education Today." *American University Law Review* 52: 1461–76.
Chesler, Ellen. 2011. "Was Planned Parenthood's Founder Racist?" Salon. https://www.salon.com/2011/11/02/was_planned_parenthoods_founder_racist/.
Christensen, Jen. 2014. "The FBI's Secret Memos Show an Agency Obsessed with 'Neutraliz(ing)' MLK." CNN, November 14, 2014. https://www.cnn.com/2014/11/14/us/fbi-and-mlk/index.html.
Clark, Kenneth B. and Mamie P. Clark. 1939. "Racial Identification and Preference in Negro Children." *Journal of Social Psychology* 10, no. 4: 591–99.
Clement, Scott and John C. Green. 2011. "The Tea Party and Religion." Pew Research Center for Religion and Public Life, February 23, 2011. https://www.pewforum.org/2011/02/23/tea-party-and-religion/.

References

Coates, Ta-Nehesi. 2010. "A Final Thought." *The Atlantic,* July 16, 2010. https://www.theatlantic.com/national/archive/2010/07/a-final-thought/59924/.

Connick, Wendy. 2018. "A Step-By-Step Guide to the Earned Income Credit." The Motley Fool. https://www.fool.com/taxes/2018/01/06/a-step-by-step-guide-to-the-earned-income-credit.aspx.

Constas, Helen. 1958. "Max Weber's Two Conceptions of Bureaucracy." *Journal of Sociology* 63, no. 4: 400–409.

Cooper, Kenneth J. 1994. "Gingrich: 'Cooperation, Yes. Compromise, No.'" *Washington Post,* November 12, 1994. https://mail.google.com/mail/u/0/#search/quote/FMfcgxwBTshdvCJwmgkbhgTcRfgLqZDx?projector=1&messagePartId=0.1.

Cooper, Michael. 2012. "Conservatives Sowed Idea of Health Care Mandate, Only to Spurn It Later." *New York Times,* February 14, 2012. https://www.nytimes.com/2012/02/15/health/policy/health-care-mandate-was-first-backed-by-conservatives.html.

Cosby, Bill. 2004. "Address at the NAACP 50th Anniversary of Brown v. Board of Education." American Rhetoric Online Speech Bank. https://www.americanrhetoric.com/speeches/billcosbypoundcakespeech.htm.

Cottom, Tressie McMillan. 2016. "The Problem with Obama's Faith in White America." *The Atlantic,* December 13, 2016. https://www.theatlantic.com/politics/archive/2016/12/obamas-faith-in-white-america/510503/.

Cressey, Eric. 2010. "Why President Obama Throws like a Girl." EricCressey, April 7, 2010. https://ericcressey.com/why-president-obama-throws-like-a-girl.

Cross, William E., Jr. 1991. *Shades of Black: Diversity in African-American Identity.* Philadelphia: Temple University Press.

Daniel, Daphney. 2012. "How Blacks Became Blue: The 1936 African American Voting Shift from the Party of Lincoln to the New Deal Coalition." PhD diss. Salve Regina University.

Davidson, Joe. 2017. "How Big Is the Federal Workforce? Much Bigger than You Think." *Washington Post,* October 3, 2017. https://www.washingtonpost.com/news/powerpost/wp/2017/10/03/how-big-is-the-federal-workforce-much-bigger-than-you-think/?noredirect=on&utm_term=.fc43a25f2623.

Dawson, Michael C. 2001. *Black Visions: The Roots of Contemporary African-American Political Strategies.* Chicago: University of Chicago Press.

deLong, Matt and Dave Braunger. 2017. "Breaking Down the Dashcam: The Philando Castile Shooting Timeline." *StarTribune,* June 21, 2017. http://www.startribune.com/castile-shooting-timeline/429678313/.

Demo, David H. and Michael Hughes. 1990. "Socialization and Racial Identity among Black Americans." *Social Psychology Quarterly* 53, no. 4: 364–74.

Dobrin, Arthur. 2014. "The Gracious Person Is Kind and Tactful." *Psychology Today,* February 11, 2014. https://www.psychologytoday.com/us/blog/am-i-right/201402/what-it-means-be-gracious.

Douglas, William. 2010. "Tea Party Protesters Scream 'Nigger' at Black Congressman." McClatchy newspapers, March 20, 2010. https://www.mcclatchydc.com/news/politics-government/article24577294.html.

Douglass, Frederick. 1848. "An Address to the Colored Peoples of the United States." September 29, 1848. http://teachingamericanhistory.org/library/document/an-address-to-the-colored-people-of-the-united-states/.

Dovidio, John F. and Samuel L. Gaertner. 2000. "Aversive Racism and Selection Decisions: 1898 and 1999." *Psychological Science* 11, no. 4: 315–19.

Draper, Robert. 2012. *Do Not Ask What Good We Do: Inside the U.S. House of Representatives.* New York: Free Press.

D'Souza, Dinesh. 2012. *Obama's America: Unmaking the American Dream.* New York: Threshold Editions.

Du Bois, W. E. B. 1897. "Strivings of the Negro People." *The Atlantic Monthly,* August 1897. https://www.theatlantic.com/magazine/archive/1897/08/strivings-of-the-negro-people/305446/.

———. (1903) 1994. *The Souls of Black Folk.* Mineola, NY: Dover Publications.

———. (1920) 1999. *Darkwater: Voices from within the Veil.* Mineola, NY: Dover Publications.

Du Ross, Michelle. 2011. "Somewhere in Between: Alexander Hamilton and Slavery." *The Early American Review* XV, no. 1 (Winter/Spring). https://www.varsitytutors.com/earlyamerica/early-america-review/volume-15/hamilton-and-slavery.

Dynarski, Mark, Ning Rui, Ann Webber, Babette Gutmann, and Meredith Bachman. 2018. "Evaluation of the DC Opportunity Scholarship Program: Impacts Two Years after Students Applied." Jessup, MD: National Center for Education Evaluation and Regional Assistance, Institute of Education Sciences, U.S. Department of Education.

Dyson, Michael Eric. 2015. "What Happened to Cornel West?" *The New Republic,* April 19, 2015. https://newrepublic.com/article/121550/cornel-wests-rise-fall-our-most-exciting-black-scholar-ghost.

Economic Policy Institute. 2012. "Characteristics Associated With Leaving the Bottom Income Fifth." The State of Working America, May 16, 2012. http://stateofworkingamerica.org/chart/swa-mobility-figure-3e-characteristics-leaving/.

Editor. 2009. "Studliest President in History Throws like a Girl." I Hate the Media!, July 1, 2009. https://www.ihatethemedia.com/obama-throws-like-a-little-girl.

The Editors of Life. 2008. *The American Journey of Barack Obama.* New York, Boston, and London: Little, Brown and Co.

Edwards, David. 2008. "Anti-Obama Sign Stirs Controversy in Florida." Raw Story, September 30, 2008. https://www.rawstory.com/2008/09/anti-obama-sign-stirs-controversy-in-florida/.

Ehrenfreund, Max. 2012. "What President Obama Really Thinks about the Police." *Washington Post,* July 18, 2012. https://www.washingtonpost.com/news/wonk/wp/2016/07/18/what-president-obama-really-thinks-about-the-police/?utm_term=.f722dfeac59a.

Ehrenreich, Barbara. 2012. "Michael Harrington and the 'Culture of Poverty.'" *The Nation,* April 2, 2012. https://www.thenation.com/article/michael-harrington-and-culture-poverty/.

Eisenstadt, Peter. 1999. *Black Conservatism: Essays in Intellectual and Political History.* New York and London: Garland Publishing.

Eligon, John. 2018. "Talking to a Man Named Mr. Cotton about Slavery and Confederate Monuments." *New York Times,* August 11, 2018. https://www.nytimes.com/2018/08/11/us/confederate-monuments-charlottesville-slavery.html.

Ennett, Susan T., Christine Jackson, J. Michael Bowling, and Denise M. Dickinson. 2013. "Parental Socialization and Children's Susceptibility to Alcohol Use Initiation." *Journal of Studies on Alcohol and Drugs* 74, no. 5: 694–702.

Entman, Robert M. and Andrew Rojecki. 2000. *The Black Image in the White Mind.* Chicago: University of Chicago Press.

Etheridge, Eric. 2009. "Rick Santelli: Tea Party Time." *New York Times,* February 20, 2009. https://opinionator.blogs.nytimes.com/2009/02/20/rick-santelli-tea-party-time/.

Everest-Phillips, Max. 2015. "Is the Private Sector More Efficient? A Cautionary Tale." Singapore: Global Centre for Public Service Excellence, United Nations Development Programme. http://www.undp.org/content/dam/undp/library/capacity-development/English/Singapore%20Centre/GCPSE_Efficiency.pdf.

Farhi, Paul. 2008. "Tavis Smiley Will Cut Ties with Joyner Radio Show." *Washington Post,* April 12, 2008. http://www.washingtonpost.com/wp-dyn/content/article/2008/04/11/AR2008041103056.html?hpid=topnews.

Fauntroy, Michael. 2011. "Republicans and the Black Vote." Huffpost, May 25, 2011. https://www.huffingtonpost.com/michael-fauntroy-phd/republicans-and-the-black_b_37731.html.

Feagin, Joe R. 2000. *Racist America.* New York and Abingdon, UK: Routledge.

———. 2006. *Systemic Racism: A Theory of Oppression.* New York and London: Routledge.

———. 2013. *The White Racial Frame: Centuries of Racial Framing and Counter-Framing.* New York: Routledge.

Festinger, Leon. 1957. *A Theory of Cognitive Dissonance.* Stanford, CA: Stanford University Press.

Fields, Corey D. 2013. "The Paradoxes of Black Republicans." In *The Social Side of Politics,* edited by Douglas Hartman and Christopher Uggen, 145–60. New York: W.W. Norton.

Finkleman, Paul. 2000. "Garrison's Constitution: The Covenant with Death and How It Was Made." National Archives. *Prologue Magazine* 32, no. 4. https://www.archives.gov/publications/prologue/2000/winter/garrisons-constitution-1.html.

Fishel, Leslie H. 1964–1965. "The Negro in the New Deal." *The Wisconsin Magazine of History* 48, no. 2: 111–26.

Fortin, Jacey. 2017. "N.A.A.C.P., Seeking a New Voice, Names Derrick Johnson as President." *New York Times*. October 21, 2017. https://www.nytimes.com/2017/10/21/us/derrick-johnson-naacp-president.html.

Fossett, Mark A. and K. Jill Kiecolt. 1989. "The Relative Size of Minority Populations and White Racial Attitudes." *Social Science Quarterly* 70, no. 4: 820–35.

Fraley, R. Chris, Brian N. Griffin, Jay Belsky, and Glenn I. Roisman. 2012. "Developmental Antecedents of Political Ideology: A Longitudinal Investigation from Birth to Age 18 Years." *Psychological Science* 23, no. 11: 1425–31.

Frazier, E. Franklin. 1957. *Black Bourgeoisie*. New York: The Free Press.

Fredrickson, George M. 2002. *Racism: A Short History*. Princeton, NJ, and Oxford, UK: Princeton University Press.

Freeden, Michael. 1979. "Eugenics and Progressive Thought: A Study in Ideological Affinity." *The Historical Journal* 22, no. 3: 645–71.

Friedersdorf, Conor. 2012. "What Americans When They Say They're Conservative." *The Atlantic*, January 27, 2012. https://www.theatlantic.com/politics/archive/2012/01/what-americans-mean-when-they-say-theyre-conservative/252099/.

Fuller, Nicole, Ted Philips, Maria Alvarex, Anthony M. Destefano, and Will James. *Newsday*, December 13, 2014. https://www.newsday.com/news/new-york/millions-march-nyc-protesting-grand-jury-decision-in-eric-garner-death-begins-in-manhattan-1.9711149.

Gallup, Inc. 2008. "Election Polls—Vote by Groups, 2008." http://news.gallup.com/poll/112132/election-polls-vote-groups-2008.aspx.

Gates, Bill. 2017. "Our Education Efforts Are Evolving." gatesnotes, October 17, 2017. https://www.gatesnotes.com/Education/Council-of-Great-City-Schools.

Geary, Daniel. 2015. "The Moynihan Report Is Turning 50. Its Ideas on Black Poverty Were Wrong Then and Are Wrong Now." *In These Times*, June 30, 2015. http://inthesetimes.com/article/18132/moynihan-report-black-poverty.

Gibbs, Robert. 2009. "Press Briefing 3/3/09." Office of the Press Secretary, the White House. https://obamawhitehouse.archives.gov/the-press-office/press-briefing-3309.

Gilens, Martin. 2003. "How the Poor Became Black: The Racialization of American Poverty in the Mass Media." In *Race and the Politics of Welfare Reform*, edited by Sanford F. Schram, Joe Soss, and Richard C. Fording, 101–30. Ann Arbor, MI: University of Michigan Press.

Glastris, Paul. 2012. "The Incomplete Greatness of Barack Obama." *Washington Monthly*, March/April 2012. https://washingtonmonthly.com/magazine/marchapril-2012/the-incomplete-greatness-of-barack-obama-2/.

Glied, Sherry and Stephanie Ma. 2015. "How Will the Affordable Care Act Affect the Use of Health Care Services?" Issue Brief, February 2015. The Commonwealth Fund. https://www.commonwealthfund.org/sites/default/files/documents/___media_files_publications_issue_brief_2015_feb_1804_glied_how_will_aca_affect_use_hlt_care_svcs_ib_v2.pdf.

Gnau, Thomas. 2014. "Officers Describe Moments Before Crawford Shooting." *Dayton Daily News*, October 14, 2014. https://www.daytondailynews.com/news/local/officer-fired-two-shots-center-mass-john-crawford-iii/gGiZUov76z5xScodwI57nI/.

Godrej, Dinyar. 2015, December 1. "Myth 5: The Private Sector is More Efficient than the Public Sector." *The Internationalist*, December 1, 2015. 488. https://newint.org/features/2015/12/01/private-public-sector#footnote-2.

Goertzel, Ted. 1994. "Belief in Conspiracy Theories." *Political Psychology* 15: 731–42.

Goldberg, Jeffrey. 2016. "The Obama Doctrine." *The Atlantic*, April 2016. https://www.theatlantic.com/magazine/archive/2016/04/the-obama-doctrine/471525/.

Goodwin, Kerri A. and C. James Goodwin. 2017. *Research in Psychology: Methods and Design*. Hoboken, NJ: John Wiley & Sons.

Gordy, Cynthia. 2011. "Welfare, Fathers and Those Persistent Myths." The Root, June 17, 2011. https://www.theroot.com/welfare-fathers-and-those-persistent-myths-1790864434.

Gore, D'Angelo. 2017. "Physician Numbers up under Obamacare." FactCheck.org, March 22, 2017. https://www.factcheck.org/2017/03/physician-numbers-up-under-obamacare/.

Granderson, L. Z. 2013. "What's Motivating Some of Obama's Black Critics?" CNN, July 26, 2013. https://www.cnn.com/2013/07/23/opinion/granderson-tavis-smiley/index.html.

Gray, Steven. 2008. "What Obama's Election Really Means to Black America." *Time,* November 6, 2008. http://content.time.com/time/nation/article/0,8599,1857222,00.html.

Greenberg, Jon. 2018. "Donald Trump Says Iran Got $150 Billion and $1.8 Billion in Cash. That's Half True." *Washington Post,* April 27, 2018. https://www.politifact.com/truth-o-meter/statements/2018/apr/27/donald-trump/donald-trump-iran-150-billion-and-18-billion-c/.

Greenwald, Anthony G., Debbie E. McGhee, and Jordan L. K. Schwartz. 1998. "Measuring Individual Differences in Implicit Cognition: The Implicit Association Test." *Journal of Personality and Social Psychology,* 74, no. 6: 1461–80.

Gregory, Paul Roderick. 2012. "Why the Fuss? Obama Has Long Been in Favor of Redistribution." *Forbes,* September 23, 2012. https://www.forbes.com/sites/paulroderickgregory/2012/09/23/why-the-fuss-obama-has-long-been-on-record-in-favor-of-redistribution/#371568e4593a.

Grunwald, Michael. 2012. *The New New Deal: The Hidden Story of Change in the Obama Era.* New York: Simon & Schuster.

Guglielmo, Thomas A. and Earl Lewis. 2003. "Changing Racial Meanings: Race and Ethnicity in the United States, 1929–1964." In *Race and Ethnicity in the United States,* edited by Ronald Bayor, 167–92. New York: Columbia University Press.

Guthmann, Edward. 2006. "Shelby Steele Has a Lot to Say about Black Society. He Calls It Common Sense. Some Call Him Uncle Tom." SFGate, May 15, 2006. https://www.sfgate.com/entertainment/article/Shelby-Steele-has-a-lot-to-say-about-black-2535245.php.

Haidt, Jonathan. 2013. *The Righteous Mind: Why Good People Are Divided by Politics and Religion.* New York: Vintage Books.

Hall, Ronald E. 2008. "Rooming in the Master's House: Psychological Domination and the Black Conservative." *Journal of Black Studies* 38, no. 4: 565–78.

Hamilton, Brady E., Joyce A. Martin, Michelle J. K. Osterman, Sally C. Curtin, and T. J. Mathews. 2015. "Births: Final Data for 2014." *National Vital Statistics Reports* (December 23, 2015) 64, no. 12. https://www.cdc.gov/nchs/data/nvsr/nvsr64/nvsr64_12.pdf.

Hammon, Jupiter. 1787. An Address to the Negroes of the State of New-York. Maiden-Lane, NY: Carroll and Patterson. http://etext.lib.virginia.edu/readex/20400.html.

Hammon, Jupiter, Stanley A. Ransom, and Oscar Wegelin. 1970. *America's First Negro Poet: The Complete Works of Jupiter Hammon of Long Island.* Port Washington, NY: Kennikat Press.

Handa, Sudhanshu, Silvio Daidone, Amber Peterman, Benjamin Davis, Audrey Pereira, Tia Palermo, and Jennifer Yablonski. 2018. "Myth Busting? Confronting Six Common Perceptions about Unconditional Cash Transfers as a Poverty Reduction Strategy in Africa." *The World Bank Research Observer* 33: 259–98.

Hanisch, Carol. 1969. "The Personal Is Political." February 1969. http://www.carolhanisch.org/CHwritings/PIP.html.

Harrell, James A. 1968. "Negro Leadership in the Election Year 1936." *The Journal of Southern History* 34, no. 4: 546–64.

Harris, Hamil R. 2010. "From Tavis Smiley, Love and Criticism for Obama." *Washington Post,* March 24, 2010. http://voices.washingtonpost.com/44/2010/03/from-tavis-smiley-love-and-cri.html.

Harris-Britt, April, Cecelia R. Valrie, Beth Kurtz-Costes, and Stephanie J. Rowley. 2007. "Perceived Racial Discrimination and Self-Esteem in African American Youth: Racial Socialization as a Protective Factor." *Journal of Research on Adolescence* 17, no. 3: 669–82.

Harris-Lacewell, Melissa. 2004. *Barbershops, Bibles, and BET: Everyday Talk and Black Political Thought.* Princeton: Princeton University Press.

Hasher, Lynn, David Goldstein, and Thomas Toppino. 1977. "Frequency and the Conference of Referential Validity." *Journal of Verbal Learning and Verbal Behavior* 16: 107–12.

Haskins, Ron. 2006. "Welfare Reform, Success or Failure? It Worked." Brookings, March 15, 2006. https://www.brookings.edu/articles/welfare-reform-success-or-failure-it-worked/.
Hekman, Susan J. 1983. *Weber, the Ideal Type, and Contemporary Social Theory.* Notre Dame, IN: University of Notre Dame Press.
Henig, Jess. 2008. "Born in the U.S.A." FactCheck.org, August 21, 2008. https://www.factcheck.org/2008/08/born-in-the-usa/.
Hess, Frederick M. 2015. "The Real Obama Education Legacy." AEI (American Enterprise Institute). http://www.aei.org/publication/the-real-obama-education-legacy/.
Higginbotham, A. Leon, Jr. 1978. *In the Matter of Color: Race and the American Legal Process: The Colonial Period.* Oxford, New York, Toronto, and Melbourne: Oxford University Press.
Higginbotham, A. Leon, Jr., and Anne F. Jacobs. 1992. "The 'Law Only as an Enemy': The Legitimization of Racial Powerlessness through the Colonial and Antebellum Criminal Laws of Virginia." *North Carolina Law Review* (April): 969–1070.
Hill, Robert A. 1985. *Marcus Garvey: Life and Lessons.* Berkeley and Los Angeles: University of California Press.
Hoberman, John. 2012. *Black and Blue: The Origins and Consequences of Medical Racism.* Berkeley and Los Angeles: University of California Press.
Hoffman, Martin L. 1975. "Moral Internalization, Parental Power, and the Nature of Parent-Child Interaction." *Developmental Psychology* 11, no. 2: 228–39.
Holan, Angie Drobnic. 2010. "Why Do So Many People Think Obama Is a Muslim?" Politifact, August 26, 2010. https://www.politifact.com/truth-o-meter/article/2010/aug/26/why-do-so-many-people-think-obama-muslim/.
Hopkins, Daniel J. and Katherine T. McCabe. 2012. "After It's Too Late: Estimating the Policy Impacts of Black Mayoralties in U.S. Cities." *American Politics Research* 40, no. 4: 665–700.
Hornsey, Matthew J. and Jolanda Jetten. 2005. "Loyalty without Conformity: Tailoring Self-Perception as a Means of Balancing Belonging and Differentiation." *Self and Identity* 4: 81–95.
Horton, James O. 2018. "Race and the American Constitution: A Struggle toward National Ideals." http://new.gilderlehrman.org/history-by-era/creating-new-government/essays/race-and-american-constitution-struggle-toward-national-ideals=.
Huffmon, Scott H., H. Gibbs Knotts, and Seth C. McKee. 2016. "Similarities and Differences in Support of Minority and White Republican Candidates." *Journal of Race, Ethnicity, and Politics* 1: 91–116.
Hughes, Christopher. 2011. "The Waiting Times Myth." Doctors For America, March 3, 2011. http://www.drsforamerica.org/blog/the-waiting-times-myth.
Hussak, Laria J. and Andrei Cimpian. 2018. "Investigating the Origins of Political Views: Biases in Explanation Predict Conservative Attitudes in Children and Adults." *Developmental Science* 21, no. 2. DOI: 10.1111/desc.12567.
Isenstadt, Alex. 2009. "'Freedom Fighters' Take a Stand in D.C." Politico, September 12, 2009. https://www.politico.com/story/2009/09/freedom-fighters-take-a-stand-in-dc-027070.
Izadi, Elahe and Peter Holley. 2014. "Video Shows Cleveland Officer Shooting 12-Year-Old Tamir Rice within Seconds." *Washington Post,* November 26, 2014. https://www.washingtonpost.com/news/post-nation/wp/2014/11/26/officials-release-video-names-in-fatal-police-shooting-of-12-year-old-cleveland-boy/?utm_term=.64110cbfcdb4.
Jackson, Brooks. 2008. "Blacks and the Democratic Party." Factcheck, April 18, 2008. https://www.factcheck.org/2008/04/blacks-and-the-democratic-party/.
———. 2009. "Truth on the Cutting Room Floor." FactCheck.org, December 4, 2009. https://www.factcheck.org/2009/12/truth-on-the-cutting-room-floor/.
———. 2012. "Obama's 'Sealed' Records." FactCheck.org, July 31, 2012. https://www.factcheck.org/2012/07/obamas-sealed-records/.
Jackson, Kevin. 2009. *The Big Black Lie: How I Learned the Truth about the Democrat Party.* St. Louis, MO: The Black Sphere.
Jacobs, Nicholas F. 2018. "Is Obama Breaking Norms as a Former President? Not Really." *Washington Post,* September 25, 2018. https://www.washingtonpost.com/news/monkey-

cage/wp/2018/09/25/obamas-returned-to-public-life-like-past-presidents-throughout-u-s-history/?noredirect=on&utm_term=.abf0c490b4cb.

Jacobs, Sally H. 2011. *The Other Barack: The Bold and Reckless Life of President Obama's Father*. New York: PublicAffairs.

Jacobson, Brian. 2009. "Chicago Tea Party." Video, February 27, 2009. https://www.youtube.com/watch?v=5Hl3WxXGys4.

James, Frank. 2013. "Boehner Blasts Tea Party Groups over Budget Deal Criticism." National Public Radio, December 12, 2013. https://www.npr.org/sections/itsallpolitics/2013/12/12/250555582/boehner-blisters-tea-party-groups-over-budget-deal-criticism.

Japson, Bruce. 2017. "Doctor Wait Times Soar 30% in Major U.S. Cities." *Forbes*, March 19, 2017. https://www.forbes.com/sites/brucejapsen/2017/03/19/doctor-wait-times-soar-amid-trumpcare-debate/#4fbaa8b22e74.

Johnson, Theodore R. 2016. "Why Are African Americans Such Loyal Democrats When They Are So Ideologically Diverse?" *Washington Post*, September 28, 2016. https://www.washingtonpost.com/news/monkey-cage/wp/2016/09/28/can-trump-win-black-votes-what-we-know-from-5-decades-of-black-voting-data/?utm_term=.099d37647ccd.

Jonsson, Patrik. 2010. "Amid Harsh Criticism, 'Tea Party' Slips into the Mainstream." *Christian Science Monitor*, April 3, 2010. https://www.csmonitor.com/USA/Politics/2010/0403/Amid-harsh-criticisms-tea-party-slips-into-the-mainstream.

Jordan, Barbara. 1994. "The Universalization of the Philosophy or Ethic of Responsibility." Texas Senate Papers. https://texashistory.unt.edu/ark:/67531/metapth611442/.

Jost, John T., Arie W. Kruglanski, Jack Glaser, and Frank J. Sulloway. 2003. "Political Conservatism as Motivated Social Cognition." *Psychological Bulletin* 129, no. 3: 339–75.

Juzwiak, Rich and Aleksander Chan. 2014. "Unarmed People of Color Killed by Police, 1999–2014." Gawker, December 8, 2014. https://gawker.com/unarmed-people-of-color-killed-by-police-1999-2014-1666672349.

Kamisar, Ben. 2017. "Obama: Someone Opposed to Immigration System Isn't Automatically a Racist." *The Hill*, April 24, 2017. https://thehill.com/homenews/news/330239-obama-someone-opposed-to-immigration-system-isnt-automatically-a-racist.

Kane, Paul. 2010. "'Tea Party' Protesters Accused of Spitting on Lawmaker, Using Slurs." *Washington Post*, March 20, 2010. http://www.washingtonpost.com/wp-dyn/content/article/2010/03/20/AR2010032002556.html.

Katznelson, Ira. 2005. *When Affirmative Action Was White: An Untold History of Racial Inequality in Twentieth-Century America*. New York and London: W.W. Norton & Co.

Kay, Jonathan. 2010. "Tea Party Movement Is Full of Conspiracy Theories." *Newsweek*, February 8, 2010. https://www.newsweek.com/tea-party-movement-full-conspiracy-theories-75153.

Kekes, John. 1997. "What is Conservatism?" *Philosophy* 72, no. 281 (July): 351–74.

Keller, Edmund J. 1978. "The Impact of Black Mayors on Urban Policy." *The Annals of the American Academy of Political and Social Science* 439: 40–52.

Kengor, Paul G. 2017. "Forgotten Conservative: Remembering George Schuyler." The Center for Vision and Values. https://www.visionandvalues.org/2017/09/forgotten-conservative-remembering-george-schuyler/.

Khazan, Olga. 2018. "In One Year, 57,375 Years Lost to Police Violence." *The Atlantic*, May 8, 2018. https://www.theatlantic.com/health/archive/2018/05/the-57375-years-of-life-lost-to-police-violence/559835/.

Khederian, Robert. 2018. "Before Private Jets, There Were Private Train Cars." Curbed, February 1, 2018. https://www.curbed.com/2018/2/1/16943216/pullman-private-railroad-car-history.

Kidd, Quentin, Herman Diggs, Mehreen Farooq, and Megam Murray. 2007. "Black Voters, Black Candidates, and Social Issues: Does Party Identification Matter?" *Social Science Quarterly* 88, no. 1: 165–76.

Killough, Ashley. 2015. "Jeb Bush Fights Lonely Battle Defending Common Core." CNN Politics, May 31, 2015. https://www.cnn.com/2015/05/30/politics/bush-common-core/index.html.

Kinder, Donald R. and Nathan P. Kalmoe. 2017. *Neither Liberal nor Conservative: Ideological Innocence in the American Public.* Chicago: University of Chicago Press.
King, Martin Luther. 1986. "A Testament of Hope." In *A Testament of Hope: The Essential Writings and Teachings of Martin Luther King, Jr.,* edited by James Melvin Washington, 313–30. New York: HarperCollins.
Kirk, Russell. 1993. "Ten Conservative Principles." https://kirkcenter.org/conservatism/ten-conservative-principles/.
Klein, Ezra. 2011. "Republicans Reject Their Own Deficit-Reduction Report." *Washington Post,* June 30, 2011. https://www.washingtonpost.com/blogs/ezra-klein/post/republicans-reject-their-own-deficit-reduction-report/2011/05/19/AGTcR2rH_blog.html?utm_term=.ec45a5a57a32.
Klos, Joseph J. 1969. "Public Assistance, Family Allowances, or the Negative Income Tax?" *Nebraska Journal of Economics & Business* 8, no. 2: 16–32.
Knowles, Louis L. and Kenneth Prewitt, eds. 1969. *Institutional Racism in America.* Englewood Cliffs, NJ: Prentice-Hall.
Kornacki, Steve. 2009. "The New Teflon President." *Observer,* June 19, 2009. https://observer.com/2009/06/the-new-teflon-president-2/.
Kotlikoff, Laurence J. and Lawrence H. Summers. 1981. "The Role of Intergenerational Transfers in Aggregate Capital Accumulation." *Journal of Political Economy* 89, no. 4: 706–32.
Kramnick, Isaac, ed. 1999. *The Portable Edmund Burke.* New York: Penguin Putnam.
Kraus, Michael W. and Jacinth J. X. Tan. 2015. "Americans Overestimate Social Class Mobility." *Journal of Experimental Social Psychology* 58: 101–11.
LaFraniere, Sharon and Andrew W. Lehren. 2015. "The Disproportionate Risks of Driving While Black." *New York Times.* October 24, 2015. https://www.nytimes.com/2015/10/25/us/racial-disparity-traffic-stops-driving-black.html.
Lartey, Jamiles. 2016. "Obama Made Progress on Criminal Justice Reform. Will It Survive the Next President?" *The Guardian,* November 14, 2016. https://www.theguardian.com/us-news/2016/nov/14/barack-obama-criminal-justice-reform-prison-sentencing-police.
Lau, Richard R. and David P. Redlawsk. 2006. *How Voters Decide: Information Processing During Election Campaigns.* New York: Cambridge University Press.
Lauter, Paul. 1991. *Canons and Contexts.* New York: Oxford University Press.
Lazarsfeld, Paul F., Bernard Berelson, and Hazel Gaudet Lazarsfeld. 1944. *The People's Choice: How the Voter Makes Up His Mind in a Presidential Campaign.* New York: Duell, Sloan and Pearce.
Leondar-White, Betsy. n.d. "Black Job Loss Déjà Vu." *Dollars and Sense.* http://www.dollarsandsense.org/archives/2004/0504leondar.html.
Levendusky, Matthew. 2013. *How Partisan Media Polarize America.* Chicago: University of Chicago Press.
Lewis, Angela K. 2013. *Conservativism in the Black Community.* Routledge Series on Identity Politics. New York and London: Routledge.
Lewis, Oscar. 1959. *Five Families: Mexican Case Studies in the Culture of Poverty.* New York: Basic Books.
———. 1966. "The Culture of Poverty." *Scientific American* 215, no. 4: 19–25.
———. 1998. "The Culture of Poverty." *Society* 35, no. 2: 7–9.
———. 2009. "The Culture of Poverty." In *Urban Life: Readings in the Anthropology of the City,* edited by George Gmelch and Robert V. Kemper, 175–84. Long Grove, IL: Waveland Press.
Lichtman, Allan J. 2008. *White Protestant Nation: The Rise of the American Conservative Movement.* New York: Grove Press.
Liebow, Elliot. 1967. *Tally's Corner.* Boston: Little, Brown and Company.
Linder, Douglas O. 2019. "Lynchings: By Year and Race." https://www.famous-trials.com/sheriffshipp/1084-lynchingsyear.
Litwack, Leon F. 2000. "Hellhounds." In *Without Sanctuary: Lynching Photography in America,* edited by James Allen, Hilton Als, John Lewis, and Leon F. Litwack, 8–37. Santa Fe, NM: Twin Palms Publishers.

Loury, Glenn C. 1995. *One by One from the Inside Out: Essays and Reviews on Race and Responsibility in America.* New York and London: The Free Press.
Lowery, Wesley. 2014. "Paul Ryan, Poverty, Dog Whistles, and Electoral Politics." *Washington Post,* March 18, 2014. https://www.washingtonpost.com/news/the-fix/wp/2014/03/18/paul-ryan-poverty-dog-whistles-and-racism/?noredirect=on&utm_term=.64afce5b57cd.
Lupez, Linette and Robert Johnson. 2011. "The Truth about Crime and Sexual Assault at Occupy Wall Street." *Business Insider,* November 8, 2011. https://www.businessinsider.com/truth-about-crime-at-occupy-wall-street-2011-11.
Lusher, Adam. 2016. "'The White Man Is the Devil': What the Nation of Islam Taught Muhammad Ali." *Independent,* June 5, 2016. https://www.independent.co.uk/news/world/muhammad-ali-nation-of-islam-michael-parkinson-interview-who-were-elijah-muhammad-a7066301.html.
Maccoby, Eleanor E. 1992. "The Role of Parents in the Socialization of Children." *Developmental Psychology* 28, no. 6: 1006–17.
Majors, Richard and Janet Mancini Billson. 1992. *Cool Pose: The Dilemmas of Black Manhood in America.* New York: Lexington Books.
Malcolm X. 1965. "Message to the Grass Roots." In *Malcolm X Speaks,* edited by George Breitman, 3–17. New York: Grove Press.
Marcus, Lloyd. 2010. *Confessions of a Black Conservative: How the Left Has Shattered the Dreams of Martin Luther King and Black America.* Belle Glade, FL: Higher Standard Publishers.
Martin, Ben L. 1991. "From Negro to Black to African American: The Power of Names and Naming." *Political Science Quarterly* 106, no. 1: 83–107.
Martin, Lucy and Virginia Hite. 2014. "How Do You Affect Your Child?" Developmental Psychology at Vanderbilt. https://my.vanderbilt.edu/developmentalpsychologyblog/2014/04/how-do-you-affect-your-child/.
Martin, Michel. 2015. "Fear of Black Men: How Society Sees Black Men and How They See Themselves." Michel Martin Going There, March 31, 2015. https://www.npr.org/2015/03/31/396415737/societys-fear-of-black-men-and-its-consequences.
———. 2017. "Racism is Literally Bad for Your Health." You, Me, and Them: Experiencing Discrimination in America, October 28, 2017. https://www.npr.org/2017/10/28/560444290/racism-is-literally-bad-for-your-health.
Marx, David M., Sei Jin Ko, and Ray A. Friedman. 2009. "The 'Obama Effect': How a Salient Role Model Reduces Race-Based Performance Differences." *Journal of Experimental Social Psychology* 45, no. 4: 953–96.
Marx, Jerry D. 2011. "American Social Policy in the 1960's and 1970's." Social Welfare History Project. http://socialwelfare.library.vcu.edu/war-on-poverty/american-social-policy-in-the-60s-and-70s/.
Marzouki, Nadia. 2016. "Islamophobia and the Tea Party." livemint. https://www.livemint.com/Sundayapp/SBohvTng6N7LZVluMQ1LHI/Islamophobia-and-the-Tea-Party.html.
Matthews, Dylan. 2015. "America's Best Program for the Poor May Be Better than We Thought." *Vox,* July 16, 2015. https://www.vox.com/2015/7/16/8974745/eitc-study-hoynes-patel.
Maxwell, Angie. 2016. "How Southern Racism Found a Home in the Tea Party." *Vox,* July 7, 2016. https://www.vox.com/2016/7/7/12118872/southern-racism-tea-party-trump.
Mayer, Jane and Jill Abramson. 1994. *Strange Justice: The Selling of Clarence Thomas.* New York: Houghton Mifflin.
Mazzetti, Mark. 2015. "Killing of Americans Deepens Debate over Use of Drone Strikes." *New York Times,* April 13, 2015. https://www.nytimes.com/2015/04/24/world/asia/killing-of-americans-deepens-debate-over-proper-use-of-drone-strikes.html.
McCord, Joan. 1983. "A Forty Year Perspective on the Effects of Child Abuse and Neglect." *Child Abuse and Neglect* 7: 265–70.
McEwen, Alvin. 2017. "So Much for No Tea Party Racism: Mark Williams Expelled from National Tea Party Federation." Huffpost, December 6, 2017. https://www.huffpost.com/entry/so-much-for-no-tea-party_b_650480.

McIntyre, Lisa J. 1999. "Hernando Washington." In *The Practical Skeptic,* edited by Lisa McIntyre, 75–80. Pullman, WA: Washington State University Press.

McMorris-Santoro, Evan. 2010. "Out Crazying the Crazy: How a Pranskster Plans to Infiltrate and Destroy the Tea Party Movement." TPM, April 13, 2010. https://talkingpointsmemo.com/dc/outcrazying-the-crazy-how-a-prankster-plans-to-infiltrate-and-destroy-the-tea-party-movement.

Meich, Richard Allen and Michael J. Shanahan. 2000. "Socioeconomic Status and Depression over the Life Course." *Journal of Health and Social Behavior* 41, no. 2: 162–76.

Menchaca-Bagnulo, Ashleen. 2018. "Conservatives Should Care about Institutional Racism." *Public Discourse,* April 23, 2018. http://www.thepublicdiscourse.com/2018/04/21367/.

Merritt Hawkins. 2017. "Survey of Physician Appointment Wait Times." https://www.merritthawkins.com/uploadedFiles/MerrittHawkins/Content/Pdf/mha2017waittimesurveyPDF.pdf.

Merry, Robert W. 2017. "How Will History Assess Obama?" *The American Conservative,* January 20, 2017. https://www.theamericanconservative.com/articles/how-will-history-assess-obama/.

Miah, Malik. 2009. "Race and Class: Obama Forgets African Americans." Solidarity. https://solidarity-us.org/atc/145/p2674/.

Milbank, Dana. 2016. "Republicans' Mindless Obstruction Has Helped Create Something Far Worse." *Washington Post,* March 11, 2016. https://www.washingtonpost.com/opinions/republicans-mindless-obstruction-has-helped-create-something-far-worse/2016/03/11/46ba9022-e723-11e5-b0fd-073d5930a7b7_story.html?utm_term=.3bae397831b0.

Miles, Matthew B., A. Michael Huberman, and Johnny Saldana. 2014. *Qualitative Data Analysis.* Thousand Oaks, CA: Sage Publishing.

Miller, Emily. 2010. "Obama's Hypocrisy on School Choice." *Human Events*, October 12, 2010. http://humanevents.com/2010/10/12/obamas-hypocrisy-on-school-choice/.

Miller, Zeke. 2011. "Maxine Waters Says Congressional Black Caucus 'Getting Tired' of Covering for Obama." *Business Insider*, August 17, 2011. https://www.businessinsider.com/maxine-waters-says-congressional-black-caucus-getting-tired-of-making-excuses-for-obama-2011-8.

Mills, C. Wright. 1959. *The Sociological Imagination.* London, Oxford, and New York: Oxford University Press.

Mitchell, Joshua. 2017. "The Identity-Politics Death Grip." *National Review,* October 26, 2017. https://www.nationalreview.com/2017/10/identity-politics-ruined-democratic-party/.

Moe, Terry M. 2012. "Teachers Unions and American Education Reform: The Politics of Blocking." *The Forum* 10, no. 1: Article 4.

Montopoli, Brian. 2012. "Tea Party Supporters: Who They Are and What They Believe." CBS News, December 14, 2012. https://www.cbsnews.com/news/tea-party-supporters-who-they-are-and-what-they-believe/.

Morial, Marc H. 2017. "50 Years of Black Mayors." Huffpost, July 31, 2017. https://www.huffingtonpost.com/entry/50-years-of-black-mayors_us_596fc9abe4b0d72667b05e19.

Moynihan, Daniel Patrick. 1969. *Maximum Feasible Misunderstanding.* New York: Free Press.

Murphy, Mark. 2011. "The Natural Law Tradition in Ethics." *The Stanford Encyclopedia of Philosophy.* https://plato.stanford.edu/entries/natural-law-ethics/.

Murphy, Tim. 2014. "Inside the Mammoth Backlash to Common Core." *Mother Jones,* September/October 2014. https://www.motherjones.com/politics/2014/09/common-core-education-reform-backlash-obamacare/.

Musgrove, George Derek. 2012. *Rumor, Repression, and Racial Politics: How the Harassment of Black Elected Officials Shaped Post-Civil Rights America.* Athens, GA: University of Georgia Press.

NAACP. 2010. "Tea Party Signs." July 18, 2010. https://www.youtube.com/watch?v=PWbmEUIQOCQ.

National Fair Housing Alliance. 2018. "Discrimination When Buying a Car: How the Color of Your Skin Can Affect Your Car-Shopping Experience." https://nationalfairhousing.org/wp-content/uploads/2018/01/Discrimination-When-Buying-a-Car-FINAL-1-11-2018.pdf.

Newheiser, Anna-Kaisa, Miguel Farias, and Nicole Tausch. 2011. "The Functional Nature of Conspiracy Beliefs: Examining the Underpinnings of Belief in the *Da Vinci Code* Conspiracy." *Personality and Individual Differences* 51: 1007–11.

New York Times/CBS News. 2010. "National Survey of Tea Party Supporters." April 5–12, 2010. https://www.nytimes.com/interactive/projects/documents/new-york-timescbs-news-poll-national-survey-of-tea-party-supporters.

Nichols, Shaun. 2011. "Is Free Will an Illusion?" *Scientific American,* November 1, 2011. https://www.scientificamerican.com/article/is-free-will-an-illusion/.

Nittle, Nadra K. 2017. "Why Racism in Health Care Is Still a Problem Today." ThoughtCo, March 18, 2017. https://www.thoughtco.com/racism-in-health-care-still-a-problem-2834530.

Obama, Barack. 2004. *Dreams from My Father.* New York: Three Rivers Press.

O'Connor, Tom. 2017. "How ISIS Got Weapons From the U.S. and Used Them to Take Iraq and Syria." *Newsweek,* December 14, 2017. https://www.newsweek.com/how-isis-got-weapons-us-used-them-take-iraq-syria-748468.

Office of Policy Planning and Research, United States Department of Labor. 1965. "The Negro Family: The Case for National Action." Washington, DC: U.S. Government Printing Office.

Office of the Mississippi Secretary of State. 2013. "In the Matter of: One Voice" Consent Order, File Number C-13-0589. http://www.sos.ms.gov/ConsentAgreementsFinalOrders/OneVoice-ConsentOrder-C-13-0589.pdf.

Office of the Press Secretary. 2011. "Remarks by the President." The White House, April 27, 2011. https://obamawhitehouse.archives.gov/the-press-office/2011/04/27/remarks-president.

Ondaatje, Michael L. 2010. *Black Conservative Intellectuals in Modern America.* Philadelphia: University of Pennsylvania Press.

Orey, Byron D'Andra. 2004. "Explaining Black Conservatives: Racial Uplift or Racial Resentment?" *The Black Scholar* 34, no. 1: 18–22.

Oshinsky, David M. 1996. *Worse than Slavery: Parchman Farm and the Ordeal of Jim Crow Justice.* New York: Free Press Paperbacks.

Owens, Mackubin T. 2007. "Emancipation as Political-Military Strategy." The Ashbrook Center. http://ashbrook.org/publications/oped-owens-07-emancipation/.

Page, Clarence. 2012. "Romney the Chameleon Debates Himself." *Chicago Tribune,* October 24, 2012. https://www.chicagotribune.com/news/ct-xpm-2012-10-24-ct-oped-1024-page-20121024-story.html.

Pager, Devah, Bart Bonikowski, and Bruce Western. 2009. "Discrimination in a Low-Wage Labor Market: A Field Experiment." *American Sociological Review* 74: 777–99.

Parham, Thomas A. and Paris T. Williams. 1993. "The Relationship of Demographic and Background Factors to Racial Identity Attitudes." *Journal of Black Psychology* 19, no. 1: 7–24.

Parker, Christopher C. and Matt Barreto. 2013. *Change They Can't Believe In.* Princeton: Princeton University Press.

Patterson, G. R. and Eleanor E. MacCoby. 1980. "Mothers: The Unacknowledged Victims." *Monographs of the Society for Research in Child Development* 45, no. 5: 1–64.

Pear, Robert and Sheryl Gay Stolberg. 2009. "Obama Says He Is Open to Altering Health Plan." *New York Times,* March 5, 2009. https://www.nytimes.com/2009/03/06/us/politics/06web-health.html

Perry, Twila L. 1995. "Race, Feminism, and Public Policy." Markkula Center for Applied Ethics at Santa Clara University. http://www.scu.edu/ethics/publications/other/lawreview/familyvalues.html#22f.

Peters, Marie Ferguson. 1985. "Racial Socialization of Young Black Children." In *Black Children: Social, Educational, and Parental Environments,* edited by Harriette Pipes McAdoo and John Lewis McAdoo, 159–73. Newbury Park, CA: Sage Publications.

Peterson, David. 2017. "Horatio Alger and the Bootstrap Myth." Signature. https://www.signature-reads.com/2017/03/horatio-alger-bootstrap-myth/.

Pettigrew, Thomas F. and Linda R. Tropp. 2006. "A Meta-Analytic Test of Intergroup Contact Theory." *Journal of Personality and Social Psychology* 90, no. 5: 751–83.

Pew Research Center. 2009. "A Religious Portrait of African-Americans." http://www.pewforum.org/2009/01/30/a-religious-portrait-of-african-americans/.
———. 2010. "Section 6: Tea Party and Views of Government Overreach." April 18, 2010. http://www.people-press.org/2010/04/18/section-6-tea-party-and-views-of-government-overreach/.
———. 2015. "10 Countries with the Largest Muslim Populations, 2010 and 2050." April 2, 2015. http://www.pewforum.org/2015/04/02/muslims/pf_15-04-02_projectionstables74/.
Philpot, Tasha S. 2017. *Conservative but Not Republican: The Paradox of Party Identification and Ideology among African Americans.* New York: Cambridge University Press.
Pipes, Sally. 2018. "Canadians Are One in a Million—While Waiting for Medical Treatment." *Forbes,* June 11, 2018. https://www.forbes.com/sites/sallypipes/2018/06/11/canadians-are-one-in-a-million-while-waiting-for-medical-treatment/#6a0371b63e7d.
Piven, Frances Fox and Richard Cloward. 1971. *Regulating the Poor: The Functions of Public Welfare.* New York: Pantheon Books.
Pollock, Mica, ed. 2008. *Everyday Antiracism: Getting Real about Race in School.* New York and London: The New Press.
Ponder, Jon. 2010. "Photo Shows Top Tea Bagger Holding Sign with N-Word (Which He Misspelled)." *Pensito Review,* January 4, 2010. http://www.pensitoreview.com/2010/01/04/photo-shows-top-tea-bagger-holding-sign-with-n-word-which-he-misspelled/.
Pournelle, Jerry. 2010. "The Iron Law of Bureaucracy." Chaos Manor Special Reports. September 11, 2010. https://www.jerrypournelle.com/reports/jerryp/iron.html.
Pratt, Douglas. 2018. *Religion and Extremism: Rejecting Diversity.* London and New York: Bloomsbury Academic.
Pullman. Philip. 2003. *The Amber Spyglass.* New York: Laural-Leaf.
Raghunathan, Raj. 2012. "Free Will Is an Illusion, So What?" *Psychology Today,* May 8, 2012. https://www.psychologytoday.com/us/blog/sapient-nature/201205/free-will-is-illusion-so-what.
Randall, Lisa. 2015. *Dark Matter and the Dinosaurs: The Astounding Connectedness of the Universe.* New York: Ecco.
Rapley, Timothy John. 2001. "The Art(fullness) of Open-Ended Interviewing: Some Considerations on Analysing Interviews." *Qualitative Research* 1, no. 3: 303–23.
Raspberry, William. 1988. "How the Underclass Came to Be." *Washington Post.* February 19, 1988. https://www.washingtonpost.com/archive/opinions/1988/02/19/how-the-underclass-came-to-be/eba3a548-2bdd-43b2-a349-1f42a0dfb4d7/?noredirect=on&utm_term=.9ebdfc176f03.
Reagan, Ronald. 1981. "Inaugural Address." The American Presidency Project, January 21, 1981. http://www.presidency.ucsb.edu/ws/?pid=43130.
redarrowguy. 2010. "Tea Party Hate and Spit Targets Blacks and Democrats." Video, April 8, 2010. https://www.youtube.com/watch?v=kYRLeJw1aG8.
Rehwald, Jackie. 2018. "On 112-Year Anniversary of Springfield Lynchings, Memorial for Victims Is Planned." *Springfield News Leader,* April 12, 2018. https://www.news-leader.com/story/news/local/2018/04/12/112-year-anniversary-springfield-lynchings-memorial-victims-planned/504031002/.
Reuters. 2017, September 8. "Most Americans Get News from Social Media." *Fortune,* September 8, 2017. http://fortune.com/2017/09/08/facebook-twitter-snap-news.
Ricketts, Erol. 1989. "The Origin of Black Female-Headed Families." *Focus* 12, no. 1: 32–36.
Riis, Jacob. 1890. *How the Other Half Lives: Studies among the Tenements of New York.* New York: Charles Scribner's Sons.
Roberts, Cokie and Steven V. Roberts. 2018. "America at Its Best." uexpress.com, October 31, 2018. https://www.uexpress.com/cokie-and-steven-roberts/2018/10/31/america-at-its-best.
Robertson, Lori. 2017. "Employer Premiums and the ACA." FactCheck.org, March 14, 2017. https://www.factcheck.org/2017/03/employer-premiums-and-the-aca/.
Robi, Jill. 2018. "A Strange Feeling of Safety for a Black American." *High Country News,* August 16, 2018. https://www.hcn.org/articles/essays-a-strange-feeling-of-safety-for-a-black-american-tribal-police.

Roff, Peter. 2009. "Obama Wrong on D.C. School Vouchers and Hypocritical, Just Like Congress." *U.S. News & World Report.* April 22, 2009. https://www.usnews.com/opinion/blogs/peter-roff/2009/04/22/obama-wrong-on-dc-school-vouchers-and-hypocritical-just-like-congress.

Ross, Catherine E. 2000. "Neighborhood Disadvantage and Adult Depression." *Journal of Health and Social Behavior* 41, no. 2: 177–87.

Rotter, Julian B. 1966. "Generalized Expectances for Internal Versus External Control of Reinforcement." *Psychological Monographs: General and Applied* 80, no. 1: 1–28.

Russell, Katherine K. 1998. "Measuring Racial Equity in Criminal Justice: The Historical Record." In *The Color of Crime,* 14–25. New York: New York University Press.

Sääfström, Carl Anders and Niclas Månsson. 2004. "The Limits of Socialisation." *Interchange* 35/3: 353–64.

Salvi, Carola, Irene Cristofori, Jordan Grafman, and Mark Beeman. 2016. "The Politics of Insight." *The Quarterly Journal of Experimental Psychology* 69, no. 6: 1064–72.

Sanders Thompson, Vetta L. 1984. "Socialization to Race and Its Relationship to Racial Identification among Americans." *Journal of Black Psychology* 20, no. 2: 175–88.

Sarlin, Benjamin. 2010. "Liberals Crash the Tea Party." The Daily Beast, April 15, 2010. https://www.thedailybeast.com/liberals-crash-the-tea-party.

Savage, Barbara D. 2008. *Your Spirits Walk Beside Us: The Politics of Black Religion.* Cambridge and London: Belknap Press of Harvard University Press.

Schamberg, Kirsten and Kim Barker. 2007. "The Not-So-Simple Story of Barack Obama's Youth." *Chicago Tribune,* March 25, 2007. http://www.chicagotribune.com/news/nationworld/chi-0703250359mar25-archive,0,3329878,full.story.

Schlenker, Barry R., John R. Chambers, and Bonnie M. Le. 2012. "Conservatives are Happier than Liberals, but Why? Political Ideology, Personality, and Life Satisfaction." *Journal of Research in Personality* 46: 127–46.

Schoenherr, Neil. 2018. "Impact of Religion and Racial Pride on Classroom Discrimination." PHYS/ORG, Washington University in St. Louis. https://phys.org/news/2018-01-impact-religion-racial-pride-classroom.html.

Schorow, Stephanie. 2008. "Wilson Perceives Social Structure and Culture as Key Causes of Poverty." *The Harvard Gazette,* October 9, 2008. https://news.harvard.edu/gazette/story/2008/10/wilson-perceives-social-structure-and-culture-as-key-causes-of-poverty/.

Schuyler, George S. (1967) 2001. "The Rising Tide of Black Racism." In *Rac(e)ing to the Right: Selected Essays of George S. Schuyler,* edited by Jeffrey B. Leak, 106–8. Knoxville: University of Tennessee Press.

Schwarz, Donald F. 2018. "What's the Connection between Residential Segregation and Health?" *Culture of Health* (blog). April 3, 2018. https://www.rwjf.org/en/blog/2016/03/whats-the-connection-between-residential-segregation-and-health.html.

Seidman, Steven. 2009. "Anti-Obama and Tea Party Movement Posters." Ithaca College Communication Management and Design, September 15, 2009. https://www.ithaca.edu/rhp/programs/cmd/blogs/posters_and_election_propaganda/anti-obama__and_tea_party_movement_posters/.

Sellin, J. Thorsten. 1976. *Slavery and the Penal System.* New York and Amsterdam: Elsevier Scientific Publishing.

Senécal, Caroline and Frédéric Guay. 2000. "Procrastination in Job-Seeking: An Analysis of Motivational Processes and Feelings of Hopelessness." *Journal of Social Behavior and Personality* 15, no. 5: 267–82.

The Sentencing Project. 2000. "Reducing Racial Disparity in the Criminal Justice System." Washington, DC: The Sentencing Project. https://www.sentencingproject.org/wp-content/uploads/2016/01/Reducing-Racial-Disparity-in-the-Criminal-Justice-System-A-Manual-for-Practitioners-and-Policymakers.pdf.

———. 2019. Criminal Justice Facts. https://www.sentencingproject.org/criminal-justice-facts/.

Seow, Choon-Leong. 1996. "Textual Orientation." In *Biblical Ethic and Homosexuality: Listening to Scripture,* edited by Robert L. Brawley, 17–34. Louisville, KY: Westminster John Knox Press.

Serwer, Adam. 2011. "Michelle Bachmann's Views on Slavery Are Worse than You Thought." *The American Prospect,* August 8, 2011. http://prospect.org/article/bachmanns-views-slavery-are-worse-you-thought.

Severns, Maggie. 2015. "Boehner's Last Fight with Obama." Politico, October 21, 2015. https://www.politico.com/story/2015/10/john-boehner-vouchers-education-schools-republicans-214984.

Shafer, Jack. 2019. "Senator Mitt Romney is the Season 3 Character We Needed." Politico, January 2, 2019. https://www.politico.com/magazine/story/2019/01/02/mitt-romney-trump-administration-223616.

Sharockman, Aaron. 2015. "PunditFact Checks in on the Cable News Channels." Politico, January 29, 2015. https://www.politifact.com/truth-o-meter/article/2015/jan/29/punditfact-checks-cable-news-channels/.

Shepherd, Def. 2012. "Racism is Alive and Well: 35 Incredibly Racist Anti-Obama Signs." October 19, 2012. http://www.defshepherd.com/2012/10/racism-is-alive-and-well-35-incredibly.html.

Shibutani, Tamotsu. 2017. *Society & Personality: An Interactionist Approach to Social Psychology.* Abington, UK and New York: Routledge.

Siciliani, Luigi and Jeremy Hurst. 2003. "Explaining Waiting Times Variations for Elective Surgery across OECD Countries." OECD Health Working Papers. http://www.oecd.org/health/health-systems/17256025.pdf.

Silver, Nate. 2011. "The Effects of Union Membership on Democratic Voting." *New York Times,* February 26, 2011. https://fivethirtyeight.blogs.nytimes.com/2011/02/26/the-effects-of-union-membership-on-democratic-voting/.

Simmel, Georg. 1950. *The Sociology of Georg Simmel.* Edited by Kurt H. Wolff. New York: The Free Press.

Simon, David, Mark McInerney, and Sarah Goodell. 2018. "The Earned Income Tax Credit, Policy, and Health." Health Affairs Health Policy Brief, October 8, 2018. https://www.healthaffairs.org/do/10.1377/hpb20180817.769687/full/.

Simpson, Alan K. 2006. *Politics is a Contact Sport.* Charlotte Hall, MD: Recorded Books.

Sitkoff, Harvard. 1978. *A New Deal for Blacks: The Emergence of Civil Rights as a National Issue: The Depression Decade.* New York: Oxford University Press.

Skinner, Allison. 2017. The Conversation, January 4, 2017. http://theconversation.com/are-americans-becoming-more-xenophobic-70509.

Skinner, Allison L. and Jacob E. Cheadle. 2016. "'The Obama Effect'? Priming Contemporary Racial Milestones Increases Implicit Racial Bias among Whites." *Social Cognition* 34, no. 6 (December): 544–58.

Skinner, Deborah Creighton. 2010. "NAACP Condemns Tea Party Racism." *Black Enterprise,* July 14, 2010. https://www.blackenterprise.com/naacp-condemns-racism-of-tea-party-movement/.

Skocpol, Theda and Vanessa Williamson. 2012. *The Tea Party and the Remaking of Republican Conservatism.* New York and London: Oxford University Press.

Smith, K. Carl and Dr. Karnie C. Smith, Sr. 2011. *Frederick Douglass Republicans: The Movement to Re-Ignite America's Passion for Liberty.* Bloomington, IN: AuthorHouse.

Smith, Mark, Robert Saunders, Leigh Stuckhardt, and J. Michael McGinnis, eds. 2013. *Best Care at Lower Cost: The Path to Continuously Learning Health Care in America.* Washington, DC: National Academies Press.

Smithsimon, Gregory. 2018. "Are African American Families More Vulnerable in a Largely White Neighborhood?" *The Guardian,* February 21, 2018. https://www.theguardian.com/books/2018/feb/21/racial-segregation-in-america-causes.

Snopes Staff. 2015. "Is Former CIA Director John Brennan a Muslim?" Snopes.com, January 22, 2015. https://www.snopes.com/fact-check/cia-director-john-brennan-muslim/.

Sowell, Thomas. 1998. "Race, Culture, and Equality." Hoover Institution on War, Revolution and Peace. Palo Alto, CA: Stanford University.

Spalding, Douglas A. 1873. "Instinct. With Original Observations on Young Animals." *Macmillan's Magazine* 27: 282–93.

Spellman, Jim. 2009. "Tea Party Movement Has Anger, No Dominant Leaders." CNN Politics, September 12, 2009. http://www.cnn.com/2009/POLITICS/09/12/tea.party.express/index.html.
Spencer, Margaret Beale. 1990. "Parental Values Transmission: Implications for the Development of African American Children." In *Black Families: Interdisciplinary Perspectives*, edited by Harold E. Cheathan and James B. Stewart, 111–30. Piscataway, NJ: Transaction.
Steele, Shelby. 1998. *The Content of Our Character: A New Vision of Race in America*. New York: Harper Perennial.
———. 1999. "The Loneliness of the 'Black Conservative.'" Hoover Digest: Research + Opinion on Public Policy. https://www.hoover.org/research/loneliness-black-conservative.
———. 2006. *White Guilt: How Blacks and Whites Together Destroyed the Promise of the Civil Rights Era*. New York and London: Harper Perennial.
Steinberg, Laurence, Julie D. Elmen, and Nina S. Mounts. 1989. "Authoritative Parenting, Psychosocial Maturity, and Academic Success among Adolescents." *Child Development* 60: 1424–36.
Steinmetz, Katy. 2015. "See Obama's 20-Year Evolution on LGBT Rights." *Time*, April 10, 2015. http://time.com/3816952/obama-gay-lesbian-transgender lgbt-rights/.
Stroud, Natalie Jomini. 2011. *Niche News: The Politics of News Choice*. New York and London: Oxford University Press.
Sue, Derald Wing. 2010. *Microaggressions in Everyday Life: Race, Gender, and Sexual Orientation*. New York: Wiley.
Suggs, Henry Louis. 1999. "The Washingtonian Legacy: A History of Black Political Conservatism in America, 1915–1944." In *Black Conservatism: Essays in Intellectual and Political History*, edited by Peter Eisenstadt, 81–108. New York and London: Garland Publishing.
Suttles, Gerald D. 1976. "Urban Ethnography: Situational and Normative Accounts." *American Review of Sociology* 2: 1–18.
Swanson, Ana. 2015. "The U.S. Court System is Criminally Unjust." *Washington Post*, July 20, 2015. https://www.washingtonpost.com/news/wonk/wp/2015/07/20/why-the-u-s-court-system-is-criminally-unjust/?utm_term=.df15ad802ffd.
Taris, Toon W. and Inge A. Bok. 1997. "Effects of Parenting Style upon Psychological Well-Being of Young Adults: Exploring the Relations among Parental Care, Locus of Control and Depression." *Early Child Development and Care* 132: 94–104.
Taylor, Jim. 2009. "Parenting: Decision Making." *Psychology Today*, October 19, 2009. https://www.psychologytoday.com/us/blog/the-power-prime/200910/parenting-decision-making.
TheLoop21. 2012. "Debate! Has School Desegregation Been Good for Blacks?" *Ebony*, March 1, 2012. https://www.ebony.com/news-views/debate-has-school-desegregation-been-good-for-blacks.
Thompson-Miller, Ruth, Joe R. Feagin, and Leslie H. Picca. 2015. *Jim Crow's Legacy: The Lasting Impact of Segregation*. Lanham, MD: Rowman & Littlefield.
Thorburn, Sheryl and Laura M. Bogart. 2005. "Conspiracy Beliefs about Birth Control: Barriers to Pregnancy Prevention among African Americans of Reproductive Age." *Health Education and Behavior* 32, no. 4: 474–87.
Tipple, John. 1959. "The Anatomy of Prejudice: Origins of the Robber Baron Legend." *The Business History Review* 33, no. 4: 510–23.
Topaz, Jonathan. 2014. "Obama: GOP Blocked 500 Bills." Politico, May 8, 2014. https://www.politico.com/story/2014/05/republicans-legislation-obama-dccc-event-106481.
Tope, Daniel, Justin T. Pickett, and Ted Chiricos. 2015. "Anti-minority Attitudes and Tea Party Movement Membership." *Social Science Research* 51: 322–37.
Travis, Shannon. 2010. "NAACP Passes Resolution Blasting Tea Party 'Racism.'" CNN Politics. July 18, 2010. http://www.cnn.com/2010/POLITICS/07/14/naacp.tea.party/index.html.
Tutu, Naomi and Rose Bator. 2006–2008. "I Don't Think of You as Black." The Linkage Leader. http://03badae.netsolhost.com/wie3/images/pdfs/I%20Don't%20think%20You%20As%20Black.pdf.
Ujifusa, Andrew. 2017. "Map: Tracking the Common Core State Standards." *Education Week*, September 18, 2017. https://www.edweek.org/ew/section/multimedia/map-states-academic-standards-common-core-or.html.

Unnever, James D. and Shaun L. Gabbidon. 2011. *A Theory of African American Offending.* New York: Routledge.

US Congress. 2009. "H.R. 1, American Recovery and Reinvestment Act of 2009." https://www.gpo.gov/fdsys/pkg/BILLS-111hr1enr/pdf/BILLS-111hr1enr.pdf.

US Department of Justice. 2015. "Department of Justice Report Regarding the Criminal Investigation into the Shooting Death of Michael Brown by Ferguson, Missouri Police Officer Darren Wilson." Memorandum, March 4, 2015. https://www.justice.gov/sites/default/files/opa/press-releases/attachments/2015/03/04/doj_report_on_shooting_of_michael_brown_1.pdf.

US Department of State. 2016. "Joint Comprehensive Plan of Action." https://www.state.gov/e/eb/tfs/spi/iran/jcpoa/.

US General Accounting Office. 1990. "Death Penalty Sentencing: Research Indicates Racial Disparities." Washington, DC: U.S. Government Printing Office.

US House of Representatives. n.d.a. "Party Realignment." History, Art & Archives. Accessed March 2, 2019. http://history.house.gov/Exhibitions-and-Publications/BAIC/Historical-Essays/Temporary-Farewell/Party-Realignment/.

———. n.d.b. "The Civil Rights Movement and the Second Reconstruction, 1945–1968." Accessed March 1, 2019. http://history.house.gov/Exhibitions-and-Publications/BAIC/Historical-Essays/Keeping-the-Faith/Civil-Rights-Movement/.

US Senate. n.d. "The Senate Rejects a Supreme Court Nominee." Accessed March 1, 2019. https://www.senate.gov/artandhistory/history/minute/Judicial_Tempest.htm.

US Supreme Court. 1968. "King v. Smith" 392 U.S. 309. https://supreme.justia.com/cases/federal/us/392/309.

Utter, Glenn H. and James L. True. 2004. *Conservative Christians and Political Participation: A Reference Handbook.* Santa Barbara, CA: ABC-CLIO.

Valenza, C. 1985. "Was Margaret Sanger a Racist?" *Family Planning Perspectives* 17, no. 1: 44–46.

Vaughn, Aundra Simmons. 2015. "The Obama Effect on African American High School Males." PhD diss. Georgia Southern University. https://digitalcommons.georgiasouthern.edu/cgi/viewcontent.cgi?article=2279&context=etd.

Vitelli, Romeo. 2015. "Can You Change Your Personality?" *Psychology Today*, September 7, 2015. https://www.psychologytoday.com/us/blog/media-spotlight/201509/can-you-change-your-personality.

Walker, Clarence E. 2011. "'We're Losing Our Country': Barack Obama, Race & the Tea Party." *Daedalus* 140, no. 1: 125–30.

Walter, Amy, Elizabeth Hartfield, and Chris Good. 2012. "Obama Fights Back against 'You Didn't Build That' Attacks." ABC News, July 24, 2012. https://abcnews.go.com/Politics/OTUS/obama-fights-back-build-attacks/story?id=16843789.

Washington, Booker T. 1895. "Atlanta Exposition Address." http://www.pinzler.com/ushistory/bookertsupp.html.

———. 1904. "A Protest against the Burning and Lynching of Negroes." *The Birmingham Age Herald*, February 29, 1904. https://www.loc.gov/item/91898237/.

Washington, Jesse. 2010. "Did Spit, Slurs Fly on Capitol Hill?" *The Seattle Times*, April 13, 2010. https://www.seattletimes.com/nation-world/did-spit-slurs-fly-on-capitol-hill/.

Watson, T. Stuart and Christopher H. Skinner. 2004. *Encyclopedia of School Psychology.* New York: Kluwer Academic/Plenum Publishers.

Weber, Max. 1947. *The Theory of Social and Economic Organization.* New York: Oxford University Press.

Weeks, Brian E. and R. Kelly Garrett. 2014. "Electoral Consequences of Political Rumors: Motivated Reasoning, Candidate Rumors, and Vote Choice during the 2008 Election." *International Journal of Public Opinion Research* 26, no. 4: 401–22.

Whatley, Stuart. 2010. "The Tea Party Movement is a National Embarrassment." Huffington Post, August 6, 2010. https://www.huffingtonpost.com/stuart-whatley/the-tea-party-movement-is_b_455883.html.

Willer, Robb, Matthew Feinberg, and Rachel Wetts. 2016. "Threats to Racial Status Promote Tea Party Support among White Americans." May 4, 2016. https://ssrn.com/abstract=2770186 or http://dx.doi.org/10.2139/ssrn.2770186.
Williams, Oscar R. 2007. *George S. Schuyler: Portrait of a Black Conservative.* Knoxville: University of Tennessee Press.
Williams, Walter E. 2011. *Race & Economics: How Much Can Be Blamed on Discrimination?* Stanford, CA: Hoover Institution Press.
Wilson, William Julius. 1993. *The Ghetto Underclass: Social Scientific Perspectives.* Newbury Park, CA: Sage.
Wilson, William Julius and Robert Aponte. 1987. "Urban Poverty: A State-of-the-Art Review of the Literature." In *The Truly Disadvantaged: The Inner City, the Underclass, and Public Policy,* edited by William Julius Wilson, 165–87. Chicago and London: The University of Chicago Press.
Wing, Nick. 2016. "Here's How the Nation Responded When a Black Militia Group Occupied a Government Building." Huffpost, December 16, 2016. https://www.huffingtonpost.com/entry/black-panthers-california-1967_us_568accfce4b014efe0db2f40.
Winston, David. 2010. "Behind the Headlines: What's Driving the Tea Party Movement?" The Winston Group, April 2010. https://winstongroup.net/2010/04/01/behind-the-headlines-whats-driving-the-tea-party-movement/.
Wolf, Patrick, Babette Gutmann, Michael Puma, Brian Kisida, Lou Rizzo, Nada Eissa, and Marsha Silverberg. 2009. "Evaluation of the DC Opportunity Scholarship Program: Impacts after Three Years." Jessup, MD: National Center for Education Evaluation and Regional Assistance, Institute of Education Sciences, U.S. Department of Education.
Wolf, Patrick, Babette Gutmann, Michael Puma, Brian Kisida, Lou Rizzo, Nada Eissa, Matthew Garr, and Marsha Silverberg. 2010. "Evaluation of the DC Opportunity Scholarship Program: Final Report." Jessup, MD: National Center for Education Evaluation and Regional Assistance, Institute of Education Sciences, U.S. Department of Education.
Wolf, Patrick, Babette Gutmann, Michael Puma, Lou Rizzo, Nada Eissa, and Marsha Silverberg. 2007. "Evaluation of the DC Opportunity Scholarship Program: Impacts after One Year." Jessup, MD: National Center for Education Evaluation and Regional Assistance, Institute of Education Sciences, U.S. Department of Education.
Worrell, Frank C., James R. Andretta, and Malcolm H. Woodland. 2014. "Cross Racial Identity Scale (CRIS) Scores and Profiles in African American Adolescents Involved with the Juvenile Justice System." *Journal of Counseling Psychology* 61, no. 4: 570–80.
Yan, Holly, Joshua Berlinger, and Faith Robinson. 2016. "Baton Rouge Officer: Alton Sterling Reached for a Gun before He Was Shot." CNN, July 13, 2016. https://www.cnn.com/2016/07/12/us/police-shootings-investigations/.
Yellin, Emily. 2000. "Lynching Victim is Cleared of Rape, 100 Years Later." *New York Times,* February 27, 2000. https://www.nytimes.com/2000/02/27/us/lynching-victim-is-cleared-of-rape-100-years-later.html.
Zaveri, Mihir. 2018. "Politicians and World Leaders Remember John McCain." *New York Times,* August 26, 2018. https://www.nytimes.com/2018/08/26/us/mccain-death-reactions.html.
Zeleny, Jeff. 2009. "Persistent 'Birthers' Fringe Disorients Strategists." *New York Times,* August 4, 2009. https://www.nytimes.com/2009/08/05/us/politics/05zeleny.html.
Zeng, Zhen. 2018. "Jail Inmates in 2016." Bureau of Justice Statistics, Office of Justice Programs, U.S. Department of Justice. https://www.bjs.gov/index.cfm?ty=pbdetail&iid=6186.
Zernike, Kate and Megan Thee-Brenan. 2010. "Poll Finds Tea Party Backers Are Wealthier, More Educated." *New York Times.* April 14, 2010. https://www.nytimes.com/2010/04/15/us/politics/15poll.html?_r=0.
Zombie. 2010. "Crashing the Crashers: Tea Party Infiltrators Outmaneuvered in S.F." PJ Media, April 16, 2010. https://pjmedia.com/zombie/2010/04/16/crashing-the-crashers-tea-party-infiltrators-outmaneuvered-in-s-f/.

Name Index

Bachmann, Michelle, 144
Borelli, Deneen, xiii, 2
Brown, Michael, 102–103
Burke, Edmund, 81
Bush, George W., 107, 112
Bush, Jeb, 126

Carson, Ben, x, 30
Carter, Jimmy, 59
Cleaver, Emanuel, 144
Clinton, Bill, 6
Conway, Kellyanne, 112
Cosby, Bill, 92
Crawford III, John, 125

Douglass, Frederick, x
D'Souza, Dinesh, 125
Du Bois, W. E. B., x, 137–138, 142

Elder, Larry, x

Frank, Barney, 144
Franklin, Shirley, 107

Garner, Eric, 125
Garrison, William Lloyd, ix
Gates, Bill, 126
Gates, Henry Louis, xiv, 107
Goldwater, Barry, 34
Gray, Freddie, 103

Hammon, Jupiter, x, xi, xiii
Hoover, Herbert, 34
Hurston, Zora Neal, 93

Jealous, Ben, 140, 151
Johnson, Lyndon, 34, 87

King, Martin Luther, Jr., xiv, 18, 58
King, Rodney, 14

Lewis, John, 144
Loury, Glenn, x, 70

Malcolm X, 36, 58
Marcus, Lloyd, xiv
Martin, Trayvon, 14, 125
McCarthy. Kevin, 108
McConnell, Mitch, 108
Mills, C. Wright, xvi, 71
Moynihan, Daniel Patrick, 86

Newton, Huey, 26
Nixon, Richard, xii

Obama, Barack, 107–135; attitudes of Tea Party supporters toward, xii, 6, 158; Christian identity of, 110, 113, 131, 143, 155; popularity among African Americans; ix; supposed ties to Islam, 113

Powell, Adam Clayton, 9, 11
Powell, Colin, x

Reagan, Ronald, x, 59, 124
Rice, Condoleeza, x, xv
Rice, Tamir, 125
Roosevelt, Franklin Delano, 34

Sanders, Bernie, 31
Sanger, Margaret, 18
Schuyler, George, x, xiii, 11
Scott, Tim, x
Simmel, Georg, 56
Smiley, Tavis, 124
Sowell, Thomas, x
Steele, Shelby, x, 1

Thomas, Clarence, x, 2, 30
Truman, Harry, 34

Voinovich, George, 108

Washington, Booker T., x, xi, 102
Waters, Maxine, 127
Watts, J. C., x
Weber, Max, 62, 80
West, Allen, x
West, Cornell, 124
Williams, Armstrong, x
Williams, Walter E., x

Zimmerman, George, 14

Subject Index

abortion, 26, 55
absent fathers, 9, 84, 85–86
absolutism, 32, 117, 144
Affordable Care Act (Obamacare), ix, 108, 118–121, 144
African Americans: attitudes toward black Tea Party supporters, 2; aversion to "African American" label, 5, 57; comparative wealth, viii; history of alliance with Democrats, 16; history of conservativism, x–xi; members of Congress, vii; pastors, 1; political kinship, ix, xiii, 35; social ties, xvi, 16; stereotypes, vii. *See also* poverty; white nationalists
American Recovery and Reinvestment Act of 2009, vii, 108
antipoverty programs. *See* entitlement programs
assimilation, 2

Bible, 27
biblical literalism, 44
birth control, 18
birthers, 109, 112, 130–131
Black Lives Matter, 103–104
Black Panther Party for Self-Defense, 26

character flaws. *See* personality traits
Christianity: and same-sex marriage, 117; as an appeal of Republican Party, 24, 26, 27, 32; as an element of identity, 32, 41, 43–44, 48, 119, 148, 155; as a rallying cry, vii, 115; as a reason to shun the Democratic Party, 27; history of presence in American politics, 44–45
Common Core, 126
Confederacy, symbols of, vii, ix
confirmation bias, 34
conservatives, types of: Afrocentric, xi; black right, xi; common-sense, 36; compassionate, 35; constitutional, 35; individualist, xi–xii; national defense, 36; neoconservative, xi–xii; progressive, 35
counterpartisanship, 34–35
crime, 10, 11, 91–105
criminal justice system: and policing, 93–94; history of racism in, 94–96
cultural norms, 10, 100–101

Declaration of Independence, 83
dehumanization, 37
Democratic Party, 16–27. *See also* African Americans

Earned Income Tax Credit, 85–86
education, 41–42, 87, 88; D.C. Opportunity Scholarship Program, 118–119; teachers' unions, 117, 118
entitlement programs, xv, 19, 75–78, 85–86, 89, 145

eugenics, 34
experimental philosophers, 61

financial literacy, 62–63
Fox News, ix, 2
free will, 61

Great Society programs, 87
group threat theory, 139
gun control, 26, 28, 104

house Negroes, 36–37
housing patterns, 138

ideal type, 62
illusory truth, 153
immigration, 19, 70
imprinting, 64
individualism, 69–70
integration, 21
introversion, 60

Jim Crow segregation, viii, x, 2, 16, 21, 63

Ku Klux Klan, ix, xiv, 7, 18

locus of control, 50
lynching, 101–102, 138, 152

microaggressions, 153
Muslim Brotherhood, 109

National Association for the Advancement of Colored People (NAACP), 91, 140
National Tea Party Federation, 140
Nation of Islam, 30
natural law, 32
New Deal, 16
news consumption, 34, 59

Obamacare. *See* Affordable Care Act
"Obama Effect," 107–108
Occam's Razor, 38
Occupy Wall Street protests, 146–147
out-of-wedlock births, 20–21, 86–87
over-regulation of business, 18–19

parenting: and the criminal justice system, 98–99; authoritarian, 42, 65; authoritative, 42; egalitarian, 65; old-fashioned, 92; permissive, 42. *See also* socialization
partisanship, 31–35
personal experience, 58–59
personality traits, 9–11, 60, 87–88, 90
personal responsibility, 69–106
personal troubles, xvi, 70, 71, 90, 105; of Barack Obama, 128–129. *See also* introversion; personal responsibility; self-hatred; work ethic
political efficacy, 22–23
poverty, 72–91, 105–106
prejudice reduction, 149
primary socializer, 38
principled choices, 48–50
privacy, 32, 33
public issues, xvi, 70, 71, 90, 105

race traitors, 124–127
racial socialization: cautious/defensive, 51; individualistic/universalistic, 52–54; integrative/assertive, 52
racism: academic definition of, 5; African American conservatives' attitudes toward, xi, 5–15, 20; at Tea Party rallies, vii, 110, 137–155; aversive, 25; deflectors, 8–11; deniers, 6–7; dismissers, 14–15; institutional, 5–8; interpersonal, 5; realists, 12–14; restrictors, 11–12; within the Republican Party, 26, 30–31. *See also* Ku Klux Klan; white nationalists
redneck, 144, 148
reference group, 2, 3
religion, 26, 109. *See also* Christianity
Republican Party, xii, 7–8, 16; critiques of poor people, 28; elitism, 32; failure to support African American candidates, 31; lack of fiscal restraint, 28; resistance to Obama, 108–109, 121–124. *See also* Christianity; racism

same-sex marriage, 117. *See also* Christianity
self-hatred, 2, 37. *See also* Uncle Tom
self-improvement, 70
self-sufficiency, 32

Subject Index

single-headed households. *See* absent fathers
slavery, x, 2, 86; law pertaining to, viii; freedom from, 16
social cohesion, 67
socialism, vii, 114–115, 159–160
socialization, 41–67; limits of, 56–61. *See also* racial socialization
sociological imagination, 71–72
Student Nonviolent Coordinating Committee (SNCC), 57, 58

Tea Party Caucus, US House, viii
Tea Party supporters: as conservative reactionaries, xii–xiii

Uncle Tom, 1, 37
underclass, 83
unemployment, 11, 71
US Constitution, vii, viii, ix, 27, 32
US Supreme Court, 95

victimhood, 9–10

welfare. *See* entitlement programs
white nationalists, viii; assumptions about African Americans, viii. *See also* Ku Klux Klan
work ethic, 69, 83; of African Americans, 9, 89–90; of interviewees' family members, 44–47; of poor people, 28

About the Author

Kirk A. Johnson is associate professor of sociology and African American studies at the University of Mississippi, where he studies race and news media. This is his first book about politics.